BLACK
CHRISTIANS
THE UNTOLD
LUTHERAN STORY

CONCORDIA
SCHOLARSHIP
Today

BLACK
CHRISTIANS
THE UNTOLD
LUTHERAN STORY

Jeff G. Johnson
Foreword by Martin E. Marty

Publishing House
St. Louis

Library of Congress Cataloging-in-Publication Data

Johnson, Jeff G., 1924–
    Black Christians—the untold Lutheran story / Jeff G. Johnson.
        p.   cm. — (Concordia scholarship today)
    ISBN 0-570-04558-4
    1. Afro-American Lutherans—History. 2. Blacks—America—
Religion. 3. United States—Church history. 4. America—Church
history. 5. Lutheran Church—America—History. I. Title.
II. Series.
BX8116.3.A37J64   1989
284.1'089'96073—dc20   91-12473

1 2 3 4 5 6 7 8 9 10 VP 00 99 98 97 96 95 94 93 92 91

Contents

List of Tables   7

Foreword   9

Editor's Foreword   13

Introduction   15

PART I: NEW WORLD COLONIAL SLAVE SOCIETIES

1. The United States Colonial North, 1669–1776   21
2. The Danish West Indies, 1713–   36
3. The United States Colonial South, 1717–1781   53
4. Surinam, 1791–   67
5. Guyana, 1818–   85

PART II: SLAVERY AND EMANCIPATION

6. The Southern Slave States, 1774–1865   105
7. Jehu Jones and the First All-Black Lutheran Church,
   1832–1849   130
8. The Old Lutherans in the South, 1865–1891   138

PART III: NEW DIRECTIONS

9. The Rebirth of Black Lutheranism, 1877–1950   151

PART IV: WHERE DO WE GO FROM HERE?

10. The Great Debates, 1930–1964   185
11. Integration, Inclusiveness, or What? 1947–1990   198

PART V: AFRO-AMERICANS INSIDE MAINLINE CHRISTIANITY:
        THE LUTHERAN EXPERIENCE

12. Summary   225
13. Conclusions   231

Appendices   239

Notes   250

Tables

1. Free and Unfree Confirmations at the Lutheran Church
   in Christiansted, 1841–1845   46
2. Baptisms on St. Thomas for the Years 1828–1837   48
3. The Black Population in Colonial Georgia, 1740–1780   60
4. 1989 Membership in the Christian Churches of Surinam   83
5. The Population of British Guiana by Race, 1891–1960   92
6. Church Growth, the Lutheran Church in Guyana,
   1931–1965   99
7. Communicant Membership of the Largest Congregations
   of the Lutheran Church in Guyana   101
8. Blacks Confirmed and Baptized in the North Carolina
   and Tennessee Synods, 1819–1824   109
9. The Number of Blacks Confirmed and/or Baptized
   in the Tennessee Synod, 1819–1865   112
10. The Slave and Free Colored Population of Charleston,
    1790–1848   115
11. Black Accessions in the South Carolina Synod, 1830–1865   127
12. Free Black, Slave, and White Population of Philadelphia,
    1790–1860   133
13. Statistical Report of the Alabama Field for the Years 1927,
    1931, 1946, and 1948   168
14. Percent of Population of Wilcox County That Was Rural
    in 1910, 1940, and 1950   171
15. Black Population of Wilcox County in 1910, 1930,
    and 1980   171
16. Black Lutheran Congregations Consolidated in Alabama
    by 1961   173
17. Black Lutheran Congregations and Preaching Stations
    in the U.S. in Rank Order of the Number
    of Confirmed Members by State, 1948–1950   177
18. Number of Black Lutherans in 1950 by Region   178

19. Total Disbursements for Negro Missions by the
    American Lutheran Church, 1886–1949   187
20. Expenditures for Black Missions by the Synodical
    Conference, 1930–1938   194
21. Congregations of the Alabama Lutheran Conference,
    1954   211
22. LCA Synods with the Largest Black Membership,
    1980   219

Foreword

In *Heart of Missouri*, historian and archivist August R. Suelflow tells of an incident in the 1860s when a son of Missouri Synod pioneer C. F. W. Walther arrived in New Brunswick, Missouri, to start a congregation. His mentor, the missionary-minded J. F. Buenger, the young Ferdinand Walther's uncle, took his charge to main street on Saturday before the man's planned ordination. "Now we have to go around and drum up a congregation for you so that I can ordain and install you tomorrow as their pastor." Buenger buttonholed every passerby who looked like a German: "You are surely a German and a Lutheran, are you not?" If he guessed right, Buenger urged the accosted person to be at a certain location for church the next day. The technique worked, a congregation was formed, and Walther spent his whole pastoral career among them.

When I reviewed the Suelflow book in 1954, I recall commenting on the ethnocentrism of the Buenger approach, which virtually became the normative strategy among most American Lutherans, if the testimony of Jeff Johnson in respect to work among black Americans is accurate. If I smiled or sneered when I read *Heart of Missouri,* I found myself a participant in the approach two years later as I began buttonholing prospective members to start a new congregation. By "the approach" I do not mean something literal about excluding all but our kind; we were looking for anyone who might come to hear the Gospel and participate in the works of love in a new Christian community. Yet "the approach" was operating: our board had calculated that a new community of middle class, white, college-bred people, 16.9 percent of whom "preferred Lutheran" (they told the developer) was a good place for a mission to our kind. It was.

During the two years before that, while doing doctoral work, I had served in both German-American and African-American circles as a supply pastor. Their congregations might be only a few blocks apart, but a sharp line was drawn between them. Almost no whites were in the largely black congregations, and no blacks were allowed

9

in the white ones. The line between these Lutheran Christian groups was almost absolute, but it was not a line drawn by Scriptures, or Christ, or the Holy Spirit. (We also "Germanified" the black churches; in one I recall the restlessness that resulted as we sang slowly, dolefully, dourfully, as was the custom of the day, all the verses of "Soul, Adorn Thyself with Gladness.")

It is a tribute to the J. F. Buengers that they were faithful with their missions in the presence of that nearly absolute line between peoples. But it is a special tribute to Jeff Johnson that he has never been content to let it rule absolutely. In the 43 years since he graduated from seminary—can it be that long already, Jeff?—he has pursued a determined, scholarly, consistent, often lonely trajectory, in an effort to change things. Neither a radical activist who would alienate the people he would convince nor a passive complicitor who would work the system to his own advantage, he followed his own course in a partly successful effort to change things. This book is an example of his understandings.

Jeff Johnson, as it will soon be made clear, has a good deal of faith that data can be effective in mission. One quickly gains confidence in Johnson's way: those many tables of statistics are not compiled and published to dazzle or benumb readers but to get them to discover on their own what has gone wrong and been wrong and what might be done to right it. This would have been a bad book, on the one hand, had its effect been to cause white Lutheran Christians to glower in self-hate, which is not the same thing as repentance, but which could easily have been the aim of an author who has a right to express frustration that turns to rage. It would also have been a bad book, on the other hand, did it not hold up the mirror to each reader who has a chance to see his or her part in an approach which has caused barriers to the work of the Gospel, and to inspire them to participate in change.

Johnson's technique is exemplified by a passage near the end:

> A forthright interpretation of integration/inclusiveness (as understood and practiced by the Lutheran Church) would state that black people may come into the church if they will hear the Gospel, speak the Gospel, and worship and live by the Gospel as *Euro-Americans do*. The black vote has been loud and clear about such a view of integration/inclusiveness. They don't want to be integrated/included so much as they want to be empowered. It comes

as no surprise, therefore, that after 300 years, there are only 132,000 black Lutherans in the United States.

After 300 years, 132,000 members: that represents a good beginning. It would put black Lutheranism, were it separatist and separated, in the top 50 in size among the 225 or so denominations in the *Yearbook of the American Churches*. But it represents only a tiny fragment of the potential.

During the next 300 years nonwhites almost certainly will make up the majority of North American citizens, just as they are coming to be the Christian majority globally. Most growth is in the southern world of sub-Saharan Africa, Latin America, the subcontinent of Asia, and Oceania, while what Johnson calls *Euro-American* Christianity comparatively languishes. No one needs such a long time scale to anticipate drama. During the next 30 years, the period for which churches plan strategies and approaches, most urban growth (and remember, today more than half of Americans live in metropolitan areas numbering more than a million people each) will be African-American, Hispanic in its many forms, Asian, and the like.

Church bodies which are one or two or three percent nonwhite will be left behind if they use only integration/inclusiveness models. Being left behind would be a stupid criterion if it meant only not wanting to be embarrassed in comparative statistics races among churches. Being left behind, as Johnson's pages make clear, means not living up to the opportunities and responsibilities which go with response to the Gospel.

Some may say that Johnson "preaches Law," not Gospel, on these pages—that the promise of the publisher and of Johnson himself that this will be "historical theology" have not been fulfilled. No author can say everything that needs saying in one book. Johnson preaches little here at all; his way in historical theology is to pay attention to the human record, the charter of the Gospel, his own involvement in the story, and the mind and heart of the reader.

As an historian I came to this book thinking "I know most of this stuff." I came away newly informed about a much longer story than I had pictured: a story of many starts, most of them false; of outrages and demeaning acts on the part of white church leaders who would not share power; and white church followers who would not share vision.

11

Most of all, however, I came away with admiration for the African-Americans who, through these three centuries, have not let frustration and rage turn them away, as it undoutedly turned off so many others. There is a certain nobility, an aristocracy of faith, a dignity in their record of relentless endeavors to find ways to put into church life the message that Lutheran preachers and teacheers, many of them their own African-American parents, kept giving them. Johnson is himself evidence of that staying power, an example of what good can come forth when a black American, informed by the Gospel, seeks and has found a measure of "empowerment."

Martin E. Marty

The University of Chicago

Editor's Foreword

The Concordia Scholarship Today series explores current issues from a theological point of view and asks how the household of faith may meet the challenge to self-understanding that comes from the surrounding culture. The hope is that we "may be able to comprehend [more fully] with all the saints what is the [extent of] the love of God" toward all His creatures (Eph. 3:17–18).

Black Christians—The Untold Lutheran Story describes the love of God towards Lutherans in the New World. But the record also shows how Lutherans have failed in their responsibility, specifically on the part of whites towards blacks. The hope is that this volume, which highlights current concerns as it relates the past, will contribute to a broader and deeper understanding of the Christian faith, that it will clarify and enrich our analysis of issues that beset us, and that in so doing it will enrich our comprehension of the love of Christ.

This volume is not for Lutherans only. It will be of interest to other Christian churches because to some degree it mirrors the history of those groups, albeit with notable differences. They may recognize themselves as they read about the Lutheran experience and profit from it.

The CST series encourages Christians to think theologically about all matters of life. Exploration of an issue must grow out of reliable probing and research of the Scriptures and of every other related, legitimate field of study. That may not always yield theological applications which differ markedly from the past. The greater value of such study lies in the learning process and in the assurance that the issue has been properly addressed.

Black Christians—The Untold Lutheran Story is unique in that it includes the history of black Lutheranism in all branches of that family of denominations in the New World. It summarizes patterns that are common to all Lutherans as well as the distinctive differences within individual groups and how they came to differ. Knowing that

13

background is basic for practical, positive action today.

Some readers may be indifferent to this story and the challenge it poses. Others may not want to be informed and may even resent any exploration of the subject. More important for the future are the genuine seekers, those who study the topic for a variety of reasons and with varying degrees of interest.

Obviously, this is not merely an academic study without implications. But the reader should not expect neat and final recommendations. Some of the principles that apply to all attempts at evangelization and communication are noted in the final chapter. They are useful for the process as blacks and whites experience the grace of God in their lives and strive to work together humbly yet positively under the Gospel, recognizing and wrestling with their specific problems and differences. The research that has led to this book also is an essential undergirding for that process.

In February 1984 Dr. Johnson, long-time professor at Valparaiso University, related part of the history of black Lutheranism in *The Cresset*, a university publication. Now retired in Los Angeles, California, he has completed here this previously untold story with the hope that blacks and whites will be encouraged anew to work together in the common cause of the Lord's kingdom.

The Publisher

Introduction

The Significance of This Study

This is a study in historical theology and, specifically, a study of black Christianity. (Historical theology is the obverse of systematic theology—theology in practice, as opposed to theoretical formulations.) Lest some novice brush history aside as irrelevant, it should be pointed out that no one can make sense of contemporary Christianity without that historical background.

Most studies of black religion tend to concentrate on black Christians who formed separate all-black denominations. Such studies are important because the vast majority of black Christians are committed to all-black denominations. This book, however, is one of a few studies dealing with black Christians who choose to stay within white denominations. It takes on added significance today because the majority of the world-wide membership in what are typically thought of as main-line white Christian denominations is, in fact, non-European. This is particularly true of the Roman Catholic and Anglican denominations. Worldwide, the Lutheran Church is currently headed in the same direction. In some parts, Lutheranism is already predominantly black and/or non-European.

While examining black Lutheranism throughout the New World, this study provides a cross-cultural look at black Christianity. Such an approach strengthens the conclusions to be drawn from the study.

Ultimately, this volume is significant not just because it is about black people, or what can be identified as the oldest, the longest, or the largest. What is significant is the insight this study offers about how one group of Christians (in this instance Lutherans) have defined themselves and their mission as they moved into the New World.

A personal word concerning the significance of this study. Doing history, as black people have traditionally done it, is to call out to

15

that great encompassing cloud of witnesses, our fathers, and say: Speak about God's work among us. For black people, there is no such thing as sacred versus secular history. God is the central actor in all history. There is no history without God. Since we are not permitted the luxury of taking either our survival or our humanity for granted, doing history hardly ever springs from idle curiosity. If we do it at all, it is because those witnesses are an important part of the centuries-old struggle to grasp both our survival and our humanity. If we do it well, history becomes an important resource for our present and our future.

Myths and Facts

Black Lutheranism is surrounded by a number of myths. Three of the most persistent are (1) the myth that Euro-American Lutherans have had very little contact with black people. Therefore, one should not expect to find many blacks who are members of the Lutheran Church. I call this the myth of No Contact. Oddly enough, professional historians seem to have had a hand in perpetuating it.[1]

(2) The Johnny-Come-Lately myth suggests that if you do happen to come across a black Lutheran, he/she is most likely a late-comer to the Lutheran Church. That is to say, blacks have no real history within the Lutheran tradition. (3) The myth of the Unbridgeable Chasm is, theologically and practically, the most serious of the three for Lutheran out-reach to the black community. It assumes that the religious tradition of black people is so different from that of Euro-American Lutherans that blacks simply won't respond to the Lutheran Church. These myths are in reality variants of the oft-repeated master-slave theory of the evangelization of black people in the New World.

If you want something more substantial than myths and go to the literature, two things dominate the work of most students of black Lutheran history. First, most students tend to approach the history of black Lutheranism as they approach the history of Euro-American Lutherans, that is, by dealing with the history of blacks in the various separate Lutheran denominations. They study black people only in the American Lutheran Church, or only in the Lutheran Church in America, or only in the Missouri Synod.

A separate denominational approach to the history of Euro-

American Lutherans is partly justifiable, because theirs is largely the study of the ingathering of separate European ethnic Lutherans in the New World. The history of black Lutherans, however, is not such an in-gathering of those who were already Lutheran. To use the same framework in the study of black Lutherans as one uses with Euro-American Lutherans has resulted in the collection, ultimately, of a number of disconnected, isolated incidents, some of them without meaning or explanation.[2]

Second, consistent with that denominational approach, many tend to view the history of black Lutheranism as having occurred in a vacuum, essentially disconnected from all other institutional or social reality. Most of these studies have been conducted by Lutherans. In their analysis black Lutheranism is never touched by or related to anything but a particular Lutheran denomination, as though there is no world apart from Lutherans—a stance that not even the most skeptical social scientist would espouse. The result is a "history" that is profoundly ahistorical.

Many researchers have been preoccupied with the extent to which their particular denomination has succeeded in transmitting or imposing its religious forms on black people. Bluntly stated, underlying most research is an attempt to get at political issues, that is, the effectiveness of Euro-American Lutheran organizations. Those are valid concerns. But the effectiveness of Euro-American Lutheran political activity does not necessarily contribute to an understanding of black Lutherans. Until now, such questions have simply diverted attention away from the central issue: black Lutherans.

The Purpose of This Study

Rather than an exhaustive or complete history of black Lutheranism, this is, at best, a tentative expanded outline with a four-fold purpose. The first objective is to propose an alternative framework for the study of black Lutheranism. Second, this volume will trace the development of black Lutheranism throughout the New World, beginning with the middle of the 17th century. Third, we will examine the development of black Lutheranism in the larger social context in which it occurred. Fourth, we will attempt to identify the strategies Lutherans have used in working with black people in the New World.

17

Some readers of this volume will be disappointed. Many names commonly associated with the history of black Lutheranism are barely mentioned, some not at all. For this we do not apologize. To achieve the purposes cited above, it seemed more appropriate to focus on events rather than on individuals. The hope is that we will lay the groundwork for developing generalizations that will be useful in the future. One of the first steps then is to identify the strategies that have emerged over the past three hundred years. That will provide a basis for further study and action.

I

NEW WORLD
COLONIAL
SLAVE SOCIETIES

1

The United States Colonial North, 1669–1776

Lutheranism was born and developed in a world that was undergoing profound change. Almost at the very moment that Luther was nailing his 95 theses to the door of the castle church at Wittenberg, the world as Europeans knew it was exploding with new peoples and new continents laid bare by the voyages of discovery. This recently-discovered new world demanded that Europeans, long isolated and insulated, rethink and revise two fundamental issues with which all humans grapple: (1) the nature of the world in which they live, and (2) their identity and place in that world.

Two of the answers that Europeans gave, the notions of race and colonialism, form the context in which New World black Lutheranism was born. Black Lutheranism was not conceived in the bright glow of missionary zeal, nor did European Lutherans come to the New World to make disciples of black people. In fact, when they got here, many did not even bother to seek out or establish the church for themselves. That was not their custom. They waited for the church to come to them.

Some contemporary Lutheran historians find the slavery (racism) and colonialism of the New World embarrassing. There has been an effort on the part of some to disclaim responsibility for those twin evils that were so much a part of the New World. As they would have it, the Lutheran nations of northern Europe, at best, entered the enterprise of colonial empire-building quite late in the game. Their disclaimers tend to obscure more than they reveal.

The critical issues in understanding the origins of black Lutheranism are not Who is responsible for colonialism? or Who is responsible for the institution of slavery? The important questions are What brought black people and Lutherans together in the first place? and What kinds of relations did they have once they met?

21

In the one-hundred-and-twenty-year period beginning in 1623, Lutherans from Europe settled in or established congregations in the following colonies in the New World:

1623   New Netherlands—now New York/New Jersey
1638/39 New Sweden—primarily along the Delaware River
1666   The Danish West Indies—now the U.S. Virgin Islands
1734   Ebenezer—in the British colony of Georgia
1741   Dutch Guiana—now Surinam
1743   British Guiana—now Guyana

Two of the aforementioned, New Sweden and the Danish West Indies, were Lutheran political entities; a third, Ebenezer, was a Lutheran community. What brought together Lutherans from Europe and blacks from Africa in all of these instances was the need for labor, that is, slaves. For almost two and a half centuries, from 1623 to 1865, slavery and colonialism were the primary context for contact, conversion, and Christian brotherhood, if indeed those labels can be used.

The roots of black Lutheranism, therefore, were planted squarely in the midst of a dilemma: To make anyone a disciple of Jesus Christ is to empower that individual with the life of God. Slavery, however, demanded above all else that slaves be kept powerless. In making disciples of slaves, Lutherans brought those black disciples into the institution of the church. But again, slavery demanded that slaves (as well as free blacks) be excluded from full participation in the institutional life of the church. Those embarrassing alternatives have not disappeared today. Slavery is one, but not the only, form of institutionalized racism.

Initially, the most likely place to look for black Lutherans was in the northern colonies. At the beginning of the colonial period, that is where Lutherans from Europe first settled, and that is also where black people were most numerous.

New Sweden

Black Lutheranism might have begun in New Sweden, but it didn't.

The Swedes were the first group of Lutherans to formally establish a religious organization and build a church in the New World.

22

In the early part of 1638, the Swedes settled along the Delaware River just southwest of the Dutch colony of New Netherland. Their first settlement, Fort Christina and the village that sprang up around it, became the city of Wilmington, Delaware. New Sweden encompassed most of what is now Delaware, southeastern Pennsylvania, and part of southwestern New Jersey.

New Sweden existed as a political entity for only 17 years, from 1638 to 1655, when the Dutch, under the leadership of Peter Stuyvesant, took control of their territory. As a religious entity, the Lutheran Church in New Sweden maintained a relationship with the Church of Sweden for 148 years, until 1786. During that time the Swedish government sent more than 30 ministers to serve the Swedish colonists at an estimated cost of between $100,000–$200,000.

The record reveals that the Swedes had relatively little communication with blacks. That may be related to several factors: (1) While in the planning stage, the colonial thrust was supposed to reject slavery. In the words of Gustavus Adolphus who originally proposed the idea of a colony in the New World, "We shall gain more by free people with wives and children" than with slaves.[1] But that did not prevent the Swedish congregation at Christiana from selling part of its church land in 1719 to purchase a Negro female slave for service in the parsonage.

(2) While the original sponsors of the colony hoped that it would become a trading enterprise, it actually emerged as an agricultural settlement. As such, it did not lend itself to the extensive use of slaves.

Continued assistance from the Swedish state church seems to have been a mixed blessing: Control from abroad, though ineffective, remained. The state church failed to distinguish between Lutheranism as a theological phenomenon and Lutheranism as a cultural expression. The state church also failed to recognize the ongoing acculturation of the Swedes in the New World. When the Church of Sweden failed to respond to the continuing assimilation of their people, many of the Swedes asked the Episcopal Church to serve them.

The early Swedish Lutherans played a minimal role, if any, in the development of black Lutheranism for at least two reasons: (1) The Swedish government prohibited the introduction of slavery while it was in control. (2) The Lutheran pastors who were sent out from Sweden thought of themselves as temporary workers, spending much of their time waiting for a better position at home.[2]

New Netherland

New Netherland is the next logical place to look for black Lutherans in the northern colonies. This is a more likely spot because Lutherans were among the first settlers to arrive in the colony in 1623 and the Dutch brought in eleven company slaves as part of the labor force in 1625. At least the stage was set for something to happen.

A critical issue for the development of black Lutheranism was the position blacks occupied in this new colony. To understand that, we shall have to look at the nature and growth of slavery in New Netherland.

It was clear to Pieter Minuit, the first Director-General of New Netherland, that in establishing the colony, the Dutch West India Company had not struck a gold mine. In 1628, the only economic benefit reaped by the company came from the export of furs. The furs yielded about $20,000.[3] Almost all the supplies needed to sustain the trading posts had to be imported from Holland. Indentured servants abandoned all agricultural pursuits as soon as their period of service ended. The cost of maintaining the outposts was so high that the return after expenses was not at all what the company had anticipated.

Pieter Minuit recommended a change in policy. Instead of trying to operate trading posts, he suggested that the company plant colonies that would support the outposts.[4] This meant that there would be a much greater need for labor. There were two possible sources for such labor, indentured servants and slaves. Indentured servants, could not fill all of the need. The population of Holland was not large. Life in the new colony was harsh and unattractive. The cost of maintaining servants was high, and as soon as they had put in their time, they were free to go about their own business.

Slaves, the other source of labor, cost only $100–$150 apiece. They would be available for service throughout their adult life. The solution to the labor problem was therefore a mix of indentured servants and more slaves. In Article XXX, "THE FREEDOMS AND EXEMPTIONS GRANTED . . . . TO ALL SUCH AS SHALL PLANT ANY

COLONIES IN NEW AMSTERDAM," dated June 7, 1629, the Dutch West India Company stipulated, "The Company will use their endeavors to supply colonists with as many blacks as they conveniently can, on conditions hereafter to be made."[5]

Because of their possessions in Brazil and on the coast of Guinea, not to mention the taking of Spanish and Portuguese prizes, the Dutch had relatively easy access to slaves. The introduction of slaves into the colony was thus accelerated.

Slavery under the Dutch

Slavery in New Netherland, as in the other colonies established by Europeans, was governed by local municipal law. For most practical purposes, there were no legal precedents to guide the colonists in the matter of slavery. Each colony was on its own.

Slavery in New Netherland differed significantly from that which was later practiced in the South.[6] The Dutch were rather pragmatic. For them, slavery was an economic expedient. What concerned them most was the outcome of the system. As a consequence, slavery under the Dutch never became the clearly or rigidly defined system that it later became in the South. The Dutch had little interest in developing theories or in rationalizing to justify the system. There was actually more religious discrimination than racial discrimination. Initially, there were no legal restrictions for free blacks. Free blacks could and did own white indentured servants; they served in the militia; and black slaves married whites. By contrast, Jews could neither own real estate nor be accepted in the militia.

Slaves had the same standing as whites in the courts. Not only could they testify against each other, they could testify in cases involving free whites.[7] In 1658 a law was passed that prohibited the whipping of Negro slaves without first obtaining permission from the city magistrates. There was not the brutalization and repression of Dutch slaves that characterized slavery in the South. Both judges and the community were even hesitant about imposing the death penalty on slaves convicted of a capital offense. In such cases, it was not unusual for the judge to stage a mock hanging.

While slaves were considered chattel, there was some hope for freedom in the Dutch policy of "half-freedom," a form of partial manumission that was granted to some slaves who had given long

25

and faithful service. They were required, however, to provide the company with a fat hog, a stipulated amount of corn, wheat, peas, or beans, as well as a limited amount of service on land or at sea. One of the earliest recorded instances of such half-freedom occurred in 1643 and again in 1648 when several Negroes and their wives were manumitted. Interestingly enough, they were also given a grant of land in order to support themselves.[8] The parcels of land given the manumitted Negroes usually was less than ten acres. They slowly developed into an agricultural settlement that provided the residents of New Amsterdam with produce, eggs, and fowl.[9]

While any child born to a half-free woman was technically a slave, the Dutch colonists were very much opposed to retaining such a child in slavery. They viewed such retention as against the law of nature. "How anyone born of a free Christian mother, could, notwithstanding, be a slave and obliged to remain such, passed their comprehension."[10] Slavery under the Dutch, and subsequently under the British in New York, was not a matter of blood. Rather, it was a matter of maternity. If the mother was free, the child of that mother was free. If the mother was a slave, the child of that mother was a slave. The status of the father was irrelevant.

Slavery, therefore, was not limited to blacks. Anyone whose mother was a slave automatically was a slave. Because of intermarriage, some people who were unmistakably black were often free, whereas a number of persons who were obviously white were slaves.

> By the 18th century, the latter had become quite numerous. Advertisements for fugitive slaves make it clear that some runaways gained their freedom simply by passing over into the white population.[11]

Two indications of the somewhat mild nature of slavery under the Dutch were the minimum use of force that maintained the system, and the absence of slave revolts. This is not to suggest that the Dutch were completely color-blind. They did in fact equate race with slavery. It was commonly assumed that any visible evidence of Negro blood was, on the face of it, evidence of slave status. Consequently, half-free Negroes were given a certificate of their status, and those free Negroes who could not produce clear evidence of their status were always subject to being enslaved.

Under the Dutch, there were incentives and opportunities for freedom. Freedom was not a distant dream, granted at the whim, caprice, or even the benevolence of one's master. The Dutch had built into the system the kinds of incentives that encouraged self-help and assertiveness on the part of slaves.

Slavery under the British

The British ousted the Dutch from New Netherland in 1664, renamed it New York, and, except for a brief reoccupation by the Dutch in 1673–1675, maintained themselves there until the Revolutionary War.

The English were decidedly more rigid in their approach to slavery. For one thing, "As sovereignty over the area passed from Dutch to English hands, slavery was altered from a *de facto* to a *de jure* institution."[12] Second, "For the first time in the colony's history, slaves were being imported for the sole purpose of providing their owners with profit opportunities on their sale."[13]

Several things tended to moderate the severity of the British approach to slavery. First, they could not eradicate all the traditions developed under the Dutch. Second, slavery under both the Dutch and the English progressively became more urban and nonagricultural. Urban slaves are less isolated, less subject to surveillance and control, and more frequently exposed to a world larger than just that of their masters. Third and most important, slaves in New York acquired a number of occupational skills in the late 17th and early 18th centuries, comparable to those possessed by free laborers. The need to retain their cooperation, therefore, became grounds for granting them concessions.

Despite the control exercised by the English, slaves in New York enjoyed considerable freedom of action. They could accumulate property for their own use, reject prospective buyers, hire themselves out for service, and bargain with their masters for their own freedom. McManus concludes:

> Such conditions produced a large number of aggressive slaves, secure in their skills and confident of their ability to bend the system to their individual needs. [In New York] ... slaves were not only boldly self-assertive but often tenaciously pursued objectives that clashed with the interests of masters.

27

The conditions under which slaves were usually freed (loyal service or payment of an agreed sum to the master or his heirs) make it clear that the bulk of manumissions had little to do with philanthropy. Rather, manumission was the price that the master class paid for the efficient operation of the system.[14]

When emancipation finally came to New York, it was not a case of benevolence. In the words of McManus, it was really a matter of "economic displacement."[15] Towards the end of the 18th century, slavery was no longer a profitable way of recruiting or organizing labor. Emancipation, however, brought the illusion of freedom. Free blacks were systematically excluded from the occupations they had held during slavery. At this point, the tensions between the emancipated blacks and white laborers erupted into riots.

Lutherans Arrive in New Amsterdam

Lutherans were part of the first contingent from Holland that settled New Netherland, but they were different. For one thing, although they had lived in Holland before coming to the New World, most of them were German or Scandinavian, not Dutch. Because the state church in Holland was Reformed, these "foreigners" living there had shed the state church mentality and habits of Germany and Sweden..

They did not expect the church to come looking for them. They were also somewhat accustomed to religious opposition. It was Lutheran laymen who organized a congregation, conducted worship services, and then sent out a request for a pastor.

By 1650 one in every six individuals in the colony was Lutheran, and

By the 1660s nearly 10 percent of the colony's population of 8,000 was black, although census reports failed to distinguish between free persons of color and slaves.[16]

In 1657, the Rev. J. Ernestus Goetwater, a Lutheran minister, arrived in New Amsterdam with a commission from the Lutheran consistory in Holland authorizing him to act as pastor of the Lutheran congregation.[17] Two Reformed clergymen protested Goetwater's presence, demanding that he be sent back to Holland. Peter Stuyvesant so ordered. It was a year before Goetwater actually left. He was too ill to make the journey. During his stay, he did not publicly function as pastor to the Lutherans.

It was not until 1664, after the English ousted the Dutch, that the Lutheran congregation was officially chartered. The charter is dated December 6, 1664. Harry Kreider contends that the Lutheran church at New Amsterdam was in fact organized at least by 1649, if not earlier in 1643, even though it did not hold a charter.[18]

In 1669, the Rev. Jacobus Fabricius (or Fabritius) arrived from Germany to serve the Lutherans. He first went to Albany. Because of difficulties with the congregation there, he was sent to New York. On Palm Sunday, 1669, Fabricius baptized and admitted to membership a black male who took the name Emmanuel. Emmanuel is said to have had a Caucasian wife and two children.

In 1683, large numbers of Germans from the Palatinate began arriving in the colony and settled along the Hudson River. Consequently, the center of the Lutheran population in the colony shifted from the urban south (New York city) to the more rural areas along the Hudson River to the north.

Insofar as the record goes, black involvement with the Lutheran Church on a somewhat continuing basis begins with the onset of the 1700s. Justus Falckner was installed as pastor of the Dutch Lutheran Church in 1703. By 1705, Falckner listed among his members, two free Negroes, Aree van Guinea and his wife Jora.[19]

In that same year, Falckner records the baptism of a daughter of Aree van Guinea and includes in the record book the following prayer:

> Lord, merciful God, who lookest not upon the person, but from whom different creatures that fear thee and do right find favor, let this child be clothed in the white robe of innocence and righteousness, and so remain through the grace of Christ, the Saviour of all mankind. Amen.[20]

In 1708, Aree van Guinea moved to New Jersey and bought some land in the Raritan Valley. The deed to that property was not transferred to his name until 1724.

In 1714, Aree van Guinea visited New York City and asked Falckner to come to New Jersey and baptize his grandchild.[21]

On August 1, 1714, Falckner baptized three children, one of whom was van Guinea's grandchild. The service was held in van

Guinea's home. That was the first Lutheran worship service held in New Jersey. Perhaps the reason that the worship service was held in van Guinea's home was that it was the largest structure available. This was also the first time that Falckner met the German Lutherans who had begun to move into that area and marks the beginning of Zion Lutheran Church, now in Oldwick, Hunterdon County, New Jersey. Aree van Guinea is subsequently said to have donated the land for the first Lutheran church building in the Raritan Valley. By 1735, van Guinea was one of the members of the church council at Raritan who signed a complaint against the pastor, the Rev. Mr. Wolf.[22]

The few blacks who had come into the Lutheran Church to date, such as Emmanuel and the van Guineas were free. The first recorded evidence of the treatment accorded a slave in the Lutheran Church came with the baptism of Tom, an Indian slave in New York City in 1708. Sachse describes the incident as follows:

> When [Tom] first expressed a wish to become a Christian, it became a question of whether if he were admitted to the Church he could still be held in bondage and treated as a slave. The master naturally objected, in the fear that he might lose his servant. The Indian, however, settled the question by stating that he was willing to remain in servitude in this world, provided he was assured that he would be free and equal in the skies beyond.
>
> Dominie Falckner, when he heard of the circumstances, examined the Indian, found him sincere, and concluded to accept him, and instructed him in the catechism and the tenets of the faith.
>
> Upon the Sunday in question, after the Holy Eucharist had been celebrated, the Indian slave, after having been duly prepared, was called up before the altar and publicly catechized in the presence of the congregation by the pastor and wardens. He was then asked by Dominie Falckner whether he solemnly promised before the omnipotent Lord and this Christian congregation that he would, after he was received into the Church, continue to serve his worldly master and mistress as faithfully and truly as if he were yet in his benighted state.
>
> Upon the Indian giving his solemn promise that he would, Dominie Falckner proceeded to baptize him, after he had driven out the spirit of evil with the ancient exorcism according to the Lu-

theran ritual: *"Darum, du vermaledeyter Teufel, erkenne dein urtheil, etc."*[23]

Behind this promise which Falckner extracted from Tom lay the fear of many slaveholders that Christianity would undermine the legal basis of slavery. It was felt that the principle of English common law which prohibited the enslavement of anyone who was baptized would be upheld in the colonies. That fear was so widespread that in 1727, the Bishop of London finally issued the opinion that baptism did not confer freedom upon the slaves.[24]

The first recorded instance of a black slave becoming a member of the Lutheran Church in the northern colonies occurred in 1712, when a thirty-year-old black man by the name of Pieter Christian became a member of the Lutheran Church at Loonenburg in what is now Athens, New York.[25] At the time of his admission to the church, he too "promised among other things that he will hereafter, as well as he had done before, faithfully serve his master and mistress as a servant."[26] Falckner recorded the following prayer in the registry book concerning this baptism:

> Grant, O God, that this black and hard Negro heart be and remain a Christian heart, and he may be numbered among those who are clothed with white raiment before the throne of the Lamb, through the merits of the Lamb of God who bore the sins of the world. Amen.[27]

This prayer was even more racially pointed than in the case of Aree van Guinea's daughter.

No one knows who was instrumental in bringing Pieter Christian into the Lutheran Church. Most likely, it was not his master, Jan van Loon. Van Loon, a Roman Catholic, did make one contribution to Pieter's baptism. He served as Pieter's sponsor, the only recorded instance where he did this.

Two years after his baptism, Pieter got married. With his master's consent and the Rev. Joshua Kocherthal officiating, Pieter married a widow, Anna Barbara Asmer, a Caucasian. Two years later, Pieter married another Palatine woman, a Caucasian named Elizabeth Brandemoes. Elizabeth bore seven children by Pieter, all of whose baptisms were recorded at the Loonenburg church. Because their mother was free, the children were also free.[28] The way in which Julius Sachse (Falckner's biographer) tells it, Pieter Christian is a

31

"sort of first fruits of Lutheran missions to the Negro race."[29] Sachse apparently was unaware of Aree van Guinea, who only seven years earlier was a recognized member of the Lutheran Church.

By 1732, Pieter (sometimes referred to simply as Piet) had become a member of the church council at Loonenburg. In the mid–1740s, there was so much gossip about one of Pieter's daughters and pastor Berkenmeyer that the whole family was put under church discipline. They were not admitted back into the church until 1749.

In 1735, the constitution of Lutheran churches formally took notice of Negro slaves becoming church members and specified,

> In regard to the Negroes, a pastor shall previously ascertain that they do not intend to abuse their Christianity, to break the laws of the land, or to dissolve the tie of obedience; yea, he must have a positive promise that Christianity will not only be entered upon, but that the same shall be practiced in life.[30]

What was missing from that church constitution drawn up by pastor Berkenmeyer are the corresponding responsibilities of the slave master.[31] The constitution also equates the term "Negro" with the status of slaves, i.e., "the tie of obedience."

Further evidence of the position of blacks in the Lutheran church at Loonenburg can be seen in the minutes of the church council meeting in January 1744. Pastor Berkenmeyer asked whether the church council would express its feelings about the allotment of a bench to the Negro slaves, baptized or unbaptized. It was decided that no definite place would be designated for the colored people since only a few white members have their own seats. Again, Negritude is equated with slave status. It was decided that those masters who send their Negroes to church should advise them not to stay in the rear, but to occupy the first bench and the stairs. If, however, whites came looking for a seat, the blacks should clear the front bench.[32]

Pastor Berkenmeyer himself owned at least two slaves. It became such a matter of discussion that he finally informed his critics that it was none of their business since he had purchased them with his own money. Berkenmeyer baptized them, married them, and later baptized their two children.[33]

One final reference by Berkenmeyer indicates the prevailing attitude towards blacks, at least in the Lutheran church at Loonenburg. In a complaint about the failure of the members of the church to support its ministry, Berkenmeyer said

> While in most situations they (the members) consider themselves as good as the squire, when it comes to this matter (of contributions), they consider themselves lower than Piet, who once signed the salary list for 7 schillings.[34]

With the arrival of Muhlenberg in the 1740s, the baptism and marriage of slaves and free blacks by Lutheran pastors from Pennsylvania to Rhode Island was a fairly common practice.

"In 1745, when the Augustus Church at Providence was dedicated, Dr. Muhlenberg (who had previously instructed them) baptized three slaves."[35]

> On October 1, 1752, Dr. Muhlenberg preached at the installation service of John Frederick Handschuh. At that same service, a black man who was instructed in the faith by Handschuh was baptized.[36]

What is noteworthy is that, according to Muhlenberg, it was blacks who sought out the church, rather than the church seeking out blacks.

As early as 1714, there is evidence that child baptism had become a customary expectation among blacks. Aree van Guinea's grandchild was the third generation in his family to be baptized in the Lutheran Church. Muhlenberg records a number of second and third generation blacks that he baptized.[37]

Church membership for blacks appears to have been quite a different matter. Muhlenberg records only one black person as being a member of the Lutheran church in his area, and that report was by way of hearsay. That unnamed black is also reported to have willed his small holdings to his church.[38] Muhlenberg does mention a Negro slave who "comes diligently to our Dutch and English services and puts many nominal Christians to shame by her life."[39] Muhlenberg does not refer to her as a member of the church.

Summary

During the early colonial period in what is now the northern part of the United States, Lutheranism was initially planted under three different European powers: the Swedes, the Dutch, and the English. The Swedish Lutherans were the first to organize. The Dutch refused to let Lutherans organize. The English finally chartered the Dutch Lutheran congregation in New York City in 1664.

With the exception of the Swedes, Lutherans did not come to the colonies with mission on their minds. The Swedes were intent on evangelizing native Americans but were prohibited from engaging in slavery.

To date, there is no evidence of an organized or systematic effort on the part of Lutherans during this period to reach out to black people. On the contrary, much of the initial contact with blacks was the result of black initiative.

One of the more formidable barriers to the evangelizing of blacks was the fear that conversion to Christianity would undermine the very existence of slavery. The widely held assumption that slave holders were primarily responsible for bringing their blacks into the Christian church is not supported by any substantial body of evidence.

The first black person of record to enter the Lutheran Church was free, not a slave. He did so in 1669 at the Dutch Lutheran Church in New York City. Black slaves did not establish a continuing relationship with the Lutheran Church until the beginning of the 18th century. This seems to be supported by two kinds of evidence. First, the request in 1708 of the Indian slave, Tom, for baptism seems to have caught the church unprepared to deal with the issue of bringing slaves into the church. There was no ready-made solution to the problem of whether one could baptize a slave, or what the consequences of that action might be. Second, the Lutheran Church did not formally document a solution to the problem of baptizing slaves until 1735 in Berkenmeyer's church constitution.

From the beginning, slaves were aware of the fact that all was not right with the church's solution to the question of their baptism. Tom's final remark makes that clear. He at least wanted the assurance "that he would be free and equal in the skies beyond."

Blacks more frequently came to the Lutheran Church for the sacrament of baptism and the rite of marriage than for ongoing fellowship and nurture. This kind of response to Christianity by blacks was not limited to the Lutheran Church. A catechist for the Society for the Propagation of the Gospel in New York City reports that of the 219 baptisms performed there between 1732 and 1740, almost 90 percent were infants. After 40 years, the SPG could only report 30 communicants.[40]

The few blacks who did establish a continuing relationship with the Lutheran Church appear to have participated somewhat fully in the life of their respective congregations, whether slave or free. Both slave and free served on the church council. It was, however, in a Lutheran congregation in the North that the question of segregated seating was first raised. Notwithstanding that obvious piece of attempted discrimination, by 1750 as many as three generations in the same family had been baptized in the Lutheran Church.

The Lutheran strategy for working with blacks during the early colonial period in the North was essentially one of "We will serve you if you come." Blacks, both free and slave, therefore had to take the initiative. There is little evidence that slave masters were publicly encouraged to send or bring their slaves into the church. At this point, the Lutheran Church had not resolved the dilemma and compromise posed by slavery.

2

The Danish West Indies
1713–

Three years before Emmanuel was baptized in New York·City, the Danes took possession of St. Thomas in the Caribbean. The initiative that opened the Danish West Indies to Europeans and black people was in some respects similar to that which opened up New Netherland. It was essentially the result of private enterprise: The Danish West Indian and Guinea Company. While the initiatives were similar, the course of development was quite different.

Denmark, through the instrumentality of the Danish West Indian and Guinea Company, took possession of St. Thomas either late in 1665 or early 1666. Five years later, in 1671, the newly organized Danish West Indian Company began the task of developing the island by sending approximately 115 Danes (soldiers, clerks, serfs, a pastor, and 61 convicts—male and female) to begin work there. The convicts—whites—had been promised their freedom, but in reality, they were slaves.

In 1673, the first shipload of black slaves arrived, 103 all told, but they were probably not from the Danish West Indies Company. According to available records, the first *company* ship to bring slaves to the island arrived 15 years later in May 1687. That ship brought a total of 80 slaves.

Because of its location, St. Thomas quickly became the world's largest slave market. The demographics of the islands had some bearing on the nature and development of slavery. Europeans, who suffered health-wise in the tropical climate never migrated to the islands in the same numbers or for the same purposes that they did to the North American continent. Before the end of the 17th century blacks outnumbered all whites on the island. Trade and trans-shipment were important, but the islands remained largely a plantation society until the Americans purchased them in 1917. The Danes exercised sovereignty over the islands, but they were highly dependent on other Europeans both for trade and the political management of the territory. Many languages were spoken in the islands, but up until the early part of the 19th century the closest thing to a *lingua franca* and language for everyday life was Dutch Creole, a fact dictated by the large number of slaves.

Fifty some years after taking possession of St. Thomas, the Danish West Indian Company annexed the nearby island of St. John in 1717. In 1733, there was a slave revolt on St. John led by members of the Amina tribe. In control of St. John for several months, the rebellious slaves were bent on murdering all the whites and taking possession of the wealth they had helped to create. It was not until a French military force came to the aid of the Danish troops that the revolt was finally put down.

During the revolt, those whites who could fled to St. Thomas. By the time the revolt ended, all the crops and plantations had been destroyed. After such a holocaust, the planters refused to return to St. John. However, because the Danish West Indian Company wanted to remain in the profitable sugar production business, and because St. Thomas was not especially suited to agriculture, the company purchased nearby St. Croix island from France in 1733.

Establishment of the Lutheran Congregation

One cannot fix the exact date on which the Lutheran congregation was established on St. Thomas, but it was sometime in 1666, the first year of the Danish West India and Guinea Company's presence there, and only two years after the Lutheran church in New York was chartered.

The Danish Lutherans had some experience at working with non-Europeans before they began working with blacks in the Danish West Indies. King Frederick IV had arranged for Bartholomew Ziegenbalg and Henry Pluetschau to be sent as Lutheran missionaries to Tranquebar in South India in 1705. Even before that, when the Danes entered the African slave trade in 1659, the Danish West India and Guinea Company hired Danish Lutheran pastors to work at the slave embarkation points on the Gold Coast of Africa. When possible, a pastor was also placed on the slave ships traveling from Africa to the Americas. When, therefore, the Danish Lutherans began working with blacks in the islands, they began that work with some experience.

The first Negro slave of record to be baptized by Lutherans in the Danish West Indies took place in 1713.[1] Shortly after that, in 1718, the second recorded baptisms of a few Negroes took place on St. Thomas.[2]

One of the early baptisms—we don't know exactly when it occurred—had a unique payoff. In 1731, Count Danneskjold-Laurvig, president of the Danish West India Company, went back to Copenhagen for the coronation of King Christian VI. As part of his entourage, the count brought along a baptized slave by the name of Anton (Anthony) Ulrich.[3] At that time, the possession of a baptized slave was a unique status symbol for the aristocracy.

Anton was very much concerned about the spiritual poverty that existed in the Danish West Indies among the slaves. During the festivities that accompanied the coronation, Anton met and talked with Count Nicolai Louis von Zinzendorf, founder of the Moravian Church. Zinzendorf was so impressed with Anton's story that he took Anton to Germany to repeat it for the Moravians. As a result of Anton's efforts, the Moravians launched their first foreign mission. It was in the Danish West Indies in 1732.

What appears to have been the beginning of an organized effort on the part of Lutherans to work with blacks was initiated by pastor Hans Jacob Ottesen Stoud in 1740/41. He started by instructing fifty or more slaves in the evening. In 1741, he asked the Company, his employer, for ministers, teachers, and students to help in this endeavor. He also asked for about three hundred catechisms and Bibles, preferably in Dutch. The reason for requesting Dutch Bibles and catechisms was that the slaves, as you recall, almost universally spoke Dutch Creole, a mixture of the Dutch and African languages. In 1746, three university students arrived from Denmark as government scribes and part-time assistants to pastor Stoud in his school for slaves. We hear nothing more of Stoud's work after the arrival of the students. In 1749, another short-lived attempt was made to work with the slaves by pastor Johan Botzau. His efforts lasted less than half a year.[4]

Systematic and continuous work among the blacks did not begin until after the Danish crown purchased the islands from the Danish West Indies Company in 1750. Frederick V issued some new regulations concerning the slaves. Three of these regulations were very important to the work of the Lutheran state church in the West Indies. First, the king ordered that the Word of God should be preached to the slaves. Second, he ordered that slaves should be instructed in the Christian religion. Third, he ordered that slave children should be baptized like other children.[5] This meant that slaves were to become members of the church. Thus, the Lutheran Church in Denmark for the first time assumed direct control of the Lutheran Church and its ministers in the islands.

In 1756, ten would-be missionaries were sent to the islands from Denmark. They were all university students, none of whom was ordained. According to the instructions given them, they were to prepare the slaves for baptism and turn them over to the pastor of the local Danish congregation for examination and further instruction, after which the slaves would be admitted to church membership.

By 1770, it was clear that this strategy was not working. Very few slaves had been baptized. One of the major problems was language. Before any slave could be admitted to the Lutheran Church, he/she had to receive catechetical instruction in the Danish language, not Dutch Creole.

The missionaries had no choice in the matter; the rules had been laid down in Copenhagen by the College of Church Inspection. Had the missionaries ignored the rules, they would have been dismissed immediately. Neither could they circumvent the local Danish pastor in this matter: final catechetical instruction had to be conducted by the pastor, not the unordained missionary. The local pastor not only had much greater status in the church, he also had a vested interest in maintaining the use of the Danish language.

What helped bring about change was the activity of the Moravian Church. When the Moravians came to the islands in 1732, they immediately began working with the slaves in their own language, Dutch Creole. Almost from the very beginning, the Moravians had considerable success in winning slaves for the Moravian Church. By contrast, you could count the converts to Lutheranism on two hands.

In 1770, the Lutheran College of Church Inspection authorized some changes in the manner in which their work among the slaves was to be conducted. First, they authorized the missionaries to begin instructing the slaves in Dutch Creole rather than in Danish. Second, they authorized the use of Dutch Creole in worship services for the slaves. Third, they authorized the missionaries to establish separate congregations for blacks. Fourth, the missionaries were also authorized to make a number of changes in the worship services for blacks (for example, discontinuance of the use of the traditional chasuble and ruff vestments), as well as changes in the Confessional, the Absolution, the Sunday and holiday texts, and the chants. Fifth and finally, the missionaries were instructed to concentrate their efforts in the towns rather than attempting to work in both the towns and rural areas. (Travel was difficult, and there were too few missionaries to work in both areas.) The decision to concentrate their efforts in the cities was dictated by practical considerations. Ultimately, it had important strategic significance.

The decision of the College of Church Inspection was essentially an attempt to catch up with the Moravians. Like the Moravians, they were going to work in the language of the people. The College of Church Inspection, by directing the missionaries to concentrate their efforts in the towns, in effect, created a healthy division of labor between the two major religious groups working with blacks. The Moravians were, by agreement, restricted to rural areas. The Lutherans were now going to concentrate on the towns.

There was one element of the Moravian strategy which the Lutherans did not duplicate. The Moravian missionaries (they were both male and female) functioned as worker priests. Most were skilled craftspersons from Germany. They lived in much the same conditions and in close proximity with the slaves. In many instances they taught the slaves the skills they themselves had learned in Germany. This strategy, coupled with a good sense of organization and piety, brought them considerable success in working with the slaves.

The decision of the College of Church Inspection did not find all of the missionaries unprepared. Johannes Christian Kingo, as many other Lutherans in Denmark, had been deeply influenced by the pietism that had swept over northern Europe. One of the important tenets of pietism was the individual's knowledge of the Scriptures through his own ability to read them.

In 1764, Kingo had already translated Luther's Small Catechism into Dutch Creole. It should be remembered that Dutch Creole was a spoken language, recently created by the slaves as they were brought out of Africa. Before anything could be translated, Dutch Creole had to be reduced to writing. In order to do that, both a new alphabet and a grammar had to be created, a monumental task.

Kingo was ready. In 1765, he translated the gospel of St. Matthew into Creole. By 1770, the following Creole works had been published: (1) Kingo's translation of Luther's Small Catechism, (2) Kingo's A-B-C Book (a grammar), (3) Wold's hymnal, (4) Wold's A-B-C Book (another grammar), and (5) Magen's Grammar of the Creole Language. In 1827 the Danish Lutherans published their last two items in Creole: Dr. Martin Luther's Small Catechism and an Evangelical Christian Reader for the use of catechists of the Danish mission.

The Growth of the Creole (Black) Congregations

The change in the Lutheran mission strategy brought dramatic results. Between 1771 and 1776, the Creole congregations on the three islands increased their membership to a thousand souls. On the average, approximately 200 souls were added to the Lutheran Church every year. The 1776 report indicates that there was such a run to the Creole services and catechizations that many people had to stand outside the church because of the lack of space inside.

Within five years of the implementation of the new strategy, black Lutherans in the islands outnumbered Danish Lutherans. By the end of the century, the Creole mission congregation on St. Thomas numbered 1,000 confirmed members. The mission congregation at Christiansted (on St. Croix) was almost as large as that on St. Thomas.

There were private schools in the islands, not only for Danes but for some free blacks. In 1787, however, Denmark took a monumental step when, for the first time in history, a government attempted to provide a system of free public education for slaves. Between 1787 and 1798, the government in Copenhagen issued regulations that further facilitated the outreach program of the church to blacks.

Public Education for Slaves. The title of this new regulation was *Instructions for the Schoolmaster or Church Clerk at the Mission in the West Indies.* The schools were to be run in conjunction with the Lutheran congregations. Four free Negroes were appointed school-

masters: two in Christiansted, one in Fredriksted, and one in Charlotte Amalie. (There were more schools and schoolmasters on St.
Croix than on St. Thomas because the slave population on St. Croix
was larger.)

The instructions were as follows. First, Creole was to be the
language of instruction. Second, no child belonging to the mission
congregation or who was expected to become a member of the
congregation could be refused admission. Third, paying pupils from
other congregations might be admitted.

The schools admitted both slave and free children. Since the
schools were to be run in conjunction with the Lutheran congregations and all the churches were located in towns, this meant that
those blacks living in rural areas did not have access to the new
schools. The majority of the black population was still rural.

The Church Clerk. The second set of regulations that came from
Copenhagen concerned the newly-created position of church clerk.
It was new in the sense that, for the first time, this position was
open to blacks. The new black schoolmaster was also to serve as
the church clerk. His duties were to open and close the worship
service with prayer, to lead congregational singing in the absence
of a choir, and to substitute for the minister (in the pastor's absence)
by conducting the service and reading a sermon or delivering a
talk. Depending on the circumstances, he might also have charge
of funerals and the upkeep of the church cemetery.

This particular regulation was another attempt to play catch-up
with the highly successful Moravians. It was an important innovation
in that it had the effect of undergirding the importance and status
of blacks within the church. It also sprang from the presence of
relatively few Danes who could perform these duties.

Prohibition on Importing and Exporting Slaves. The third regulation was a royal decree, effective in 1792, that banned both the
import and export of slaves but did not affect the sale of slaves
within the islands.

This regulation grew out of (1) the debate going on in Denmark
concerning the emancipation of slaves, (2) the somewhat rapidly
increasing number of free blacks in the islands, and (3) the political
and social realities facing Danish nationals in the islands. The Danes
were a numerical minority almost from the day they took control

of the West Indies. By the close of the 18th century, their numerical and potential political position had worsened.

The End of Missionaries to the Blacks

In 1798, the responsibilities of the College of Church Inspection were transferred to the Ministry of Finance in Denmark. With that transfer the work of the Lutheran missions in the islands (that is, the Creole/black missions) was assigned to the pastors alone— meaning that the church in Denmark would no longer be supplying the extra help of the unordained missionaries. Copenhagen did send out catechists now and then, but the basic policy had the result of causing more vacancies and overwork for the pastors as well as a reduction of pastoral care for the congregations.

This regulation, however, did not slow down the growth of the Creole congregations. In Frederiksted, when there was a pastoral vacancy and the minister from Christiansted could not come to conduct worship services, the Creole congregation would meet anyway, led by the church clerk, Michael Samuelsen, a slave. (The Danish congregation at Frederiksted, however, would not hold worship services if the pastor from Christiansted could not be present.)

Until 1793, the Danish congregation at Charlotte Amalia, St. Thomas, had been worshiping in a room at the fort, and the Creole congregation was worshiping in a warehouse. In that year, a new church building was erected. Both congregations used the same building and both had the same pastor. However, each held separate worship services because of the different languages used.

The completion of the new church building at Charlotte Amalia would have been delayed had it not been for the generosity of Mr. Jean Reneau, a free Negro, who loaned the congregation about $2,000. Even though it was a loan, Reneau collected no interest for over 16 years.

The generosity of the black Lutherans was demonstrated in a number of different ways. In 1796, a public collection was taken up in the islands for the victims of the great fire that swept Copenhagen that year. The black Lutherans on St. Thomas collected three times as much money as that collected by the whites, who were the wealthy merchants in the islands.

The Golden Age: 1800–1850

The 19th century began on a sour note so far as the Danish West Indies were concerned. The British occupied the islands briefly during 1801 and again from 1807 to 1814. The British occupation marked an important turning point. During their brief stay, the British made a determined effort to Anglicize the islands. While they did not complete the job, they did establish an irreversible trend.

Notwithstanding British occupation, for the first half of the 19th century St. Thomas was the commercial center of the Antilles, one of the great ports of the world. It was a paradise for fortune hunters. Numerous individuals, including Americans, made huge fortunes there.

There were, however, mounting internal problems. Given the comparatively few Europeans who would stay in the islands, free blacks, over time, had come to constitute the middle class. The continued growth of that class had just about exhausted opportunities for middle-class employment, so that there was growing unrest among free blacks. The restiveness and ferment among free blacks was beginning to infect the slave class.

At the beginning of the 19th century, there were two congregations in each parish, that is, a Danish (white) congregation and a mission (black/Creole) congregation. Each parish had the same pastor and each used the same building, albeit at different times. The pastor was also the supervisor of both the Danish as well as the Creole school. For the most part, the churches paid their own expenses (secured from offerings, money received from church cemeteries, pew rent, and court fines). The Danish State Church in Denmark provided only a minor portion of the churches operating expenses.

There was an anonymous proposal in 1826 to admit free blacks to membership in the Danish congregations. On the face of it, it appeared to be another move in the direction of egalitarianism.

Nothing could be further from the truth. The proposal, which originated in Denmark, had several objectives. In part it was an attempt to deal with the overwhelming numerical majority of blacks in the Lutheran church in the islands. But most of all, it was an attempt to preserve the use of the Danish language and Danish culture, which were clearly in danger of being overwhelmed by

English. One of the important elements of the proposal to admit blacks to the Danish congregations was a language test. Those seeking admission had to be able to speak fluent Danish.[6] The proposal was never adopted.

The following year, 1827, Peter von Scholten was appointed governor general of the islands. He is generally recognized as the emancipator of the slaves, but he did much more than just that. Von Scholten appointed many free blacks to government service. He also initiated the practice of including blacks at official and informal government functions, and he was the first Danish governor to invite blacks to dinner as well as to society balls.

Von Scholten had a black mistress and several children by this woman. She had some wealth in her own right. It is said that von Scholten wanted to marry her, but that was not publicly acceptable. He did live with her quite openly. During his tenure as governor general, she served as the official hostess at most government functions. It is reported that she did so very graciously.

Free Public Education Expanded and Made Compulsory

At first, in 1787, public education was restricted to the towns. In 1839, it was extended to the rural areas and made compulsory. Slave owners and parents could be penalized if the children under their supervision did not show up for school. Because of the cost of expanding the educational system, the Moravians (whose work was mostly in the rural areas) were asked to staff the new system. To make the offer more attractive, it was decreed that all those who converted to Christianity through the schools would have to join either the Lutheran or the Moravian church. Governor general von Scholten was one of those behind this initiative. As he saw it, education was a necessary precursor to the emancipation of the slaves.

When emancipation finally did come, it only affected a minority of the black population because most of them were already free. For example, in the Creole congregation on St. Thomas, during the three-year period prior to the emancipation in 1848, only about one-sixth of the children baptized were not free. One of the reasons that a high proportion of black confirmands during the same period

45

at Christiansted were slaves is that St. Croix had a higher proportion of slaves than did St. Thomas.

Table 1: Free and Unfree Confirmations at the Lutheran Church in Christiansted, 1841–1845

Year	Free	Unfree
1841	28	14
1842	16	23
1843	19	23
1844	14	16
1845	38	38

Source: Jens Larsen, *Virgin Islands Story* (Philadelphia: Fortress Press, 1950), 186.

Transition to the English Language

Even before the British occupation there had been a number of British plantation owners in the islands, especially on St. Croix. They adamantly refused to speak anything but English. During the British occupation, they made a determined effort to Anglicize everything possible. (To this day, the Virgin Islanders drive on the lefthand side of the road.) At the time that the country schools were opened in 1839, English was so widely used that it was adopted as the language of instruction in those schools. The mission congregations, however, did not have official permission to use English in their worship services until 1841. Even with that permission and with the growing use of English in daily life, the Creole congregation on St. Thomas was still conducting worship services in Dutch Creole as late as 1854.

One of the problems in making the transition to the English language in the mission congregations was the lack of religious material in English. In 1857, an American hymnal was adopted for use in the black congregations. It was not until 1872, however, that a fully adequate English hymnal was available with a full roster of liturgical features. It was used in the mission congregations until the islands were transferred to the United States in 1917.

In 1843, it was suggested that the two congregations at St. Thomas (Creole and Danish) merge. The proposal was not adopted. The reasons given for turning down the merger proposal are worth noting. The first was the language problem. Second, the Danes argued that the discipline in the mission (black) congregations was lower than that in the Danish congregations. Third, the Danes were fearful that the merger would inevitably lead to the discontinued use of the Danish language—and that was viewed as disastrous. However, in 1852, the Danish congregation on one of the other islands, St. John, did join the mission congregation. The reason seems clear: there simply were too few Danes on the island to keep a separate Danish congregation going.

The Emancipation

Von Scholten, almost from the day he took office, worked for the emancipation of the slaves. Finally, in the mid-1840s, Copenhagen decided on a gradual approach to emancipation that would cover a twelve-year period. A riot on St. Croix in 1848, however, brought an abrupt change in that timetable. Governor von Scholten concluded that the only way to stop the rioting was to proclaim immediate emancipation. While most of the white leadership in the islands vehemently opposed von Scholten's proclamation, the rioting had been so severe that it was impossible to revoke his actions. Von Scholten was forced to flee the islands in disgrace. He never returned.

Church Growth

At the beginning of the 19th century there were approximately 2,000 black members of the Lutheran Church in the Danish West Indies. In 1835, the combined mission and Danish congregations numbered 6,399. Of that number, 4,000 were free blacks. In the ten-year period from 1826 to 1837, Lutherans consistently had the second largest number of accessions by baptism of any Christian church in the islands (See Table 2). Indicative of that growth was the formation (in 1837) of the first choir on St. Thomas, composed entirely of young black males.

In 1850, there was a total of 6,628 Lutherans on St. Thomas and St. Croix, not counting St. John. The Lutheran Church continued to grow, partly because of a policy change by the Reformed and Moravian Churches. In the early 1860s, both of those church bodies forbade the baptism of children born out of wedlock. The Reformed Church based its new policy on doctrinal grounds, and the Moravian policy was an effort to force people to get married. Both church groups suffered a large drop in membership. when many of the people who were refused baptism turned to the Lutheran Church. Between 1860 and 1880, the Moravians reportedly lost half their membership.

Table 2: Baptisms on St. Thomas for the Years 1828–1837

Year	Lutheran	Catholic	Reformed	Episcopal	Moravian	Hebrew
1828	70	206		33	25	9
1829	72	264	12	41	18	21
1830	78	301	15	33	65	12
1831	73	326	17	38	50	76
1832	55	243	23	33	78	4
1833	67	309	27	36	81	3
1834	81	238	16	37	28	4
1835	54	318	15	38	74	2
1836	81	214	34	30	41	
1837	136	256	31	27	29	
TOTAL	767	2,675	190	338	459	131

Source: Jens Larsen, *Virgin Islands Story* (Philadelphia: Fortress Press, 1950), 153.

The End of the Golden Age

While the Golden Age (economically) of the islands is popularly believed to have lasted until the early 1850s, economic decline had set in by the mid-1830s. Following the company's purchase of St. Croix in 1733, that island became the center of the Danish West Indies economy. It was much more fertile than St. Thomas. Its principle crop was sugar cane. With the development of sugar beets in Europe, the sugar plantations of St. Croix began to decline after 1815. After the middle of the 19th century, with the development of steam sailing vessels, Charlotte Amalia on St. Thomas began to decline as a refueling station. By 1870, the Danish West Indies were caught up in a serious economic depression.

By the late 1880s, the economic depression and poverty were staggering. The infant mortality rate was 50 percent, that is, half of the children died before reaching the age of five. Malaria and yellow fever ravaged the islands. Abortion was widespread. It was reported that as many as 75 percent of the women were single parents. The impact of all this on the island's population was unmistakable. In 1835, the total population of the islands was 43,178. By 1880, the island population was 33,761, a decline of 22 percent in 45 years. Another factor in that population decline was outward migration. Some Danish West Indians were coming to the United States as early as the 1870s (see chapter 9).

The islands' economic problems were intensified by political problems in Denmark, which had come out on the losing side of the Napoleonic War. It had neither the human nor the economic resources to assist the islands. Instead, it attempted to sell the islands to the United States. Beginning in the last quarter of the 19th century, Denmark made five attempts to sell the islands to the U.S.

Social Ministry Programs

Conditions on the islands were so poor that in 1904, with the assistance of the royal family, a social service program was established that was geared to work with pre-school children, sick and neglected school-age children, as well as new mothers. The first facility was located in Fredricksted. It was so effective that a second one was opened in Christiansted. Both of these programs were staffed by deaconesses from the Lutheran Church in Denmark. Given the high maternal mortality rate, a third facility, the Ebenezer Home for Girls, was opened in 1908. It was staffed by Sister Johanna Siversten from Denmark and Sister Emma Francis, the first black deaconess in the islands.

Sister Emma Francis. Emma Francis, born in 1876, was reared on St. Kitts Island. Both her father and oldest brother were Moravian ministers. When Emma finished her course in teacher training at the Moravian college on St. Kitts, she went to the Estridge mission to teach in the parochial school connected with the church where her father served as pastor. Emma was an especially devout person. When she was confirmed at the age of 15, she knew that her life must be dedicated to the Lord's work. After her mother died, Emma went to Germany to begin her training as a missionary. The first part of her training was at Freinwalde, where she studied the Bible. Next she went to the Elizabeth Hospital in Berlin for training in nursing. While in Berlin, she received the "call" to do missionary work in Africa with another student from the Bible House. Those plans fell through when her friend became seriously ill. The mission board of the Moravian Church was embarrassed because of Sister Emma's color. They didn't know what to do with her.

Emma's studies in Europe opened up a whole new world. She not only saw what deaconesses were doing in Germany, it was clear that women (both Protestant and Roman Catholic) managed some of the great European institutions of mercy, even though it was generally held that this was a man's world.

In 1908, Sisters Emma Francis and Johanna Sivertsen opened the Ebenezer Home for Girls at Fredricksted. Sister Sivertsen had very little experience of this type, so most of the planning was in Sister Emma's hands.

After the Danish West Indies were purchased by the United States in 1917, the Lutheran Church in the Virgin Islands was affiliated with the United Lutheran Church in America, and Sister Emma Francis became a member of the ULCA deaconess organization. In 1921, she came to the states and was asked by the mission board of the ULCA to assist in the organization of a black church in Harlem, since large numbers of black Lutherans from the islands had been coming to New York since before the turn of the century. A mission was organized (Transfiguration Lutheran Church), and Sister Emma served as the parish deaconess. She provided the money to make the initial payment on the new building.

In several senses, Sister Emma was an accident as far as the Lutheran Church is concerned. She was initially a committed Moravian headed for missionary service in the Sudan. But for her sex, she would have gone to Africa. But for her race, she might have stayed in Germany.

Sister Edith Prince. Edith Prince, like Emma Francis, was a native of St. Kitts. She was brought to St. Croix by her widowed mother. Shortly after her mother died, Edith Prince was brought to the home for girls and fell under the guidance of Sister Emma. Edith Prince studied to become a deaconess at the ULCA's motherhouse in Philadelphia. After serving for a short period in Harlem, she returned to Fredricksted, where she spent the majority of her professional career.

The training young people received from the deaconesses in the islands was so outstanding that many of them, after leaving the orphanage, went on to become professionals in the island society. In the states, people looked down on those who were raised in an orphanage; in the Virgin Islands, those who were raised by the Lutheran deaconesses speak of it with great pride.

Summary

The Danish West Indies, now the U.S. Virgin Islands, was the first place in the New World where Lutherans pursued an organized and systematic program to bring black people into the church.

Lutherans in the Danish West Indies used a number of different strategies. (1) Until 1740, they opted for a strategy of baptizing those blacks who sought it. (2) The first organized effort to work with blacks was initiated in 1740/41 and lasted approximately four years. The central item of that strategy was the use of the Dutch language. Thirty years before it became official policy, at least one pastor recognized the need to break through the cultural barrier that stifled effective outreach, i.e., abandon the use of the Danish language and use Dutch Creole with blacks. (3) In 1749, Pastor John Botzau initiated another effort that lasted less than half a year. (4) The second organized effort to work with blacks began in 1755. It lasted fifteen years. It failed because blacks had to become culturally Danish before they could become a member of the Lutheran Church. (5) A third organized effort to work with blacks began in 1770 and consisted of the following elements: use of Dutch Creole, the organization of separate black (Creole/mission) congregations, concentrating the outreach program in urban areas, assigning blacks positions of responsibility and authority in carrying out the ministry of the church, a system of free public education for both slave and free persons of color, an effective social ministry program, and finally disbanding the separate mission congregations and integrating all Lutherans in a given parish into one congregation.

The work of the Lutheran Church in making Dutch Creole a written language and its use in the church had important consequences. It was a major factor in uniting black people who came from diverse backgrounds into a common community. It also gave black people a sense of legitimacy and pride as a people.

The system of free public education run by the Lutheran Church was instrumental in helping many slaves gain their freedom and in helping many free blacks gain middle-class status and employment.

One of the towering black personages of Lutheranism in the Virgin Islands to date is Sister Emma Francis, the first black deaconess within the Lutheran Church in the New World.

Given the small number of Danes who ultimately stayed in the Virgin Islands, it is doubtful whether the Lutheran Church would still exist today had they not been successful in winning blacks for the church.

By 1982, the membership of the Lutheran Church in the Virgin Islands totaled 3,600, gathered in seven congregations. Most of the members of the Lutheran Church in the Virgin Islands today are black. In fact, the Virgin Islands have exported more black Lutherans to the continental U.S. than there are blacks remaining in the Virgin Islands.

3

The United States Colonial South, 1717–1781

The third major area where Lutherans settled in the New World was in the U.S. Southern colonies. Virginia and Georgia thus became the fifth and sixth colonies in the continental U.S. in which the Lutheran Church was planted.

This marks an important turning point for black Lutheranism. For one thing, Lutheranism was being introduced into that part of the country where blacks ultimately became most numerous and where black Lutheranism was to predominate for the next two centuries. Second, the kind of slavery that existed in the South was in a number of respects quite different from that which existed in the North. Third, in the following century and a half, Lutherans developed a number of different strategies for working with black people.

Virginia

The first group of Lutherans to settle in the South and form a permanent Lutheran congregation came to Virginia in 1717. They came as indentured servants, bound to serve for eight years. Though only 20 families, about 80 individuals,[1] they were the vanguard of a fairly large number of German Lutherans who migrated from Pennsylvania and the Hudson Valley. By the end of this period (1781), at least seven congregations with approximately one thousand members had been established in the colony. When they first arrived, the colony's total population was 87,000. In 1781, the colony of Virginia had a population of slightly over a half million. In 1720, 30 percent of the colony's population was black; in 1780, 40 percent.

The actions of that first group of Lutherans are not necessarily typical of those who followed. However, they do signal that the South was a different world. In 1734, the Virginia Lutherans at Hebron in

Madison County sent a committee of three individuals to Europe, soliciting funds to build a church and support their pastor. On that mission in Europe, Pastor Stoever, shepherd of the Hebron congregation, published a pamphlet describing his church. One of the reasons for requesting funds from European Lutherans, as Stoever put it, was so that

> every effort [could] be made to lead the heathen, who still walk in darkness, to Christ [and that those who receive the pamphlet should] send contributions across the ocean for the quickening of the poor fellow believers and the conversion of the heathen.[2]

We cannot say with certainty whether Stoever, in his use of the term *heathen,* was referring to native Americans or blacks. He did not have an opportunity to clarify that statement because he died on the return trip from Europe.

The committee returned from Europe with approximately $10,000. Part of the money was used to purchase a 685-acre farm. Some of the money was used to purchase Negro slaves to work the land. In 1743, the church owned seven slaves. By 1748 the church owned nine slaves. This is the earliest evidence we have of the contact that blacks had with the Lutheran Church in colonial Virginia.

It is not clear whether the recipients of that money ever made an effort to lead the heathen to Christ—native American or black—or even thought of trying to convert them. It is clear, however, that they had no compunction about using black people for the economic support of the church. One cannot help but wonder what those Lutherans in Europe would have thought had they known that the money they gave for mission work was actually used to purchase slaves.

The money received from those European Lutherans provided a very comfortable life-style for Stoever's successor, the Rev. Georg Samuel Klug. It was quite similar to the establishment clergy of that time. Muhlenberg was quite critical of it and held Klug at arms length. That life-style, coupled with professional incompetence, was one of the things that led the English Society for the Propagation of the Gospel to become involved in mission work in the colonies.

The record of black Lutheranism in Virginia during this period is quite sparse. There are very few references to black people in the Lutheran Church other than that a few were baptized, given rudimentary instruction, admitted to church services, received as church members, and here or there provided with a special place to sit in the church.

One notable exception to this was the work of the Rev. Jacob Franck who served as the pastor of Hebron church in Madison County from 1775 to 1778. He is said to have taken a lively interest in and given instruction to the Negro slaves.[3]

Georgia

The second organized and systematic effort by Lutherans to evangelize black people in the New World was undertaken by the so-called Georgia Salzburgers in the early 1750s. This was shortly after Lutherans began similar efforts in the Danish West Indies.

The Salzburgers began arriving in Georgia in mid-1734. On January 1, 1735, the trustees of the colony banned the importation of slaves into the colony and prohibited the use of blacks within the colony as slaves. After vigorously opposing the introduction of slavery for a number of years, the Lutherans changed their minds and consented to the legalization of slavery within the colony. The circumstances which led the Salzburgers to work with blacks and the strategy they employed warrant a more detailed examination of how they came to this position.

The Salzburgers' journey to the New World, according to one authority, began as the result of a serious miscalculation.[4] In 1731, the Archbishop of Salzburg, Austria, the religious and political head of state, decided to rid his domain of all heresy.[5] For him, Protestantism was the heresy. He ordered all Protestants either to give up their faith or their homeland. He assumed that there were just a few troublemakers. To his surprise, he found that at least 25 percent of his subjects were ready to give up their native land rather than their faith. It is estimated that between 20-thousand and 30-thousand people were driven from their homes in one of the bloodiest religious persecutions of the 18th century. West Europeans were outraged at the archbishop's actions. After all, this was supposed to be the Age of Enlightenment. West Europeans also found themselves with a monumental refugee problem on their hands.

Two groups quickly came to the aid of the Salzburgers: the London-based Society for the Promotion of Christian Knowledge

(SPCK) and the trustees of the newly chartered colony of Georgia.[6]

There was an important connection between these two groups in the person of the Rev. Frederick Michael Ziegenhagen, the German Lutheran chaplain to the king of England. Ziegenhagen was a member of both the SPCK and the Georgia trustees. The SPCK was intensely interested in the maintenance of Protestantism, not only in England but wherever it got a foothold. The trustees were desperately looking for settlers to send to Georgia. What better candidates for Georgia than these Protestants who had been driven out of Salzburg!

In 1732, Ziegenhagen wrote a letter to Henry Newman, secretary of the SPCK, indicating that the SPCK had already assumed responsibility for aiding the Salzburgers.[7] In 1732 and 1733, the SPCK expended 3,400 English pounds for the support of the Salzburgers. According to G. F. Jones,

> At first, the SPCK's motivation seemed to be pure charity. However, by December 1732, the SPCK made it clear in a letter to Rev. Urlsperger (in Augsburg) that the money they sent him could only be spent on those persons who intended to become citizens of Great Britain (i.e., those who would consent to go to Georgia).[8]

There were all kinds of motives at work here: religious, economic, political. The SPCK together with the trustees were engaged in "hard sell." The SPCK promised the Salzburgers that if they would go to Georgia, the SPCK would pay the salary of a minister to serve their spiritual needs. The trustees not only promised them free transportation but free land, seeds, etc. In fact, the trustees sweetened the offer by giving the Salzburgers more land than was normally given to people already provided with free transportation. The Salzburgers were not unaware of the hazards of the offer, nor were they easily convinced.[9] Only 40 people volunteered to make the first journey. On their way from the continent to Georgia, they stopped off in England for a few days and were given the royal treatment.[10]

Initially, Georgia was a trusteeship, not a crown colony. It was not ruled by the crown but rather was governed by a group of trustees chartered by the English crown and periodically given funds by the English Parliament.

The charter gave the trustees absolute ownership over all land in the colony as well as extensive political authority. . . . The structure of the charter government insulated the trustees from many local Georgia pressures because, unlike the charters of other colonies, the Georgia charter did not require the establishment of a local colonial legislature, and only one trustee, Oglethorpe, lived in Georgia.[11]

As the trustees saw it, Georgia was to be another Pennsylvania, that is, a place for the unemployed and refugees who would farm small plots as did the English yeomen. Georgia was not to be like Carolina, a place of land speculation and slaves. In Georgia, the prohibition against slavery was closely tied to land restrictions.

The Salzburgers came to Georgia in four different "transports," as they were called. The first group arrived in 1734; the last contingent in 1741. With the arrival of the last group of migrants, the Salzburgers numbered slightly over 1,000. Georgia was more Austrian than English. The Salzburgers came as a well-organized theocracy that simultaneously served as a mission outpost of the SPCK and the German Evangelical Lutheran Church.[12]

The Salzburgers' first stop on reaching the New World was Charleston, SC. After a few days rest, they went on to Savannah, established just the year before their arrival. There they met General Oglethorpe, who escorted them to their new settlement, which they promptly named *Ebenezer*. Two years later, they relocated their settlement to obtain better farm land and better access to Savannah.[13]

Ebenezer was about 25 miles northeast of Savannah in what is now Effingham County. A few Salzburgers stayed in Savannah and some settled at Frederica on St. Simon's Island. At its height, the main settlement (Ebenezer) contained 500 inhabitants. These Austrians built a number of churches and schools. The main church, Jerusalem, was built at Ebenezer; Zion was four miles south of Ebenezer; Bethany was five miles northwest of Ebenezer; Goshen was built ten miles south of Ebenezer; and Ascension in Savannah. Ascension, organized in 1741, is still a functioning congregation today.[14] The Salzburgers were thus the first religious organization to build a church in what is now the state of Georgia. They were initially served by two pastors, the Rev. Johann Martin Boltzius (chief pastor and business agent for the community) and the Rev. Israel Gronau.[15] Neither of the two men were from Salzburg.

The Salzburgers' first contact with blacks occurred at Charleston.[16] At that time, there were an estimated 30,000 blacks in Carolina. The Salzburgers were overwhelmed by what they saw. Blacks vastly outnumbered whites. Without extensive contact with blacks or knowing much about their condition as slaves, the Salzburgers began to manifest what in the ghetto today is called "an attitude." As the Salzburgers saw it, the blacks in Carolina "are not faithful to the Christians and are very malicious."[17]

The Salzburgers had more direct contact with blacks when they arrived in Savannah. Fourteen black slaves (Boltzius calls them "servants") were assigned to them for six months to help with the initial task of getting settled at Ebenezer.[18] Technically, the possession of slaves was not illegal at that time. The law prohibiting the use of slaves in the colony was not passed until after they arrived. These were company slaves which the trustees had stationed at Savannah as laborers.

Boltzius quickly learned two things about slaves. First, a slave would steal anything that was not nailed down. Second, many of the slaves would kill themselves if not carefully watched.[19] Perhaps it was naivete, but Boltzius failed to see any connection between slavery and stealing. At that time, thievery was one of the things that made the system of slavery work; not just for the slaves but for the slave owners as well. The "hiring out" system, then in vogue, compelled slaves to steal. As for suicides, which Boltzius condescendingly calls "superstition," it was a desperate attempt for the African to grapple with the meaning of his existence. It was also an act of self-affirmation.[20]

In his complaints about the slaves, Boltzius seems to have forgotten that it was slaves who helped them clear the land. It was slaves who helped erect the shelters over their heads. It was slaves who taught them how to survive in their new environment—what plants were edible, how and where to find them—even how to function in that hot and humid climate.[21]

The Question of Slavery

When the Salzburgers first arrived in Georgia, their opposition to slavery in the colony was beyond doubt. They steadfastly opposed it both on theological and practical grounds. It was their opposition to slavery that made them so appealing to the trustees and General Oglethorpe.

The ink on the colony's charter was hardly dry, however, before the ban on slavery was being challenged. As Jones sees it, the trustees brought this challenge on themselves:

> The reasons for forming the colony were "mixed" if not conflicting. That is, it was a haven for debtors and the unemployed, a refuge for distressed Protestants, a military outpost to fight off the Spanish and the French, and a source of raw material for the industrial needs of Great Britain.[22]

No policy could have been developed to fit those conflicting purposes.

John Vat, a representative of the trustees who brought over the second transport in 1735, in a letter to Henry Newman, made the following comments about the difficulty of agricultural pursuits in that area, obliquely admitting the desirability of slavery:

> I apprehend [that success in farming will be difficult to achieve because it is] observed that in Carolina the Negroes, as the only proper planters ... are made use of, and that whenever white people are employed in that way of working, they die like flies, as being unable to endure [the work] much less the heats of the greatest part of the day in summer time, the clearing [of] such swamps being more difficult and labourious, than the dry land, be it ever so much overrun with large or small wood of any kind. And considering these people [the Salzburgers] were born and bred in high and rocky lands, which are as different from the nature of these here as the day is from night, some knowing people say, it would be better to shoot the people at once than to put them into such a way of planting.[23]

By 1738, opposition to the ban on slavery broke out into the open. One hundred and seventeen of the colony's settlers petitioned the trustees for the right to own slaves.[24] Boltzius, on the other hand, sent a letter in which he asked the trustees to maintain the ban on slavery. Some of the colonists were so dissatisfied with the policy about slavery that they left the colony and settled in Charleston.

Before Boltzius wrote his letter in 1739 urging the trustees to maintain the ban on slavery, he knew that some of the Salzburgers at Ebenezer already had slaves. (At least two years previously, he had seen some "Moors" on one of the settler's farms. In his letters to Urlsperger in Germany, Boltzius consistently refers to slaves as "Moors." The editor of Boltzius' correspondence suggests that, in using the term *Moor,* either Boltzius or Urlsperger was trying to suppress the fact that these were indeed Kiefer's slaves.[25])

The debate about slavery was so heated that

> The whole province dwelt, as it were, on the brink of a volcano, whose intestine fires raged higher and higher threatening at no distant period a desolating eruption.[26]

It was under these explosive circumstances in 1750 that Boltzius finally wrote to the trustees on behalf of the Salzburgers and himself, withdrawing his objection to the introduction of slaves in Georgia.

That was not an easy decision for Boltzius. In fact, it was made with great pain and reluctance. (Keep in mind that he was both chief pastor and business agent for the community.) The issue as he saw it was not, Shall we or shall we not have slavery? Rather, for Boltzius, the issue was, Either permit slavery or preside over the demise of Ebenezer. The Salzburgers were the last to withdraw their objection to the introduction of slavery. Georgia became a slave colony in 1750, and slavery grew rapidly.

Table 3: The Black Population in Colonial Georgia 1740–1780

Year	Black Population	Total Population
1740		2,021
1750	1,000	5,200
1760	3,578	9,578
1770	10,625	23,375
1780	20,831	56,071

Source: Bicentennial Edition, *Historical Statistics of the United States. Colonial Times to 1970.* U.S. Department of Commerce. Rogers C. B. Morton, Secretary. James L. Pate, Assistant Secretary for Economic Affairs (Washington, D.C.: Bureau of the Census. Vincent P. Barabba, Director, 1975), Part 2, 1168.

Having withdrawn his objection to the introduction of slavery, Boltzius was now faced with the question, How do I now justify that which I so vigorously opposed? That justification was ultimately provided by the Rev. Samuel Urlsperger, Boltzius' mentor in Germany. Urlsperger counseled, "If you take slaves in faith, and with the intent of conducting them to Christ, the action will not be a sin, but may prove a benediction."[27] Provided with that rationale, Boltzius was now compelled to reach out to blacks. Thus began the Salzburgers unique experiment of mission work with slaves.

The Salzburgers' New Mission Strategy

Boltzius was an organized, methodical person, not the kind of man to go off half-cocked. If one examines some of the correspondence of that period, it is clear, first of all, where some of the key elements of his strategy came from; and second, that over the years, Boltzius had given some thought to working with non-Europeans. In a letter dated May 19, 1735, Boltzius says,

> If there should be any opportunity to teach Indian children, it is supposed it would be easier to instill the principles of Christian knowledge into their minds than into those of grown [Indian] people.[28]

In a letter that Henry Newman wrote to the Rev. John Wesley, who had just arrived in Savannah on June 8, 1736, Newman says,

> The people of New England seem now convinced after 100 years' experience that the shortest way to instruct the Indians is to teach them English and good manners in order to instruct them in the Christian religion. The adult people will hardly be capable of this but the young of both sexes may by a method of instruction be led into a way that may gradually diffuse the language and common civility among themselves till ... the old wild language may fall into oblivion. [It is hard] to refrain inveterate habits or correct a byass [bias] which nature hath interwoven in their very constitution.[29]

If Boltzius and Newman seem to propose such similar ideas about working with non-Europeans, it should be remembered that Boltzius and Newman were in regular communication with each other. Boltzius regularly sent reports on the progress of the Salzburgers to Newman in London. Newman, as secretary of the SPCK, was responsible for monitoring those reports and seeing to it that Boltzius' salary was paid. It seems most likely, therefore, that Boltzius (who had no experience at working with non-Europeans) was indeed influenced by the SPCK's work with Native Americans in New England. They had been at it for 100 years.

Boltzius decided that the best way to circumvent similar problems was to begin the process of evangelizing blacks by teaching them German and starting the process with the very young—that is, raise and train them as Christians, using the German language from infancy. According to both Weatherford and Muhlenberg, Boltzius began his mission to blacks by first appealing to friends in Germany to provide him with money to purchase young black children directly from slave ships so that he could raise them as Christians.[30]

The church records give us a somewhat more precise picture of what happened at Ebenezer. From 1753 to 1781, the Ebenezer record book indicates that at least 59 young blacks were baptized. During the same period, 9 young blacks were given a Christian burial.[31] Since we do not have the complete record, there may have been additional baptisms and burials.

The first fully-dated and recorded baptism took place in 1757. The record book indicates, however, that at least two baptisms took place before 1757. Catherine, burial #477, was baptized on June 27, 1753 (cf. Appendix). Mary, burial #316, was baptized on December 14th, without the citation of the year in which her baptism took place (Appendix). Given what follows in the record book, Mary could have been baptized no later than 1756.

As far as the record goes, the Salzburgers' mission to blacks reached its peak in the six-year period 1761–1767. More black baptisms were recorded during this period than at any other time: 32 baptisms, or 54 percent of those recorded between 1753 and 1781. The relatively large number of blacks baptized during this period is consistent with the growth of the black population of Georgia during the decade of the 1760s. During this period, the black population of Georgia tripled.[32] It should be noted that all of the recorded burials of blacks took place from 1760 to 1771 (Appendix).

How the Salzburgers' Strategy Worked

Under the Salzburgers, the slaves were given freedom from labor on Sunday and other church festival days. Nothing was required of them that would prevent them from attending any week-day service.[33] Muhlenberg gives some additional information about this experiment at Ebenezer. He indicates that it was somewhat common among the members of the community to bring young Negroes to church and to school. Muhlenberg, who visited Ebenezer on several occasions, also gives somewhat contradictory accounts of the outcome of the Salzburger efforts. On one occasion, he says

> [The Salzburgers] have little success in giving them [blacks] Chris-tianity. [Referring to efforts to teach them to write, he continues,] it is like writing Hebrew text with points and accents on coarse blotting paper.[34]

On another occasion, however, Muhlenberg gives this account of how the experiment was working:

> A devout housefather raised a Negro boy from infancy and had him baptized and instructed so that he was able to read and write well. During the intolerably hot summer months there is never-theless a great deal of work to be done on the land. The master preferred to sit at home in the shade, but the Negro had to work outside in the heat of the sun. He often came into the house and saw his master reading the Bible or other edifying books and praying and writing. The Negro began to do the same thing and wanted to spend half the day in the shade over his devotions; and when the master instructed him from God's Word that one must work if one would eat, he [the Negro] made a wry mouth and declared that that kind of Christianity was not becoming or suitable to him.[35]

The Salzburgers were doing two things which, given the times, were thought to be near revolutionary. They not only actively sought to convert slaves; as part of that effort, they deliberately taught some of their slaves to read and write. One of the provisions of the 1755 Georgia slave code prohibits

> teaching a slave to read or write—an act that elicited a penalty of fifteen pounds sterling. [In fact] . . . the financial penalty for teach-ing a slave [to read and write] was 50 percent greater than that for willfully castrating or cutting off the limb of a slave.[36]

The plan which Boltzius envisioned for evangelizing non-Eu-ropeans was more ambitious than any experiment attempted by 20th century social scientists. It called for the separation of young children from their socio-cultural heritage and their subsequent induction into a new socio-religious world. Theoretically, the plan had some merit. It was bold, imaginative, not to mention radical. It was doomed to failure, however, before it got started. The Salzburgers were trying to pursue fundamentally conflicting goals.

Before looking at the details of the strategy, there remains the question where the young would-be converts came from. Weatherford and Muhlenberg contend that Boltzius purchased young blacks from in-coming slave ships. Jernegan also contends that Boltzius "expressed joy when his first purchase proved to be a Catholic Christian."[37] However, the record of those blacks baptized at Ebenezer shows that all but three were born of black parents who lived within the community. There is no evidence in the record book to suggest that any of those baptized at Ebenezer were purchased from slave ships.

As for the strategy itself, one of its central items consisted of separating young blacks from their evil socio-cultural heritage. That goal was never achieved. In fact, it was the Salzburgers themselves who brought that evil into their community when they brought in the institution of slavery. Additionally, while we do not have extensive information on the child-care arrangements surrounding those young black infants, it is highly unlikely that they were ever isolated from their biological parents. It was the Salzburgers as well as adult slaves who socialized young blacks in their role as slaves. It was the Salzburgers who on the one hand talked about the evils of slavery, but on the other hand imposed the very evil they supposedly wished to do away with.

There is another problem with those infant baptisms. A week-old child is in no position to give or withhold its consent with regard to baptism. Given the absence of any adult black Christian in the community throughout this experiment, it is hardly likely that the biological parents consented to the baptism of their children. One is left with the conclusion that baptism was simply commanded by the slave master, perhaps in the same manner that they commanded slavery itself.

As was initially true of the Danes in the West Indies, the Salzburgers failed to make the necessary distinction between the Gospel and culture. They did not just seek to share the Gospel. Rather, even more than the Danes, they sought to extend the Gospel through the medium of a transplanted Austrian culture. The Salzburgers' highly ethnocentric view of Christianity, coupled with their efforts at cultural conversion, meant that they were attempting to impose a European identity on the would-be black converts. The simultaneous imposition of slavery meant that any black who acceded to the Salzburgers efforts would be forced to live with radically conflicting identities. A black was "European" when in school and church, but a slave when he or she left the church service or laid aside the textbooks. One's identity also changed at certain points in the life cycle. In the 25 years for which records exist, not one black person (even those baptized Christians) was permitted to involve him/herself in a Christian marriage.

What brought the Salzburger experiment to an end was the Revolutionary War. The British occupied Georgia in 1779 and were finally driven out in 1783. During this period, the town of Ebenezer was deserted. When the British left, the SPCK ended its financial support of the Salzburgers. With the last entry in the Ebenezer Record Book in 1781, we hear nothing more of black Lutherans in Georgia until approximately the middle of the 19th century.

Summary

Lutherans began settling in the South almost a century after they had arrived in the northern colonies. Southern Lutherans were massively rural. One of the few exceptions to the pattern of rural settlement was that portion of the Salzburger contingent that remained in Savannah.

In colonial Virginia and Georgia, black Lutheranism (what there was of it) was in reality an extension of slavery. So far as the Salzburgers were concerned, the evangelizing of blacks became their rationalization for the introduction of slavery.

If there is any truth to Jones' assessment, the Salzburgers were the one religious group best positioned to evangelize blacks when Georgia opened its doors to slavery. As Jones puts it, "Of all the settlements made in Georgia during the trustees administration, that of the Salzburgers was by far the most successful."[38]

However, Christianity and all that went with it, at least the Salzburgers' version of it, seems to have had no impact on blacks whatsoever.

The introduction of slavery did have an impact on the Salzburgers. The most noticeable effect of the introduction of slavery was a change in the leadership's morality about slavery. Before the introduction of slavery, there was no question in Boltzius' mind but that slavery was immoral. Yet we find that in 1758, pastor Boltzius' Negro Mary gave birth to a girl named Christine (Appendix, baptism #460). Boltzius became a slave owner. Two of the community's other pastors, Rabenhorst and Lemcke, owned twelve of the 59 slaves baptized between 1753 and 1781.[39] By all accounts, Rabenhorst and Lemcke must have been two of the largest slave holders in the community during the 1760s and 1770s. The sexual immorality of slavery that Boltzius found so offensive took place between Rabenhorst's slave Daniel and Triebner's slave Anna.[40] Pastor Triebner seems to have taken special pride in that event because he notes in the Record Book that Christian Candace, the daughter of Daniel and Anna, was the first heathen child he ever baptized. Both he and his wife were sponsors for Candace. Sexual immorality was not, however, limited to blacks. Onesimus, the son of Hangleiter's female Negro, born December 8, 1764, was a mulatto (Appendix, baptism #670).[41]

The Salzburgers also brought into the community the discontent of the slaves. Both pastor Rabenhorst and his wife almost died at the hands of slaves who tried to poison them. Two of Rabenhorst's slaves got into a disagreement, and the whole affair ended with one killing the other, also by poison.

This first organized, systematic effort by Lutherans to evangelize blacks on the North American continent barely lasted thirty years. The Salzburgers were methodical and punctilious in performing all the ritual obligations of Christianity, i.e., baptisms, instruction, Christian burials, church attendance, even teaching slaves to read and write. Their efforts failed for at least two reasons. First, they were seduced by the political/economic turmoil surrounding the introduction of slavery into the colony. Second, while they performed what were thought to be all the necessary Christian duties in reaching out to the slaves, they were in fact blinded by a highly ethnocentric view of Lutheranism.

4

Surinam, 1791–

Dutch Guiana (now Surinam) and British Guiana (now Guyana) were the first two colonies in South America in which Lutheran congregations were established. Culturally, politically, and religiously, they are not a part of Latin America. They should more legitimately be considered a part of the Caribbean.

Europeans first started settling in Dutch Guiana in significant numbers in 1651, when about 100 English pioneers arrived from Barbados. This new English colony reached the height of its development fifteen years later in 1665 with 40–50 sugar estates, a white population of approximately 1,500, a slave population of 3,000, and 400 Amerindians.

The Dutch took Surinam from the British in 1667. Shortly thereafter it was formally ceded to the Dutch by the Treaty of Breda. The Dutch promptly named the colony Dutch Guiana. The British, however, were not gone for good. They reoccupied Surinam from 1799 to 1802, and again from 1804 to 1816. That action of the British was part of the fallout of the Napoleonic Wars in Europe. The British had no intention of staying in Surinam and made little effort to anglicize it as they had done in the Danish West Indies. During their stay in Surinam, the one major accomplishment—though not entirely successful—was to restrict and finally prohibit the importation of slaves. In spite of that, records from 1818 indicate that 2,500 slaves were being smuggled into the colony annually.[1]

Dutch Guiana reached the height of its prosperity during the middle of the 18th century. Its prosperity was based on the slave-labor production of sugar, coffee, tobacco, lumbering, and cotton.

Initially, only members of the state church (Dutch Reformed) were permitted to become colonists.[2] This proved to be counterproductive. Since the Dutch were noticeably unsuccessful in getting Europeans to migrate to the colony, its population was made up overwhelmingly of African slaves.

From 1667–1800, more than 300,000 slaves were brought to Surinam from Africa. It is estimated that at the height of the colony's prosperity, there were more than 80,000 slaves in Dutch Guiana. Less than one-third of them worked on the plantations. More than 30,000 worked as craftsmen at such trades as carpentry, bricklaying, plumbing, and blacksmithing. The rest were domestics.

> In Pramaribo, the capital of Dutch Guiana, the average family of some standing had at least ten house slaves. There were in 1790, more than 8,000 slaves in [that city's] population of only 2,500 whites.[3]

Life for slaves was most difficult on the plantations. Price describes their condition as follows:

> Those slaves lucky enough not to have to work a full seven-day week nevertheless had to utilize their Sundays to cultivate their own little gardens, if they wanted to eat. Conditions on the sugar and cotton plantations may have been somewhat better than at the logging plantations.

> Like their island [the Dutch Antilles] counterparts, the Dutch Guiana slaves had few human rights to speak of. Marriage did not exist; at a whim of their master couples could be separated, their children sold. Dutch Reformed ministers did not deem it worth their while to proselytize them. The Moravians, who rose to prominence in 1734, performed what little christening was done. An attractive female would become the concubine of the master or overseer as a matter of course, until she became pregnant; after that she was given to another slave to breed her master more slaves. In general the colored offspring were treated better than the blacks and were employed in domestic services. Conditions were also somewhat healthier for the town slaves.[4]

Two conditions contributed to the harshness of slavery in Dutch Guiana. The first was the high rate of absentee ownership of the plantations. The vast majority of the plantations were owned by persons who lived in Holland. Only 20 to 25 percent of the plantations were run by resident owners. Overseers who ran plantations in the absence of resident owners had little taste for country living. Another condition that contributed to the harshness of slavery was the intense speculation in plantations on the part of absentee landlords, who had seriously overpriced their holdings. The huge increases in capital investments in Dutch Guiana did not lead to greater increases in the exportation of cash crops. They rather led to an economic collapse in 1773 when bankers in Holland refused to extend any more credit. With the economic decline, Dutch Guiana progressively became less important to Holland. By 1840, Java was producing 20–30 percent of the total income of metropolitan Holland, whereas Dutch Guiana produced only one and one-half percent of the Dutch GNP.

Between 1668 and 1823, 300,000 to 325,000 slaves were brought into Dutch Guiana. By 1823, the total black population of the colony was only 50,000. During the same period, approximately 450,000 slaves were brought into the North American colonies. By 1825, however, the U.S. had a black population of approximately two million.

> In terms of wasting human life, Surinam appears to have the dubious distinction of standing near one extreme among the major plantation colonies of the new world.

> The large discrepancy between deaths and births of Surinam slaves coupled with the very high rate of importation produced a slave population with an unusually high proportion of Africans at almost every period in its history. During the 60 years following the Dutch takeover in 1667, the number of Africans imported in each ten-year period amounted to between 110 and 220 percent of the total slave population at the beginning of the same period.[5]

Maroon Societies

The high rate at which slaves were imported coupled with the harshness of slave life had long-term consequences for the development of the colony. Suriname was a classic plantation colony. What one author has called "the chronic plague" of plantation colonies were the so-called "maroon societies" that developed in many parts of the New World such as Brazil, Columbia, Cuba, Ecuador, Espanola, Jamaica, and Mexico. In Surinam they are more popularly known as the Bush Negroes. They were created by and consisted of runaway slaves who lived in the interior forests, but close enough to create havoc with the plantations. Surinam is over 90 percent rain forest.

According to one investigator,

Increasingly, scholars are recognizing that maroons and their communities hold a special significance for students of slave societies. For while maroons represented, from one perspective, the antithesis of all that slavery stood for, they were at the same time everywhere an embarrassingly visible part of those systems. Just as the very nature of plantation slavery implied violence and resistance, the wilderness setting of early New World plantations made maroonage and the existence of organized maroon communities a ubiquitous reality. Throughout Afro-America such communities stood out as a heroic challenge to white authority, and as the living proof of the existence of a slave consciousness that refused to be limited by the whites' conception and manipulation of it.[6]

Dutch Guiana was an ideal setting for the development of maroon communities. They became so troublesome that in 1684, Governor van Sommelsdyck abandoned the old strategy of sending out expeditions to subdue them and opened negotiations that led to a policy of the tacit recognition of the free status of the maroons and mutual toleration. The slave owners found the new policy unacceptable. After 50 more years of warfare against the colonial authorities, the three initial maroon communities signed another peace treaty in the 1760s. This still did not bring peace to the colony. In 1770, Governor Nepveu established the Corps of Free Negroes to deal with the maroons and protect the plantations. The Corps was made up of 150 blacks and mulattoes. They too were unable to deal with the maroons effectively. In 1772, the Corps of Black Chasseurs (300 slaves) was organized and trained by the colonial government to fight the maroons—again to no effect.

During the 1800s, additional maroon communities were formed in Dutch Guiana. Even though they developed in relative isolation, they were always dependent on the coastal society for such manufactured items as cloth, pots, axes, and guns.

Today the Bush Negroes in Surinam number about 70,000. Some live on the outskirts of Paramaribo, but the vast majority still make their home in the forest.

Despite the abolition of slavery, Bush Negroes today still oppose the central government, especially the army. Their opposition is based on efforts of the army to control them as well as the historic distrust Bush Negroes have for the Creoles (cf. chapter 1). The Bush Negroes of contemporary Surinam feel that the Creoles were and still are brainwashed by the Europeans and have surrendered to the European ethos. As part of that surrender, the Creoles did not fight colonialism and slavery as they should have. Therefore they are considered inferior and untrustworthy.

For their part, the Creoles look down on the Bush Negroes as primitive, untutored, inept, and inferior. And somewhat in the tradition of Uncle Tom, the Bush Negroes prefer to be thought of as primitive and inept. However, in most encounters between the two groups, including the army, the Bush Negroes emerge as the more effective negotiators and managers of the relationship.

Afro-Surinam Culture

Another consequence of the importation of large numbers of slaves and the harshness of life was the development of a new Afro-American culture in Dutch Guiana.

The Dutch, unlike the French, Spanish, English, and Portuguese, were unable and, clearly at some points, unwilling to share and/or impose either their language or their religion on the colony. This was particularly true with regard to religion during the first century-and-a-half of their control of the colony.

Within twenty years of the founding of Dutch Guiana, that is, by the mid–1680s, creole had become the *lingua franca* of the slaves. That language has been given many different names—e.g., Negro English, Sranan, and Surinaams—but is most commonly known as Taki-Taki. It is an English-based creole.

Price contends that the slaves early developed a unique and distinct Afro-Surinam culture, particularly on the plantations. He refers to this as the creolization of Afro-Surinam life, concluding that its growth was much more rapid and thoroughgoing than in many of the other New World colonies. It also became the base from which all subsequent variants of Afro-Surinamese culture developed.[7]

The evidence of this "complex, integrated, and distinctive" cultural system is more indirect than direct. The new culture was not related to the fact that a number of slaves shared or came from the same cultural groups in Africa. Rather, as Price sees it, it is based more on loyalty to other slaves with whom one shared a common physical and institutional setting in Surinam. The evidence he cites is that

> A specific group of [blacks] will commonly visit, worship with, and exchange specialized ritual information with those Creoles who are precisely the descendants of slaves who lived on the same plantation from which the ancestors of that particular group of [Bush Negroes] fled, over two and a half centuries ago.[8]

The Abolition of Slavery

The first serious blow to the continuation of slavery in Dutch Guiana was unintentional and indirect: the economic decline that set in during 1773. The planters, notwithstanding the decreased need for slaves, saw no alternative to slavery as a workable labor-supply system. But the profitability of slavery declined so much that by 1844, the government recognized that the abolition of slavery was inevitable. It took the planters another decade to face that reality. For the slave owners, the important question was, What sort of compensation would the government give them for their slaves? When abolition finally came in 1863, the Dutch government paid the slave owners 12 million guilders. The slaves got nothing.

Early Evangelization Efforts

When the Dutch took over the colony in 1667, the Dutch Reformed Church was the only officially recognized religious body in the land. It was almost totally indifferent to any kind of mission activity among the slaves. As for the colonists generally, one historian describes them as

> ... raw, poorly educated, given to passion, fighting, adultery and immorality, while meanness, arrogance and stupid pride abounded. They were spoiled by slavery.... It was almost impossible to instill the fear of God in them.[9]

A wealthy young Austrian-German baron named Justinian Ernst von Welz did attempt to share the Gospel with the heathen of Dutch

Guiana between 1664–1668. He was the first Lutheran missionary to work in Surinam. Little is known, however, about where he worked, what he accomplished, or where he is buried.[10]

During the early years of the colony, there was a clearly accepted prohibition against ministering to the black population. In the mid–1750s, the Classis of Amsterdam repeatedly urged the governor of Dutch Guiana to provide the mulattoes and Amerindians with some kind of religious instruction. Indicative of where the church stood at that time are the many complaints the governor's office had received about the unseemly behavior of the local clergy. The mind of the clergy was not on things spiritual. The same was true of the slaveholders. Their treatment of the slaves reached new heights of cruelty by the beginning of the 19th century.

The Moravians

The first Christian group to engage in a systematic and organized program of evangelizing blacks was the Moravian Church. Notwithstanding the prohibition on evangelizing blacks, the Moravians were permitted to begin working with blacks in Dutch Guiana in 1734/35. This permission came as the result of the intervention of a friend of Count Zinzendorf. Formal permission to work with blacks did not mean that the Moravians were welcome. They were harassed by the government and the churches, as well as the plantation owners. One kind of harassment took the form of forcing the Moravians to move from one plantation to another before they could establish a foothold. Despite the harassment, the Moravians did succeed in winning the respect of the Bush Negroes. The government tried to co-opt the Moravians by making them the colony's official agents to work with the Bush Negroes. The Moravians would have none of it, preferring to maintain their credibility with the Bush Negroes.

It was not until 1771, after 36 years, that the Moravians won their first convert. In 1901, the first black Moravian pastor was ordained in Dutch Guiana. By 1989, there were 30 black pastors serving in the Moravian Church in Surinam. Brother John Kent (a Bush Negro) serves as Prexes (Executive Secretary and the highest official) of the Moravian Church today. Part of the effectiveness of the Moravians stems from their decision to work in Taki-Taki. They have translated both the New Testament and the Psalms into that language.

Development of the Lutheran Church in Surinam

The origins of the Lutheran congregation in Dutch Guiana are similar to those of the first Lutheran congregations in New Netherland (New York) and in Guyana, in that all three were initially organized by laymen. A number of Lutherans repeatedly petitioned the colonial government for the right to organize a congregation. At the time, the Dutch Reformed Church was the only Christian group granted the right to so organize. The petition of those Lutheran laymen was turned down partly because of the objections of the local Reformed clergy. Despite government prohibitions, the laymen, like their brothers in New Netherland to the north, held meetings until November 15, 1741, when they were finally granted a charter. One of the conditions of the charter was the obligation of the Lutherans to contribute 600 guilders annually to the Reformed Deaconess Hospital in Paramaribo. A congregation was duly organized and functioned under the jurisdiction of the Consistorium of the Lutheran congregation in Amsterdam, Holland, until 1819.

Lutheranism in Surinam has a unique history. While it has the oldest continuously functioning Lutheran congregation in South America, throughout most of the two and a half centuries of its existence it has been more isolated from the world of Lutheranism than any other New World Lutheran congregation. It did not effectively begin breaking out of that isolation until after the middle of the twentieth century.

This Lutheran congregation in Paramaribo, the capital of Surinam (Dutch Guiana), might also be considered one of the least Lutheran congregations in the New World; some might say it was Lutheran in name only. For some period of time, it was indirectly influenced and controlled by the Dutch Reformed Church. During its early existence, all monies collected by the Lutheran congregation in Paramaribo had to be channeled through the local Reformed Church. Its programs, therefore, were subject to the approval of the Reformed Church. When Reformed clergymen served as pastor of that Lutheran congregation, a not uncommon occurrence, the distribution of Holy Communion was reduced from four to two times a year. In the 1930s and 1940s, under the pastorate of the Rev. D. S. Hoekstra (Reformed), the congregation for most practical purposes ceased to be Lutheran. He did away with the ecumenical

74

creeds as well as the Augsburg Confession. The worship services follow the Reformed emphasis of making the pulpit *the* central element of worship—so much so that one pastor removed the altar from the sanctuary. (When a succeeding pastor tried to replace it, the women of the church took it outside and burned it.) Add to this that from 1820 to 1959 the Lutheran congregation in Paramaribo was under the supervision of the Netherlands Commission for the Affairs of the Protestant Churches in the East and West Indies. Pastors were appointed and paid by that commission, an agency of the Dutch government. (The pastor's salary is still being paid by the government today.) Finally, throughout most of its history until 1960, this congregation in Paramaribo was the only Lutheran church in Surinam.

The Growth of Black Lutheranism in Surinam

When one refers to black people in Surinam, the reference is to three groups: (1) Creoles—those of mixed African, Dutch and/or other ancestry; (2) blacks—those of African ancestry who did not join the Bush Negroes and are largely urban dwellers; and (3) Bush Negroes—those of African ancestry who fled to the forest and for the most part have remained there.

Determining precisely the number of blacks and when they first came into the Lutheran Church in Surinam is a somewhat uncertain task. Church records never differentiate new accessions by ethnicity, ancestry, or social status. The task is further complicated by two fires, one in 1832 and the other in 1980, that destroyed many church records.

Naffier reports that at the end of the great slave revolt in 1765, the Reformed and Lutheran Churches were still not allowed to evangelize African slaves,[11] and slaves and Negroes were still barred from holding membership in the Lutheran Church.[12] Lutherans were finally given permission to baptize slaves and their children in 1791. Adult slaves could also be confirmed on condition that their masters would promise to set them free and that this would be duly reported to the government attorney.[13]

If Dominie King is correct, those blacks most likely to come into the Lutheran Church under such conditions were (1) the offspring of European fathers and African/Creole mothers, and (2) those African/Creoles who were most thoroughly assimilated into European culture. The first Negro to be granted membership in the Lutheran Church at Paramaribo was named Louis. This took place in 1800.[14]

The major dimensions of the strategy Lutherans first used, therefore, were dictated by the colonial government, not the church. Conversion, for all practical purposes, was tied to manumission, so that, ultimately, conversion was in the hands of the slave master, who would have to pay the price. Whether the government was engaged in a not-so-subtle effort at making the work of the church difficult and costly, one cannot say. It can be said, however, that the government was maintaining its position that there would be no slaves in the Christian church.

After 59 years, the Lutheran Church in Dutch Guiana turned a corner. At the beginning of the 19th century, in the face of a worsening of the status of slaves, the pastor of the Lutheran Church, Pastor Koops (whose pastorate lasted from 1793 to 1819) made it his business to minister to the sick and condemned slaves and even married blacks. His efforts led the colonial government to award him special recognition.

Evidence that it was not just Lutherans who had turned a corner came in 1828 when the Lutheran pastor together with other interested parties established the Society for the Promotion of Religious Instruction among the Slaves and other Heathens.

It may have been Paramaribo's entrance into black ministry which led the Lutheran congregation in neighboring Berbice (British Guiana) to write the congregation in Paramaribo

> . . . asking advice concerning whether colored people and Negroes could be members of the church and officers of the vestry. No answer was received, but in 1834 colored people were allowed to become members of the vestry of the congregation in Paramaribo, Surinam.[15]

Before blacks were permitted to serve on the vestry at Paramaribo, the Surinamese Lutherans wrote to the congregation in Berbice asking the same question. The Berbice Lutherans did not respond to that inquiry.

During the pastorate of the Rev. C. M. Moes (1840–1862), a sizeable number of blacks joined the Lutheran church in Paramaribo. Moes was an especially mission-minded pastor.[16] As the president of the ecumenical mission society in Paramaribo, he convinced his own congregation to make regular contributions to the Moravians' work among the Bush Negroes. That support continued through the 1970s.

With some caution, one can estimate the growth of black Lutheranism. Naffier reports that in 1860 there were approximately 300 European members of the Lutheran Church in Paramaribo.[17] A 1909 religious census reported 3,022 Lutherans of all races.[18] Assuming some continued growth in the number of European Lutherans, that is, that their number doubled in the 50–year period 1860–1909, blacks would then constitute 2,400 of the 3,022 Lutherans reported in 1909. This is an extremely conservative estimate given the fact that, after the emancipation of the slaves in 1863, large numbers of the Europeans, some of whom were Lutheran, went back to Holland. We would also estimate that blacks, in all probability, outnumbered European Lutherans in the congregation at Paramaribo as early as 1870.

In 1989, the pastor of the congregation in Paramaribo reported its membership at 3,500; but several hundred of these currently reside in Holland, and another 1,000 are reportedly inactive. There is then an active congregation at Paramaribo today of approximately 2,000, composed overwhelmingly of Creoles—not surprising, given the 1791 decision about working with blacks. Until very recently, most Surinamese reportedly perceived the Lutheran Church in Paramaribo to be primarily for Europeans (of which there are precious few) and light-skinned, upper-class Creoles. This (valid) perception has begun to change.

Surinam seemed set to get its first Creole Lutheran pastor when the Rev. M. J. Hanneman (pastor from 1949 to 1960) convinced Sony Hof, a young member of the congregation to study for the ministry. Hof completed his degree in theology in the Netherlands. He was ready to return to Paramaribo and serve the congregation. However, the church council could not make up its mind to call him. Hof continued his theological studies in Germany where he received the doctorate. In 1989 he was serving as a full professor at the University of Amsterdam and the Lutheran seminary.

The end of Surinamese Lutheranism's isolation began in 1959 when the Dutch government disbanded its commission on Protestant religious affairs. After 130 years the congregation at Paramaribo was now responsible for securing its own pastors. This search ultimately led them to seek membership in the Lutheran World Federation and a working relationship with the Caribbean Lutheran Conference as well as the Lutheran Church in America.

Another sign of change beginning in 1960 was the formation of three mixed (Lutheran/Reformed) parishes. After two and a quarter centuries, there was now more than one Lutheran congregation (albeit mixed) in Surinam. With the formal organization of Bethlehem congregation, the Lutheran Church in Surinam was reorganized and took the name, The Evangelical Lutheran Church in Surinam (or the ELKS). Before this, it was known simply as the Evangelical Lutheran Congregation at Paramaribo.

In 1969, another Creole Lutheran began studying for the ministry at the Moravian Theological Studies Center in Paramaribo. He passed the examination as evangelist (the first stage of study towards entering the ministry) and went to the Netherlands for more advanced study. There he switched his major to social work. He is now back in Surinam working for the government in the interior of Surinam.

When Surinam gained its independence from the Netherlands in 1975, thousands of Surinamese migrated to Holland. Concern about the country's future was intensified by a military coup in 1980, which ousted the democratically elected government. A number of Surinamese again went to Holland, this time in order to maintain their Dutch citizenship as well as access to a number of social welfare benefits. As a consequence of this outward migration, the Lutheran Church in Surinam lost approximately 25 percent of its membership.

The same year that Surinam gained its independence, 1975, the Lutheran Church finally got its first native pastor, the Rev. Leo King, a Creole. Dominie King entered the ministry after retiring at age 63 from a career in social work.

The top priority of the Lutheran Church in Surinam seemed to be achieved when the Lutheran Church in America sent its first missionary to Paramaribo in 1981—the development of a self-sustaining church in Surinam. After a three-year training period, ten lay liturgists and preachers were commissioned. Five Surinamese have begun studying for the parish ministry, one of whom, Miss Lucretia Ommeren, has already been ordained. Dominie Ommeren is currently serving as the pastor of Martin Luther congregation in Paramaribo.

Most of the young people preparing for the Lutheran ministry spend their first two or three years of seminary training at the Moravian seminary in Paramaribo. If they demonstrate that they are capable of doing seminary work there, they are then sent to the United Theological College of the West Indies in Jamaica. They usually do not expect to be ordained until they are about 30 years old.

In 1985 the Rev. Charles Leonard, a black pastor from Philadelphia (LCA), arrived in Surinam to work with the ELKS.

Another major change in the ELKS, beginning in the 1980s, has been the role of women in the church. This is best symbolized by Donimie Ommeren, ordained in 1987, the first female pastor to serve the Lutheran Church in Surinam. Two other Surinamese women are currently studying for the pastoral ministry. The Martin Luther congregation also has a female president. It is taken for granted in the ELKS that a woman may and will hold any position in the church.

The Lutheran Church in Surinam: Its Worship and Programmatic Life

The Lutheran Church in Surinam, its people, and its worship life are sufficiently distinct and unique to warrant comment.

Martin Luther congregation, founded in 1741, is located on a main downtown thoroughfare, Waterkant Straat, across from the city's central market in the heart of the city's business district. The church compound consists of the sanctuary, rebuilt in 1834 after being destroyed by fire; a modern parish house immediately behind the sanctuary, also rebuilt after a fire in 1980; and a housing complex for senior citizens located immediately behind the parish house. During the middle of the week, Waterkant Straat in front of the church is one of the most congested areas in the city, so much so that the brick yard on all four sides of the sanctuary is used as a commercial parking lot. On Sunday morning, Waterkant Straat is one of the most deserted streets in the city.

The sanctuary is a typical 19th-century Dutch Georgian structure. Inside the sanctuary, a huge pulpit dominates one end of the building. At the other end is one of the largest pipe organs in the Caribbean. (The organ was in a warehouse across the street from the church when that structure burned down in 1832.) In front of the pulpit is a very plain altar that almost goes unnoticed. Between the altar and the pulpit are two chairs where the pastor and the liturgist sit. They always face the congregation from behind the altar. On both the left and right sides of the pulpit and altar are three rows of pews facing the pulpit and altar, set aside for officers and deacons of the congregation as well as visiting dignitaries.

The parish house consists of living quarters for the church sexton, who is present at all times to open and close church facilities; two offices; a large meeting hall with a stage; and an open air kitchen.

The housing complex for senior citizens consists of six buildings, all but one of which are one-story structures, containing essentially one-room apartments that house 22 individuals. In the rear of the complex is a larger apartment (built by a couple that intended to spend their retirement there but never did). It is now owned by the congregation and used as office space for the pastor.

Sunday Morning Worship. The sexton opens and readies the church for Sunday morning worship. The position of sexton appears to be hereditary; the present sexton's great-grandfather, grandfather, and father (he proudly tells you) were all sextons at the church.

The worship service begins at nine o'clock with a not-too-formal procession consisting of at least two church officers with the pastor in the middle. When the procession arrives in front of the altar, the pastor turns and shakes hands firmly with each of the church officers. If the church officers accept the pastor's hand, it means that the pastor is functioning with the authority and blessing of the church council. If the officers were to refuse the pastor's hand, it would mean that the pastor is trying to function without their authority and permission.

The order of service (*Orde van de Dienst*) is printed in the bulletin. The hymns are mimeographed in a cooperative hymnal produced by the Lutheran, Moravian, and Reformed Church in Surinam. The service attended by the author was a special family service and included the baptism of three youngsters, preceded by a lively children's sermon and a musical selection by the Sunday school children. After the baptisms, there was a selection by the Diakonea, a gospel choir. One of the teenagers read the Old Testament lesson from the lectern. The liturgist (a seminarian) read the Gospel lesson from behind the altar. Following the sermon, also delivered from behind the altar, the congregation sang a hymn familiar to most American church-goers, *"Jezus mint mig salig Lot,"* ("Jesus Loves Me This I Know"). The church, which seats at least 250, was almost full. The service lasted one and a half hours.

At least 90 percent of those attending the service were Creole, that is, a mixture of African, European, Javanese, and East Indian ancestry. Most have Dutch names. Historically, Creoles have constituted the vast majority of those who joined the Lutheran Church in Paramaribo.

Three or four of the older black (not Creole) females attending the service wore the traditional "talking hats," sometimes referred to as "Let them speak" hats. These hats were part of the old female slave uniform that consisted of the *kottimisse* (a floor-length, wide dress) and the *anjiesa,* (the hat). The hat, made of cotton cloth, is wide in the back and tied in the back with a series of knots. Depending on how the knots were tied, they convey a message of love, a curse, notice of a death, etc. Today, these hats are usually worn by very senior black women when attending church or out on the street. On this particular Sunday, the only women to wear them were residents of the senior citizens complex. Younger women and those who are proud of their Creole heritage usually do not wear them, except on some very festive occasion when one wants to take note of the history of Surinam.

Customarily, shortly after a baptismal service, an open-house or reception is held either at the parents' home or that of a close relative. Before entering the house (usually with a present for the child), most guests remove their shoes. A light meal will be served consisting of a large helping of flavored rice, chicken, a well-seasoned root-vegetable, a salad, punch, and cake. Ordinarily, the child's mother gives each departing guest a small piece of cake to take home.

In addition to the Sunday morning worship service, five of the congregation's more visible programs are the Sunday school, confirmation classes, the Martin Luther Circle, the senior citizens housing program, and the Fonds Kantoor.

Sunday School. Sunday school is usually held on Sunday morning at 10:00 in the parish hall. Approximately 70 pupils are enrolled, and attendance ranges from 35 to 40 pupils. Usually six teachers are present, including an organist. Because the Surinamese love to sing, the singing was hearty, with some hand-motion songs thrown in for good measure. The teachers are well-prepared, no-nonsense, positive persons, who elicit a good deal of participation from the pupils. The teacher who took up the collection went about receiving contributions in the usual straightforward manner of the Dutch. Those who came after the collection had been received were met at the entrance, welcomed, and immediately asked to hand over the money parents had given them for the collection. Several times it seemed as though the teacher in charge of receiving the collection was ready to go into the youngsters' pockets to get their contribution.

Confirmation Instruction. Two confirmation instruction classes for teenagers, with an overlapping membership, meet on Saturday and Monday evenings. Confirmation instruction begins at age 15, the senior year in high school, and lasts for nine months. If all goes well, the students are confirmed on Palm Sunday. If a student does not make satisfactory progress, the pastor does not hesitate to withhold confirmation.

The Prayer Group. The Martin Luther Circle is a prayer group of about 30 women who meet every Wednesday at 6:00. Though not originally intended exclusively for women, women are the only ones who attend the prayer meetings.

Senior Citizen Housing. The housing program for senior citizens was initiated in 1940 and is largely directed at assisting the poor or those who have no family to care for them. It was expanded in 1959. The complex houses 22 individuals, each with his/her own one-room apartment. The complex also includes a recreational center and an apartment for a resident nurse/director. Individuals may live in the complex as long as they are able to care for themselves. A person who becomes bedridden for more than two days must leave the complex. Meetings are held with the residents on Tuesday evenings. Ordinarily, only the women residents attend.

The Burial Society. The Fonds Kantoor is a burial society run by the church. Most Christian churches in Surinam have such a society, much like many U.S. black churches in the late 19th and early 20th century. Most people are enrolled in the burial society when they are very young, and, when they become adults, take over the monthly payments for a cemetery plot in one of the two cemeteries owned by the congregation. The Lutheran Fonds Kantoor is one of the few burial societies in Paramaribo that accepts nonchurch members. On any weekday morning, a steady stream of people comes into the office to make monthly payments. Most funerals are held entirely at the cemetery. The exception is the funeral service for a pastor or church officer who dies while holding office. Such rites are conducted in the church sanctuary.

Table 4: 1989 Membership in the Christian Churches of Surinam

Roman Catholic	80,000
Moravian:	
Blacks/Creoles	36,000
Bush Negroes	9,000
Javanese	3,000
Amerindians	1,500
Chinese	500
Dutch Reformed*	9,000
Lutheran:	
Martin Luther Church	3,500
Bethlehem Church	500
New Nickier	?
Wageningen	?

*The Dutch Reformed Church in Surinam has only one black pastor despite the fact that over 90 percent of its membership is black.

Source: The Rev. John Kent, Prexes of the Surinam Moravian Church, and the Rev. Charles Leonard, pastor of Bethlehem Lutheran Church in Paramaribo.

Summary

The first Lutherans in South America to work with black people were those who organized the Lutheran congregation in Paramaribo, Dutch Guiana. The initial strategy of the church was largely dictated by government policy. That policy led Lutherans in Dutch Guiana to work principally with free Creoles, not slaves or Bush Negroes. The policy has deeply affected the Evangelical Lutheran Church in Surinam for almost two centuries. The ELKS today is over 90 percent Creole, with a sprinkling of blacks, East Indians, a few Chinese and Javanese, and very few Bush Negroes.

In the decade of the 1980s, the ELKS began to move in what is for them a radically new direction: becoming a church for all people and very much open to change, though it was bound by tradition for so much of its history.

Of all Lutheran churches in the New World, the ELKS, more than any other Lutheran body, has gone further in encouraging women to participate in all areas of its life. In 1989, a black woman, Dominie Lucretia Ommeren, was serving as the pastor of the largest black Lutheran congregation in the New World.

5

Guyana, 1818–

Early History

Guyana began in modern history as a collection of three colonies (Berbice, Essequibo, Demerara), another venture of the Dutch East India Company in the New World. The British took these colonies from the Dutch in 1803 and renamed them British Guiana. British Guiana gained its independence from Britain in 1966 and since then has been known as Guyana. Both Guyana and Surinam remained colonial plantation societies much longer than either the United States or the Danish West Indies.

A small group of Lutherans came to the colony while the Dutch still ruled. They formally organized a Lutheran congregation on October 23, 1743, and thus established the second Lutheran congregation in South America. Paradoxically, the Lutheran Church was organized amid a colonial society which, even though predominantly black, was convinced that blacks and slaves should not have the Gospel of Jesus Christ. At the time that the congregation was organized, there were only 200 whites in the colony, a few more slaves, and about 113 estates or plantations. One hundred and thirty years later that attitude almost brought the Lutheran Church in British Guiana to the brink of extinction.

The Lutheran congregation in Berbice (as it was originally titled) was initially located at Fort Nassau, 60 miles up the Berbice River from the present city of New Amsterdam. The organization of that congregation was the work of laymen. At the outset, there was some doubt as to whether the colonial authorities would grant them a charter. In the Netherlands, even though Lutheran congregations were tolerated in cities and towns, they were generally prohibited in rural areas such as Fort Nassau. The laymen were nevertheless encouraged to proceed with their request for a charter inasmuch as one had been granted to Lutherans in the neighboring Dutch colony of Surinam just three years earlier.

When the Lutherans finally received permission to organize, one of the conditions imposed on them was that

> ... all persons who presented free colored children [to the Lutheran Church] for baptism were required to sign an agreement that these children [would] never become a charge to the community or to the public.[1]

That condition imposed on the Lutherans is important in two respects. First, it was tacit recognition that miscegenation was already widespread in the colony and that those European fathers who had children by slave women might possibly bring them to the church for baptism. But more important, it was recognition that miscegenation was the opening wedge for the entrance of black people into the Lutheran Church. Second, "This regulation was the cause of converting the Lutheran community of Berbice into what has aptly been called 'a mutual benefit society.' "[2] One hundred and thirty years later, the consequences of this regulation almost proved to be the downfall of the Lutheran Church in Guyana. At the time that it was first issued, however, it did not signal a change toward general disfavor of evangelizing slaves.

A slave revolt in 1763 went a long way towards hardening the attitude of whites against the slaves. The cause of the slave revolt is revealed in a letter sent by the Bush Negroes of neighboring Surinam to the Berbice colonial authorities who had contacted them to find out what could be done to stop the uprising. The leaders of the Surinam Bush Negroes responded

> We desire to tell your governor and your court that in case they want to raise no new gangs or rebels they ought to take care that the planters keep a more watchful eye over their own property, and not to trust them so frequently in the hands of drunken overseers and managers, who by wrongfully and severely chastising the slaves, debauching their wives and children, neglecting the sick, etc., are the ruin of the colony, and willfully drive to the woods such members of stout active people who by their sweat earn your subsistence without whose hands your colony must drop to nothing; and to whom at last, in this disgraceful manner, you are glad to come and sue for friendship.[3]

What sparked the revolt was the generally accepted policy of absentee landlords and the consequent mismanagement of the plantations. Since Guyana was largely an impenetrable rain forest, Europeans who did live in Guyana were restricted to the coastal area. A dissatisfied slave could easily escape into the jungle—and a number of slaves had done just that and banded together for self-protection. They posed a serious threat to the Europeans on the coastal region.

During the 1763 revolt, slaves were in control of Berbice for over ten months. One of the factors that weighed against the success of the rebellion, however, was the assimilation of the mulattoes into the European way of life. The mulattoes sided with the Europeans. The bitterness generated by that uprising was publicly revealed by a sign posted in front of the Lutheran Church. It read, "Slaves and dogs not allowed."[4] Someone had forgotten that during the burning and pillaging at Fort Nassau, the only property spared was that which belonged to the Lutheran Church.[5]

Following the revolt, Lutherans turned again to the business of building the congregation. In an effort to support their church financially, they petitioned the Dutch East India Company for a grant of 500 acres. They received the land and in 1778 launched what was initially known as Die Kleine Maripaan. At a later date it was called Plantation Augsburg. The principle crop raised on the plantation was coffee. The plantation was worked by slaves owned by the church. Paradoxically, the initial formal relationship that the Lutheran Church had with black people was that of slave-owner and master, not the bearer of the good news of the Gospel.

The British Occupation

The British takeover of the colony in 1803 marked the beginning of a number of changes. By and large, most of the changes were neither abrupt, nor were they revolutionary. In 1812, for example, English became the official language of the colony. The Dutch Lutherans, however, found it difficult to make the transition. The arrival of the British marked the beginning of a decline in Lutheranism in British Guiana.

Another change concerned the religious makeup of the colony. When the British arrived, there were only two churches in the land—

one Lutheran and the other Dutch Reformed. With the British came the Anglican, Scottish, and Congregational Churches, not to mention the London Mission Society. With the exception of the London Mission Society, the attitude of these churches towards evangelizing blacks did not change. It is said that when Anglican prayers were read

> in a small room in the Old Courthouse, Georgetown [which served as the meeting place for the Christians], the black people used to be driven from the door when any of them ventured to look in upon the few—sometimes not more than six—worshippers there assembled.[6]

Most of the European

> ... colonists, who, during their temporary sojourn here as planters, merchants, lawyers, and doctors, all had a common interest in upholding the system of slavery and ... were in no wise interested in the spiritual welfare of the slaves.[7]

Not unexpectedly then, in 1805, when a Wesleyan missionary, on his own, came to the colony to work with Negroes, he was promptly told to leave.

One of the first persons who attempted to evangelize the Negroes with some approval was a representative of the London Mission Society, the Rev. Mr. John Wray. Wray arrived in Georgetown in 1808. His work was made possible because he came at the specific invitation of a Mr. Post, a plantation owner. Even though Mr. Wray had the blessing of Mr. Post, his was not an easy lot. Many whites made it difficult, throwing stones at his church and prohibiting him from entering certain plantations.

Yet another change came, 75 years after the Lutheran congregation was organized, when for the first time some non-Europeans were given membership in the church. The first colored and free blacks to be confirmed and granted membership in the Lutheran Church in British Guiana reportedly took place in 1818. Note that, despite these new accessions, the European Lutherans had not suddenly adopted an open door policy towards all blacks. Indeed, given the events that followed, even these few non-Europeans were not received with overwhelming joy. Those first coloreds and free blacks to gain membership in the Lutheran Church were the offspring of

European fathers and black mothers, entering through the door of miscegenation.

These colored (mulattoes) and free blacks were usually individuals who had been manumitted by their European fathers. It was not uncommon for such fathers to send their offspring to Europe to be educated. The colored also formed the majority of the militia in Berbice. Free women of color were much in demand as concubines, sometimes being brought into the colony from as far away as Barbados. Their scarcity placed them in a favorable bargaining position. The free colored formed a separate class in a society based on color.

The Dutch Lutherans clearly had second thoughts about receiving non-whites as members of the church. In July 1821, the officers of the Lutheran Church at Berbice wrote to the Lutheran congregation in neighboring Paramaribo, Surinam, seeking advice as to whether the colored and the Negroes could indeed be members and officers of the vestry. Their neighbors to the south never responded to that inquiry.

The relationship between blacks and the church was again called into question by the slave revolt of 1823. This uprising was not as serious as the 1763 rebellion, but it did remind the Europeans that slavery was a potentially explosive institution, and it rekindled fears concerning their ability to control the slaves. It also raised suspicions about those who might try to evangelize the slaves. Characteristically, the planters blamed not the institution of slavery but the missionaries for the uprising. They were particularly suspicious of those missionaries sent out by the London Mission Society. They decided that the thing to do was to control the church by making sure that the churches hired only "safe" ministers. The planters did this by dividing the colony into parishes, assigning either an Anglican or Scottish minister to each parish and then controlling both the raising of as well as payment of the minister's salary. Control was the key.[8]

At any rate, following the uprising, there was some semblance of general public approval and support for evangelizing slaves, even if for ulterior motives. By 1825, one Church of Scotland pastor reported that his church, which held about 1,000, could not contain half the blacks who came to worship.[9]

The Dutch Lutherans in British Guiana were not a part of this about-face with regard to evangelizing the slaves. In 1826, when the pastor of the Lutheran Church (the Rev. Mr. Vos) started instructing slaves for church membership, the vestry of his church publicly disapproved of his actions. They harassed the pastor and finally dismissed him in 1829.

The European Lutherans attempted to circumscribe the position of those few blacks who were members of the church. In 1828, nine colored and free black members of the Lutheran congregation wrote to the governor of the colony, explaining that, even though they were duly confirmed members of the church, they had been prevented from attending and voting at a recent congregation meeting. One of the Europeans challenged the blacks, claiming that no colored person had the right to interfere in the affairs of the church. The blacks based their petition on the law that no one in the colony could be barred from voting on public affairs on the basis of his/her physical complexion. In 1830, the governor ruled in favor of the blacks, approving their right to vote on all congregational matters.

The 1830s stand out as a landmark decade in the number of blacks brought into the Lutheran Church in New Amsterdam, British Guiana. At this distance, one cannot say that the governor's ruling had a decisive impact on the European Lutherans. More likely, it was the work of a new pastor, the Rev. Mr. Junius. In any case, during the 1830s, the largest number of blacks to date joined the Lutheran Church. On one day alone (in January 1836), Pastor Junius baptized 47 people, most of them from the Plantation Augsburg, and during that month a total of 188 blacks. In his eleven-year tenure from 1830 to 1841, Pastor Junius baptized 793 persons, almost all of them black.

Given the work of Pastor Junius, the demographics of the colony, and the slow migration of Europeans to British Guiana, by 1841 it was unmistakable that the direction of the Lutheran Church in British Guiana was toward becoming nonwhite. That fact should have been obvious a century earlier when the congregation was first organized.

The Abolition of Slavery

In 1833, the British Parliament passed a bill abolishing slavery throughout the British colonies and also providing for an apprenticeship, all of which was to begin on August 1, 1838. Two additional parts of the emancipation act were, first, government provision of funds for the religious and moral education of the slaves, and second, the reimbursement of slave owners on the average of 114 pounds 11 schillings per slave. The funds for the religious and moral education of the slaves was the beginning of a joint state-church system of education in British Guiana that lasted well past the middle of the 20th century. A number of writers refer to this relationship between the government and various churches as the "period of establishment."

Given the inevitability of emancipation and the fact that they constituted only 3 percent of the total population, the European planters were convinced that the best way to insure their continued domination of the colony lay not just in the evangelization of the ex-slaves but in their education as well. Consequently they voted large sums of money to augment the funds of the British government. So far as the planters were concerned, emancipation would not mean freedom but a change in the instruments and mechanisms of control.

Emancipation provided the Lutheran Church with a financial windfall. Since they held approximately 180 slaves on Plantation Augsburg, they received over 9,000 pounds as their reimbursement at emancipation. This was, to the best of our knowledge, the beginning of the church endowment frequently referred to as The Berbice Lutheran Fund. Forty years later, the mismanagement of this fund led to a decisive change on the part of the Lutheran Church in British Guiana. More immediately, one author argues that this fund was the basis for hiring a teacher at the church.[10]

Given the impending end of slavery in 1838, the British began importing indentured laborers in 1835. The first wave of indentured workers came from Portugal. This was the beginning of the process by which British Guiana became known as the "land of six peoples," a phrase still in common use today. By the end of the 19th century, the British had brought in Chinese, East Indians, and Javanese as indentured laborers. Within half a century, the British, in their drive for cheap labor, succeeded in completely reformulating the population of the colony, creating one of the most heterogeneous populations in the New World (see Table 5).

The British did not just rely on indentured labor to maintain their control after emancipation. They retained part of the old Dutch colonial constitution of which, in the 1840s, one English planter

Table 5: The Population of British Guiana by Race 1891–1960

Race	1891	1911	1921	1931	1946	1960
East Indians	105,000	126,517	124,938	130,540	163,343	267,840
Negroes	115,588	115,846	117,169	124,208	143,385	183,980
Mixed	20,000	30,251	30,587	33,800	37,685	67,189
Portuguese	3,714	2,623	2,722	2,952	3,567	4,074
Portuguese	12,166	10,084	9,175	8,615	8,543	
Other Europeans	4,558	3,937	3,291	2,127	2,480	11,873
All Except Amerindians	261,026	289,140	288,540	302,585	359,379	534,956
Amerindians	7,463	6,901	9,105	8,348	16,322	25,450

Source: Beatty, Appendix VII, p. 133. No explanation is given for two categories for Portuguese. A footnote states, "Figures for 1891ff. are from census returns."

... praised the Dutch for devising a legislative system which effectively kept out the laboring classes. The system included property ownership and annual income level as qualifications for voters.[11]

The attitude and designs of the British were slow to change. When the first full-blooded Afro-Guianian began to campaign for a seat in the colonial legislature in the 1880s, an Anglican minister began a public racial attack against him, asserting

... we owe it to the Negro to think for him, to help him by placing over him trustworthy men, armed with almost feudal authority to enforce such social duties as devolve upon him, and so save him from himself . . . . We legislate as men for men; and so far as men are concerned all is well, but the Negro is a child."[12]

Things were not appreciably better in the church.

The Anglican Bishop at that time was opposed to having "native" ministers, and those who did make their way into the Anglican ministry were placed in remote rural churches, because, the Bishop said, he could not allow them to preach to white congregations.[13]

The Near Demise and Rebirth
of the Lutheran Church

When Pastor Junius ended his ministry in 1841, the Lutheran church at Berbice began a 35-year period of decline. After Junius left the congregation, the Lutheran Consistory in the Netherlands informed the congregation that it would no longer be in correspondence with them. With the brief exception of the services of the Rev. Mr. Riach, a Presbyterian minister, the congregation was without a pastor until 1875.[14]

This prolonged vacancy seems strange because throughout most of this period the congregation was in excellent financial condition. After the Presbyterian minister's departure, the congregation sold its plantation and invested the money in shares of the British Guiana Bank, thus adding to the principle of the already existing endowment fund. One report revealed that "there was a time when the dividends amounted annually to five thousand dollars."[15] Less than half the amount of the annual dividend would have been enough to support a very respectable ministry. Instead, from 1850 to 1875, the congregation permitted the Wesleyans to use both the church and the parsonage and gave them 50 to 100 pounds a year to boot.

After the sale of the plantation, two administrators appointed by the congregation were in charge of managing the congregation's endowment fund. During the long vacancy, the administrators were not only in control of the money, they were accountable to no one. Over the years, they used both the dividends and some of the principal for their own personal purposes. The death of one of the administrators in 1775 brought this matter partly into the open. The surviving administrator attached the deceased administrator's life insurance policy in order to collect the money owed to the church by the deceased. He only succeeded in collecting $15,000 of the $20,000 debt. Once the matter was out in the open, an effort was made to put a good face on the whole arrangement by distributing $5,000 to the 12 surviving members of the congregation.

This led to even more greed and avarice. Some of the members who received part of that $5,000 distribution complained that they had not received their fair share. They took the matter to court, and the court ruled that all the funds either had to be used for the purpose for which they were originally designated, that is, the support of a pastor, or both the money and all church property would have to be turned over to the government.

The congregation decided in favor of supporting a pastor and immediately called on the pastor of the closest Lutheran church for assistance: the Rev. John Sauder, who was serving the Lutheran Church in Paramaribo, Surinam, 500 miles away. The Wesleyans were asked to leave, and pastor Sauder started holding Lutheran services again. However, since he could not continue to serve two congregations 500 miles apart, Pastor Sauder suggested to the congregation at Berbice that they get a local minister to serve them— specifically, the Rev. J. R. Mittelholzer, who had been ordained by the London Mission Society in 1872. The congregation agreed, and Rev. Mittelholzer began conducting the ordinary services almost immediately. In the summer of 1878, the Rev. Mr. Mittelholzer was called and ordained as the pastor of the Lutheran Church in Berbice, British Guiana.

At a later date, when Rev. Mittelholzer sought membership in the East Pennsylvania Synod, he was asked to submit a biography.[16] He mentions only his father's side of the family. His grandfather was a German who came from Switzerland, and he refers to him as a high military official in the Dutch colonial government. He is silent about his maternal ancestors. Others refer to Mittelholzer as a Creole (which can mean any number of things, depending on who the speaker happens to be). The fact is, however, that somewhere along the line, he was of mixed parentage. That was clear to anyone who saw him.[17] Beatty reports that his mother was a native Dutch Creole.[18] In any case, Pastor Mittelholzer turned out to be the first colored pastor of the Lutheran Church in Guyana.

Pastor Mittelholzer reported that the congregation was quite happy in calling him to be their pastor. One of the reasons was that he was "directly descended from the old German colonists, a good connection between the past and the present."[19] There was even a more direct connection. The record book of the Lutheran Church at Berbice indicates that Mittelholzer's brother was baptized there in 1830.

Despite the seemingly good connections, things turned sour for Mittelholzer in 1888. He referred to the ensuing three years as "The Great Persecution."[20] What apparently gave rise to the "persecution" was his request addressed to the administrators that a report of the church's finances be made to the church vestry. The church property was in need of repair and Mittelholzer wanted to know what resources were available. At first the administrators said that they would give the vestry a report. But they kept putting the matter off. Mittelholzer kept asking for a financial report. Nothing was forthcoming because Mittelholzer's request not only meant that the administrators would have to reveal precisely what had happened to the church funds over the past forty years, it also meant that they might lose control of the funds. In an effort to prevent such disclosure, the administrators hired a lawyer and then tried to fire Mittelholzer.

The fat was in the fire. The administrators, long in control, thought that everyone, including Mittelholzer, would cave in. They didn't. Mittelholzer galvanized the congregation. The congregation dismissed the two administrators and got a court order prohibiting the bank from paying out any more of the church's money to the administrators. The administrators retaliated by getting a court order blocking the church's access to their money. The matter was drawn out for three years, finally ending up in the colonial legislature.

The church funds were so thoroughly tied up in litigation that Mittelholzer received no salary for three years. The legislature finally ruled in favor of Mittelholzer and against the old administrators. Mittelholzer admitted that it was a mystery to him how he survived without a salary.

Part of Mittelholzer's strategy in dealing with the recalcitrant administrators led him to seek membership in the East Pennsylvania Synod. In all likelihood, he chose to join that group because

> (1) [it] already had a policy of receiving isolated congregations outside its territory, (2) [it] was among those Lutheran synods making extensive use of the English language, (3) [it] held a doctrinal position considerably more flexible than some in determining who was Lutheran.[21]

The last point was important because the argument used by the displaced administrators to fire Mittelholzer was that he really wasn't a Lutheran minister. The East Pennsylvania Synod had no difficulty in certifying Mittelholzer as Lutheran and as a member of that body in 1890. At the same time it also granted his congregation membership in the synod. Mittelholzer refers to his acceptance into the

East Pennsylvania Synod as the *coup de grace* in his struggle with the dissenters. Equally important, northern Lutherans in the U.S. found themselves formally involved in black ministry.

Mittelholzer was an energetic and resourceful church builder. When he became pastor of the Lutheran congregation at Berbice in 1878, there were 11 communicant members. In 1890, there were 195 communicant members, and just before his death in 1912, there were 378. Between 1878 and 1890, five congregations, sometimes referred to as the River Churches, were added to the roster of Lutheran parishes in British Guiana. One of those River Churches was designed to serve the Amerindians, the indigenous people of the country. Part of the strategy Mittelholzer used to staff the growing number of churches consisted of the extensive use of catechists.[22] In 1892, he was instrumental in renovating the church building at Berbice, at which time its name was changed to the Ebenezer Evangelical Lutheran Congregation at New Amsterdam.[23] While all of this was taking place, Mittelholzer personally conducted a secondary school in New Amsterdam known as the Geneva Academy. Some of the most prominent men of Berbice received their education in that institution.[24]

Mittelholzer's ministry ended in 1913. One commentator sums up his career by suggesting that he established himself as one of the most successful Creoles of the colony.[25] If any individual was responsible for the rebirth of Lutheranism in Guyana as well as leading it out of its colonial mentality, it was Mittelholzer.

Mittelholzer should also be credited with another major accomplishment, that is, starting the Lutheran Church in British Guiana down the road to inclusiveness. When he became pastor of the congregation, all of its members were European. Mittelholzer first brought in black and colored members. He then initiated work among the Amerindians. He also brought the first East Indians into the church. When the Rev. R. J. White ended his ministry at Ebenezer congregation in 1922, he remarked,

> Our congregation in New Amsterdam (Berbice) is made up of blacks, colored and East Indians. The blacks are the descendants of the old-time slave population. The colored are those of mixed blood. And the East Indians are from India. There are no people entirely white connected with the congregation, but there are many who could pass for white should they so desire.[26]

The American Takeover of the Lutheran Church in British Guiana

During the pastorate of Mittelholzer, the Lutheran Church in British Guiana became a vibrant, innovative, self-sufficient entity. Following his death, it slowly became a heavily subsidized mission, subjugated to and firmly controlled by the United Lutheran Church in America.

The transformation began when the vestry of Ebenezer congregation wrote to the East Pennsylvania Synod, informing them of Mittelholzer's death and asking that the Synod send them a pastor. On March 25, 1915, the Board of Foreign Missions of the General Synod "Resolved, that the Board of Foreign Missions hereby take over the New Amsterdam Mission as part of its regular work."[27] That resolution brought about a fundamental change in the Lutheran Church in British Guiana. First, its membership was summarily transferred from the East Pennsylvania Synod to the Board of Foreign Missions. Second, a church that had previously stood on its own financial feet was defined as a mission and placed in a state of dependency. Beatty contends that

> Up to this point, the [Lutheran] church in British Guiana had never received ... any financial support from abroad, and was surely not thinking in terms of any need for subsidy [when they requested a pastor]."[28]

Beatty finds it

> surprising that the Ebenezer vestry, which in the past had so epitomized "Kerkeraad," independent spirit of the traditional Dutch so readily accepted the new situation.[29]

The Board of Foreign Missions, General Synod of the Evangelical Lutheran Church in the United States immediately sent a representative to look over the field. He was followed by a succession of American pastors.

> Consistently for the next quarter of a century the Board handled all its dealing with the church in British Guiana through "the missionary in charge."[30]

The Present Situation: The Church and Education

A state-church system of education (mentioned previously) was initiated in conjunction with the 1838 emancipation of the slaves. At that time the state provided the finances and the churches operated various educational programs, many of which were largely religious in nature.

The Lutheran Church in British Guiana first began receiving government money for educational purposes when Mittelholzer was pastor. While there is some reason to believe that the Lutheran Church in New Amsterdam employed a teacher as early as the 1830s and that Mittelholzer himself operated a private school (the Geneva Academy), evidence of the church's involvement in secular educational programs is much clearer.

The Lutheran Industrial School, dedicated in 1925, was one of the first efforts in British Guiana at training in manual arts and commercial studies. Within the year, the industrial school had enrolled 150 boys. The following year a dormitory was built for those youngsters who lived outside the city of New Amsterdam. The school was finally closed in 1933 because of the depression.

While the date for the initial Guyana organization is not clear, by 1939 the Lutheran Church in British Guiana was operating four primary schools with 122 pupils. In 1944 the church began operating the Modern Educational Institute in Georgetown. This school was closed in 1948. A second high school was also opened in 1944. By 1961 the church had 19 primary schools and one secondary school with a total enrollment of 5,147 pupils.[31] Additionally, the church paid the tuition for a number of high school students as part of its leadership training program. One of the religious weaknesses of this educational endeavor was that most of the teachers in the church schools had little commitment to the church's programs or its beliefs.

Up to 1964, all those Guyanese Lutherans who sought to enter the ministry were trained either in American or Canadian Lutheran seminaries. In 1964 the Lutheran Church in British Guiana was one of the church bodies that came together to form the United Theological College of the West Indies in Jamaica. Since that time, most of those persons in both Guyana and Surinam who seek training for the office of the holy ministry attend the theological college in

Jamaica. Between 1947 and 1957, the Lutheran Church also ran a catechists' training school.

Church Growth

In 1911, shortly before his death, Mittelholzer reported that there were 362 communicant Lutherans in British Guiana. By 1917 that number had dwindled to 238. By 1938 the number had climbed to 415. In 1939 it was 560. By 1940 it was 652.

Lutheranism in British Guiana grew most rapidly during the 1940s (See Table 6). There was very little planning as to where the church ought to establish new missions. It was not until 1938, for example, that a mission was finally established in the capital city of Georgetown. While there was no clear vision as to where they ought to begin work, church workers, many of whom were catechists, were quite clear as to how to proceed. The first step was to open a Sunday school. Once that was established, they started holding worship services. (The Sunday school would continue even if there was little

Table 6: Church Growth, the Lutheran Church in Guyana 1931–1965

| Year | Communicant Membership | Congregations | Parishes | Sunday School | | Pastors | | Catechists | Receipts in Guyana Dollars | |
				Schools	Pupils	Foreign	National		Church Offerings	Board Subsidy
1931	362	6	1	8	567	1	—	4	831	6,942
1935	338	6	1	7	397	1	—	4	723	3,468
1938	415	6	2	7	448	1	2	4	901	6,097
1942	804	12	3	24	988	1	2	—	3,111	16,259
1943	1,023	19	6	27	1,440	2	2	13	3,725	27,047
1945	1,440	27	6	36	1,938	3	2	16	4,872	58,115
1946	1,615	29	6	55	3,010	3	3	17	6,890	57,814
1949	1,657	34	6	62	3,267	3	3	19	13,977	71,342
1953	2,137	40	10	—	—	4	3	26	15,015	123,184
								30	29,999	
1957	2,442	44	11	84	4,782	3	2	29	20,469	176,349
				87	5,189	7				
1961	3,213	49	18	78	4,642	3	7	27	43,250	191,942
										239,170
1965	3,145	52	16	74	3,573	4	6	20	42,289	170,168

Source: Beatty, Appendix V, 132

success in getting worship services started.) After worship services were established, the next step was to organize confirmation classes. When confirmation instruction was completed, a congregation would be organized, at times with as few as four communing members.

The base from which Lutherans worked was the Sunday school. Between 1936 and 1952, the total number of Sunday school pupils rose from 277 to 4,235. Between 1943 and 1953, the increases in the other areas of church organization were:

a 75 percent increase in pastors

a 100 percent increase in catechists

a 110 percent increase in the number of congregations

a 109 percent increase in the number of communing members

a 309 percent increase in local offerings

a 355 percent increase in the amount of the subsidy received from the United States.

> [This] growth of the Lutheran Church was a source of amazement. None of the other Christian Churches of any size were growing [so] rapidly. Almost all had grown rapidly only in the previous century. A Presbyterian missionary pastor remarked, "The other denominations watch the Lutheran explosion with awe and some trepidation, wondering where it will all end."[32]

There were other changes. In 1943 the Lutheran Church in British Guiana celebrated its bicentennial. That same year, it was formally constituted as The Evangelical Lutheran Church in British Guiana. Formally, it was no longer a mission (which it never asked to be), but its authority to administer its own affairs was limited. The foreign mission board in the U.S. retained the right to fill the position of church treasurer. Beatty comments, "The church [in British Guiana] was free to act on its own initiative as long as it acted in a way which the board could accept."[33]

The rapid growth began to wane by the end of the 1950s. Between 1961 and 1965, communing membership, pastors, catechists, local offerings, the number of Sunday schools, and the number of Sunday school pupils all began to decline. The only area of church life that did not show a decline was the number of organized congregations. During this period, they showed a slight increase (See Table 7 for the largest congregations in British Guiana).

Table 7: Communicant Membership of the Largest Congregations of the Lutheran Church in Guyana

Year	Ebenezer New Amsterdam	St. Paul Berbice River	Epiphany Georgetown	Christ Seafield	Transfiguration Canje	St. John Williamsburg	Calvary Georgetown	Redeemer Campbellville	Emanuel Skeldon
1950	404	83	96	79	73	67	37	22	43
1951	346	108	98	92	41	99	37	22	55
1952	267	103	108	95	32	131	44	28	25
1953	327	107	75	47	33	134	47	77	30
1954	331	100	83	52	47	75	65	81	41
1955	335	90	120	52	61	93	80	54	25
1956	385	106	108	54	54	90	88	45	20
1957	472	94	124	43	56	71	85	52	38
1958	408	90	146	65	63	83	101	70	41
1959	401	91	122	47	96	93	108	86	60
1960	446	85	136	37	73	110	160	64	53
1961	514	86	120	64	70	143	166	89	74
1962	410	86	108	67	59	147	146	121	72
1963	438	85	116	57	44	135	146	156	49
1964	442	76	87	50	39	130	151	163	120
1965	420	64	83	46	44	130	193	211	118
1966	392	54	90	85	45	134	240	234	121
1967	424	68	114	43	50	142	262	256	130
1968	406	60	108	45	50	130	274	241	119

Source: Beatty, Appendix VI, 134

Three major events occurred in 1966. First, British Guiana gained its freedom from England and became the nation of Guyana. Second, a new church constitution was adopted that same year, and Lutheranism took the name The Lutheran Church in Guyana. While the Lutheran Church in Guyana is constitutionally free from the control of the Board of World Missions of the LCA (now ELCA), the continuing subsidy from that body enables the mission board to exercise considerable control. Third, Ebenezer congregation became the first parish to achieve full self-support. Along with that, the Lutheran Old Folks' Home was organized in New Amsterdam. This is the first institution of the church, in more than 100 years, to be operated on the basis of local offering without subsidy.

In 1966, when Guyana became independent, racial inclusiveness was still an integral part of the church's life. Beatty comments,

> In a land in which racial divisions and tensions permeate virtually all the structures of society, the Lutheran Church is almost unique in its racial makeup. Except for the Lutheran Church, there is no church or religious group and scarcely any social institution that does not evidence a considerable degree of racial exclusiveness, imbalance, or disharmony. The Lutheran Church is far from ideal in this respect; but it has reached all of the six people of the land, its life is comparatively free from racial disharmony, and its racial balance reflects that of the population.[34]

Inclusiveness has not necessarily led to the indigenization of the Lutheran Church. In fact, inclusiveness may constitute somewhat of a barrier. Currently, the worship forms and organizational life of the Lutheran Church in Guyana are largely transplanted American forms. At the present time, "efforts toward Guyanization on anything more than a superficial level run[s] the risk of attracting [to the church] certain sections of the Guyanese people and alienating others."[35]

Summary

For 135 years (1743–1878), Lutheranism in Guyana can best be described as a private club for European colonials. Until 1878, the Lutheran Church was more opposed to the evangelization of non-Europeans than most of the Christian churches in Guyana.

Lutherans in Guyana used three different strategies in working with the black population: (1) the admission of free blacks and colored people, but insisting that they remain second-class members of the church; (2) the admission of slaves. Both of these strategies were initiated by the pastor of the congregation at New Amsterdam and were generally opposed by the European members of the congregation. (3) With the re-establishment of the congregation in 1875, blacks were admitted on a continuing basis.

A Creole pastor not only succeeded in re-establishing Lutheranism in Guyana, he also initiated the practice of racial inclusiveness. Today, the Lutheran Church in Guyana is the most inclusive of all Lutheran church bodies in the New World.

I I

SLAVERY
AND
EMANCIPATION

For the two centuries before 1783, the most powerful forces that shaped the lives of Africans who were brought to the U.S. were colonialism and slavery. Those forces, in fact, began the process of creating a new people—African Americans.

For this newly emerging people, the Revolutionary War ended neither slavery nor colonialism. The importation of slaves was supposed to end in 1808, but it continued. The United States, now the world's oldest constitutional democracy, came to life as a slave state.

> The American "Revolution" was . . . a movement of political emancipation by a section of the white settlers against control from England. [Because many of its leaders were exposed to the French Enlightenment and used the rhetoric of freedom], the American Revolution [has officially been interpreted] as a democratic, equalitarian, and libertarian movement. . . . [The truth is that to most] whites of the time, [the term] "people" [as it appears in the revolutionary documents] meant "whites." . . . The economic life of the infant republic was so heavily dependent on slavery and the

slave trade that most whites in the North as well as in the South regarded abolitionism as irresponsible and mischievous radicalism, much in the same way that their descendants later anathematized Socialism and Communism.[1]

Black people could not look to the federal government for the amelioration of their burden. Instead they turned to the church. More and more, Christianity became one of the key elements of the emerging African American culture, not always a carbon copy of Euro-American Christianity, but Christianity nevertheless.

The first Great Awakening was the point at which American blacks began joining the Christian church in significant numbers. Not until the Second Great Awakening, however, did blacks begin joining the Lutheran Church in significant numbers.

Part II focuses on black Lutheranism from the close of the Colonial Period in 1774 to the final effort of the Old Lutherans in the South to work with blacks in 1891. Chapter 6 examines black Lutheranism in the South from 1774 to 1865. The beginning of this period overlaps slightly with the efforts of the Salzburgers to work with black people in Georgia, but it represents a new and entirely different endeavor. In chapter 7, the scene shifts to Philadelphia and the first all-black independent Lutheran congregation in the U.S. Part II ends with chapter 8, the aftermath of the emancipation and the growing crisis of black Lutheranism in the South from 1865 to 1891.

6

The Southern Slave States
1774–1865

In the early part of the 18th century, Lutherans began moving into the southern colonies via two routes. One was overland, south from Pennsylvania, following the mountains through the Shenandoah Valley towards the Piedmont of North Carolina. The other route was inland, largely from the sea ports of Savannah and Charleston, following the rivers.[1]

> The two tides met in the mid-eighteenth century just above the present city of Columbia, South Carolina. Their course may still be traced in the locations of Lutheran churches founded there before 1800.[2]

This two-pronged pattern of movement had several consequences. First, "it laid out the geographical boundaries within which the church would develop."[3] Second, this pattern of settlement had social and economic consequences.

> The immigrants had been farmers in Germany, and they naturally preferred to continue as farmers in the southern colonies. This desire for land had forced them to leave Pennsylvania behind, moving on and on to the agricultural frontier. Once they had taken up land, they tended to remain rural, leaving the settlement of towns and villages to others. Their churches were rural, and so they remained. In Virginia, the towns of Winchester and Woodstock are the only county seats where Lutheran congregations are as old as the town. In North Carolina, the only Lutheran church in a town of any size was St. John's, Salisbury. In South Carolina and Georgia, only the port cities of Charleston and Savannah had Lutheran churches before the Revolution.[4]

A Five Point Plan for Evangelization

The initial effort of Lutherans to work with blacks in the South seemed to suggest that the same strategy followed in the northern colonies would be repeated in the South, that is, the emphasis would be on baptisms. Henry Muhlenberg, for example, records two of the earliest black accessions to the Lutheran Church in South Carolina in 1774. The first was the baptism of an adult Negro woman by the Rev. Mr. Tennent in Charleston. The second was a two-year-old boy named Marcus, the son of a Negro woman named Sucky. Sucky was the slave of Joseph and Maria Kimmel (Kuemmel), both members of St. John's Lutheran Church in Charleston.[5] Muhlenberg himself performed the second baptism.

Before southern Lutherans seriously took up the task of evangelizing blacks, they spent a number of years scratching their heads and talking about it. Between 1809 and 1814, the North Carolina Synod (then the only synod in the South, which encompassed most of the Lutheran congregations in South Carolina, Tennessee, Virginia, as well as North Carolina) passed a series of ever more pointed resolutions concerning its work with the black community.

The 1809 resolution states,

Resolved, that pastors have permission, on the wish and pledge of their Christian masters, to baptize their slaves.[6]

The 1810 resolution is stronger and speaks of the responsibility of the Christian slaveholders:

It shall be permitted to every preacher to baptize the children of slaves of all Christian masters, if they, the masters and mistresses, bind themselves to care for the Christian education of such children.[7]

The 1814 resolution refers to the responsibility towards all blacks, not just slaves. In addition, it speaks not just of baptism but of the inclusion of blacks within the local congregation:

Resolved, It is our duty to preach the Gospel to the Negroes, and after proper instruction to admit them to all the means of grace of the church, and for this purpose to make room for them in the churches. That masters are, in love, requested to grant liberty to their slaves for this purpose, and herewith it is placed on record that it is the duty of the master to have them instructed.[8]

Pastors serving congregations in South Carolina appear to have encountered some opposition to these resolutions.[9] The opposition was not so much to the idea of working with blacks as it was to the vagueness of the resolutions—e.g., that the property rights of southern planters would clash with some long-standing principles and practices of the church. The 1809–1814 resolutions of the North Carolina Synod did not resolve those issues. Early in 1815, a group of South Carolina pastors met and came up with a more detailed plan for the church's work with black people. These efforts led to the so-called Five Point Plan for working with blacks which was adopted by the North Carolina Synod in 1817.

Point one of the Five Point Plan contained three elements. Most important, it stated that Negroes, both slave and free, should be "prepared and fitted for full acceptance in our church, according to their situation in society." It appears to leave the door open as to whether blacks should be included in existing congregations or whether some other arrangement might be worked out. This last issue seems to have been left or assigned to the elders of the congregations.

Point two lays on blacks a requirement for admission to the Sacrament of the Altar, which was not required of whites. Blacks were not only required to be instructed before admission to Holy Communion, they were also required to demonstrate by their conduct a desire to lead a holy life. Adult whites who had been instructed and baptized were usually admitted to the Lord's Table immediately.

Point three expands on point two, adding a probationary period before slaves could be communed (and then only at the church where their masters were members). Pastors were given the right to refuse communion to blacks if the pastor was convinced that there was some question about the kind of life a given black was leading. On this last point, it was normally the responsibility of church elders to make such a determination.

Point four places on Christian slaves' parents the obligation of having their children baptized, and for the first time gives blacks the right to serve as sponsors at a baptism.

Point five tackled the thorny problem of slaves being married by the church. The church requires anyone who enters a Christian marriage to remain faithful to his/her partner and never to sever the marital tie. Slaveholders, however, wanted to maintain their right to sell individual slaves as they saw fit. The North Carolina Synod did not succeed in resolving the conflict. They simply required that Christian slaves married by the church remain faithful to each other as long as they were not separated by their master. If they were separated, neither could enter a second marriage without the consent of the minister, master, or mistress. In a less backhanded manner, the Lutheran Church sanctioned the right of a third party (slaveholders) to terminate a Christian marriage without and even against the will of the married parties.

In 1818, the Rev. Gottlieb Schober published a summary of the Five Point Plan in a book popularly referred to in his day simply as "Luther." Whenever a question arose as to how the church should work with black people, they would refer to Schober's "Luther" instead of the 1817 Five Point Plan. Perhaps this was because Schober's "Luther" was more widely disseminated than the synodical plan. Two things are interesting in Schober's summary. One cannot say whether he is articulating the sense of the Five Point Plan or whether he has taken some liberties in his summary. However, he is, first, much more emphatic that the Lutheran Church should work with both free blacks as well as slaves. Second,

> It is the duty of the elders of such congregations among which Negroes are living, as slaves or free, to provide a place for them in our churches; or when that cannot be done to build them a house adjoining or near to the church.[10]

Schober seems to be suggesting that, where necessary, Lutherans do what the Baptists and Methodists did, namely, organize separate churches for blacks. Lutherans in the South never followed Schober's suggestion. Paradoxically, however, they continued to cite him as the authority of what should be done with regard to blacks. Several years later, he made a somewhat similar proposal (as we shall see) to the North Carolina Synod. It is doubtful if any action was ever taken on his proposal.

Most important, for the first time a Lutheran synod expressed itself on the church's responsibility to work with black people. The articulation of its position took eight years, culminating in the issuance of the Five Point Plan. There was not, however, overwhelming unanimity among southern Lutherans about whether and/or how they should evangelize blacks. The upper South (North Carolina,

Tennessee and Virginia) went in one direction. The lower South (South Carolina, Alabama, Georgia, and Mississippi) went about evangelizing blacks using different strategies and at a noticeably different pace.

The Upper South

At the end of the 18th century, 1790 to be exact, German slave-holders in the South were most numerous in the Salisbury district of North Carolina. However, while 30 percent of all families state-wide held slaves in North Carolina, only 12 percent of the German families in North Carolina were slave owners. It has been reported that one Lutheran pastor, Rev. Johann Arends, was the owner of numerous slaves.[11]

Some of the earliest black accessions to the Lutheran Church in the upper South took place at Frieden's Lutheran Church in Gibsonville, North Carolina in 1803, the same year in which the North Carolina Synod was founded.

It was not until after a period of protracted discussion, 1809–1817, that blacks began to appear in the parochial reports of Lutheran congregations in the upper South (see Table 8).

Table 8: Blacks Confirmed and Baptized in the North Carolina and Tennessee Synods, 1819–1824

Year	Baptisms Confirmations
1819	54
1820	40
1821	7
1819–1821	69
1822	55
1823	13
1824	24

Source: Socrates Henkel, *History of the Evangelical Lutheran Tennessee Synod,* (New Market, Virginia: Henkel & Co., 1890).

Table 8 contains the parochial reports from six congregations. Fifty percent of the accessions were in only two congregations. The split in the North Carolina Synod in 1820, which led to the formation of the Tennessee Synod, did not appear to affect the church's work

109

with blacks. Both Synods were made up of congregations in roughly the same geographic area—North Carolina, Virginia, and Tennessee.

While the split in the North Carolina Synod came about because of theological and personal issues, there was throughout the upper South open questioning of the legitimacy of the institution of slavery. During the 1820s, three of the six antislavery leaders in the North Carolina legislature were Germans. Slavery was even less popular in eastern Tennessee. At the third annual convention of the Tennessee Synod in October 1822, a lay delegate by the name of Conrad Keicher asked the question,

> Is slavery to be considered an evil? In reply, the Synod unanimously resolved, that it is to be regarded as a great evil in our land, and it desires the government, if it be possible, to devise some way by which this evil can be removed. Synod also advised every minister to admonish every master to treat his slaves properly, and to exercise his Christian duties towards them.[12]

This was the first time a southern synod made such a pronouncement against slavery. In the end, however, the Tennessee Synod concluded that this was a political issue to be resolved by the government.

In 1822, the Rev. Gottlieb Schober brought the following information to the North Carolina Synod:

> A society of ladies in Salem have constituted and united themselves for the express purpose of supporting missionaries of the brethren among the Negroes, and of forming congregations of them according to their ritual and manner—a question was proposed by the president, whether this synod would give to the brethren's missionaries full privilege, and to invite them to establish Negro congregations according to their own plan, in all its diocese. Resolved, That the ministers of this synod have no objection to the proposal, where the masters of the slaves consent.[13]

What Schober brought to the North Carolina Synod was, in fact, a proposal from the Moravians (he refers to them as "the brethren") to do two things: (1) work with the slaves of Lutheran masters, and (2) form separate black congregations for such slaves (these would be recognized as Moravian churches). Salem (the area around Winston-Salem, North Carolina) had a comparatively large Moravian population. Schober felt somewhat comfortable in bringing this to the North Carolina Synod for two reasons. First, Schober himself had grown up as a Moravian in Salem and still maintained important ties with them, notwithstanding his ordination as a Lutheran minister. Second, Schober was much concerned about the shortage of Lutheran ministers and saw this as one way of evangelizing blacks. What the Moravian Ladies' Society wanted was the right to work among the slaves of Lutheran slaveholders. The North Carolina Synod had no objections as long as the Lutheran masters had no objections.

Blacks are not mentioned in the parochial reports of the North Carolina Synod from 1825 to 1857. In 1858, 11 blacks were reported as communicant members of St. John's Lutheran Church, Mt. Pleasant in Cabarrus County, North Carolina; and even that appears as a footnote to the regular parochial report. The last time blacks were included in the parochial reports of the North Carolina Synod was in 1864, before the end of the Civil War. That year, of the 37 congregations submitting a report, only 3 reported on blacks: 4 infant baptisms, 4 adult baptisms, 6 confirmations, and a total of 6 communicant members.[14]

The 34-year hiatus of reporting on blacks in the North Carolina Synod (1825–1857) does not accurately reflect the efforts of that synod to reach out to blacks. In 1837, the North Carolina Synod adopted the following resolution:

... that congregations have some place provided in each church for the colored people within the bounds of the same, and that part of their sermons be particularly addressed to them.[15]

Clearly, that resolution aimed at more than just inviting blacks to attend church services. One cannot say how representative it was, but when completing its new building in 1859, the members of Friendship Lutheran Church in North Carolina

... voted unanimously that colored [black] people should have seats in the church. Since they voted in that way, it is possible that some colored [black] people are buried in the old cemetery. St. Luke's [Lutheran Church] is not as old as Friendship and some colored [black] people are buried there. Slaves were buried on farms.

Most of the early colored [black] people at Friendship were servants of the Boston and Loppard families.

Brose Boston, a black, was a member of Friendship in 1914. Records show that at several times there were six or eight blacks on the communicant rolls.[16]

The best records we have of black Lutheranism in the upper South come from the Tennessee Synod (see Table 9). Most of the work with blacks reported by the Tennessee Synod was actually conducted in the state of North Carolina where the majority of the Tennessee Synod congregations were located.

Table 9: The Number of Blacks Confirmed and/or Baptized in the Tennessee Synod 1819–1865

Year	Number Baptized
1819–1821	69
1822	32
1823	13
1824	18
1825	19
1826	28
1827	
1828	
1829	205*
1830	
1831	37
1832	41**
1833	17
1834	
1835	41
1836	14
1837	13
1838	42
1839	25
1840	20
1841	
1842	1
1843	2
1844	14
1845	11
1846	
1847	
1848	5
1849	
1850	
1851	5
1852	30
1853	
1854	15

Year	Number Baptized
1855	
1856	24
1857	21
1858	29
1859	65
1860	29
1861	18
1862	8
1863	14
1864	26***
1865	2***

*Total for the decade

**In this year, one of the pastors submitted a report for three years.

***In the years 1864 and 1865, blacks were called "colored," not "slaves."

Source: Socrates Henkel, *History of the Evangelical Lutheran Tennessee Synod* (New Market, Virginia: Henkel & Co., 1890), 53–164.

One writer indicates that the Tennessee Synod " . . . parochial reports . . . are by no means full; perhaps not more than two-thirds were really reported."[17] For the years 1819–1865, the Tennessee Synod officially reported 754 black accessions. The Western Virginia Synod began to include the number of black communicants in its statistical reports in 1859, a practice that was continued until 1869. The number of colored communicants varied from a low of eight to a high of 44.[18]

Given the admitted under-reporting of the Tennessee Synod and the nonreporting of the North Carolina Synod from 1825 to 1857, coupled with the spotty reporting of the Western Virginia Synod, it would not be unreasonable to assume that, during the period under consideration, at least one thousand to fifteen hundred blacks were brought into Lutheran churches in the upper South. If the Tennessee records reveal a pattern of consistency, Lutherans in the upper South were most active in reaching out to blacks between 1820 and 1840.

The Lower South

Lutherans in the lower South were for the most part members of the South Carolina Synod, founded in 1824. The South Carolina Synod consisted of congregations located in Georgia, Alabama, and Mississippi as well as South Carolina. Some of the Lutherans in

Georgia, for example, those in Savannah, were descendants of the Salzburgers who founded Ebenezer.

Lutherans in the lower South developed more diverse strategies for working with blacks than did upper South Lutherans. We shall therefore have to examine the lower South strategies separately.

The Urban Strategy. To the best of our knowledge, Lutherans implemented an urban strategy only in the city of Charleston, South Carolina. Certainly, that is where Lutherans developed the strategy most fully.

There were a number of conditions that made Charleston a special place during the first half of the 19th century. While the kind of slavery imposed on blacks in the United States involved very rigid conditions of life, that rigidity was most strained and vulnerable within the confines of the city.[19]

One of the conditions that began to loosen the control over slaves in the city was the so-called "hiring-out system," a practice which the Salzburgers found in operation when they first landed in Charleston in 1734.[20] Some slave owners found it more profitable to let their slaves find their own employment. Blacks called it "hiring their own time." A slave found his own work and was obliged to give his owner a certain amount of money each week or each month. It was even possible for one slave to employ another. Even though some cities attempted to outlaw this system of employment, it was more profitable than a slave owner going the usual contract route.

> One owner received nearly $1,900 over an eight-year period for a single bondsman, when the prevailing hiring rate ranged around $100 annually, and seldom reached $200. The ledger indicating the $1,900 over the eight-year period of "hiring out" one's own time concludes with the remark: "Dec. 11, 1853. Ran away."[21]

This system of employing slaves created a certain degree of independence, not to mention a new kind of relationship with one's owner. The system became so widespread that some cities created what were really hiring halls where employers and employees (slaves) could come together. Because of the problem of controlling slaves who hired out their own time, some cities instituted a licensing system for such slaves. In 1849, the city of Charleston collected $14,000 from the sale of such licenses.[22]

The hiring out system in turn produced a so-called "living out system." In cities, the usual living arrangement for slaves was within a walled compound behind the slave owner's home. Some slave owners found that they could be relieved of the expense and trouble of housing their slaves by letting those slaves who hired out their own time also find or make their own living arrangements. The 1860 census of Richmond, Virginia reveals that there were over 400 slaves whose owner was unknown.[23] As a result,

> Scattered around the city, in sheds, basements, attics, small houses and single rooms, bondsmen improvised shelter. Never elegant and usually quite shabby, it nevertheless provided a privacy and independence seldom possible at the owner's place.[24]

Cities were also highly favored by free blacks. In the South, approximately one-third of the free black population was to be found in the larger urban centers.[25] From 1790 to 1830, free blacks increased from 8 to 14 percent of the total black population of Charleston (see Table 10). As early as 1790, the free blacks of Charleston began to forge organization, based on color, economic status, and high moral standards.[26] This was the group that possessed the social skills, know-how, and opportunity to provide the black community with leadership.

Table 10: The Slave and Free Colored Population of Charleston, 1790–1848

Year	Slaves	Free Colored
1790	7,684	586
1800	9,819	1,024
1810	11,671	1,472
1820	12,652	1,475
1830	15,354	2,107
1840	14,673	1,558
1848	10,772	1,492

Source: Horace Fitchett, "The Origin and Growth of the Free Negro Population of Charleston, South Carolina," *Journal of Negro History*, Vol. 26, 1941, 435.

The Rev. John Bachman is usually credited with introducing the urban strategy in Charleston. The following communication from Bachman to the vestry of St. John's Church in Charleston would indicate otherwise:

> Gentlemen. Application has been made to me as Pastor of the

Church by Several persons of colour, who wish to be instructed in the doctrines of the Christian Church, and to commune with us. It appears that this has never been done in our Church. I beg leave to ask your advice on this head & Sincerely hope you will cordially unite with me in providing every means in your power to instruct that class of Society in the most important of all duties. Perhaps it would be well to open the Gallery or other parts of the Church to them, on Sunday morning an hour before our regular Service begins. I remain Gentlemen.

Respectfully Yours,
(Signed) John Bachman

4th February 1816

The vestry took the following action:

On motion resolved that the Minister of the Church be empowered to receive, instruct and administer the usual ordinances of the Church to Such persons of Colour as may apply to him and whom he may deem duly qualified to partake of those important rites and ceremonies; and that when he may conceive it expedient, So to administer to them, that he be required to report the Same, together with the names of the parties, to the Vestry at least two days previous thereto; and that all free persons of Colour making Such application be required to produce to the Vestry of the Church the recommendation of at least two respectable white persons, that Such free persons be worthy of the object of Such application, and the Slaves be required to produce the like recommendation from his or her owner or the person having them in charge.[27]

Blacks started joining St. John's Lutheran Church just as its new building was nearing completion. During the first ten years of this new approach there was, on the average, an accession of 10 black converts each year at St. John's. The black communicant membership of St. John's reached an all-time high of 200 in 1845. There was a separate black Sunday school with an enrollment of 150 pupils and an all-black teaching staff of over 30. The black Sunday school was larger than its white counterpart. By 1860, blacks constituted 35 percent of the communicant membership of St. John's church.

The attendance of blacks at the worship services was constantly growing. In 1818 the St. John's vestry had to enlarge the original space set aside for blacks, and again in 1832 and in 1842.[28]

The black members at St. John's were both slave and free. In 1823, the account book at St. John's notes that one Jehu Jones paid his pew rent in January. Jones was a free, independent, black trades-man. His membership as well as that of other free blacks indicates that black members at St. John's were not simply the result of masters bringing their slaves to church. Rather, blacks independently elected to join St. John's, and in doing so, demonstrated their willingness and ability to carry their own weight.

The payment of pew rent raises another issue. There were three kinds of membership at St. John's: First (the lowest level), baptized members; second, confirmed members who were eligible to par-ticipate in the sacrament of Holy Communion; third, those who were members of the church corporation, formally entitled "The Lutheran Church of German Protestants." Those who paid pew rent were members of the third category and were entitled (if they were male and Caucasian) to vote on matters affecting the corporation. An examination of the treasurer's records for the ten year period 1834–1844 indicates that the majority of the blacks who paid pew rent were females.

It was widely recognized that, organizationally, there were in fact two congregations within St. John's—one black and the other white. The Rev. Benjamin Kurtz, editor of *The Lutheran Observer,* wrote of St. John's, "A large colored congregation [exists] in addition to [a] church of white members."[29] In a letter to *The Missionary,* the Rev. J. Bachman, pastor of St. John's Church, said,

> In our churches, the ministers appoint the intelligent, best edu-cated and most pious among the slaves to the superintendence and instruction of their fellow servants, under the name of leaders. These read and expound to them the Bible, and visit them in sickness and in trouble.[30]

Bachman's letter was written at the height of the slavery con-troversy and may reflect a greater concern for impressing the op-ponents of slavery than for factual accuracy. His suggestion that this mode of dual organization was generally operative in other Lutheran congregations is an exaggeration. His inference that only slaves were appointed to the position of "leader," is misleading. Both slaves and free blacks served in the position of leader at St. John's. And his open admission that "slaves [publicly] . . . read" to other slaves is outrageous. Bachman was obviously out to make some points for the continuation of slavery.

The nature of the black organization at St. John's Church in Charleston was as follows: (1) Blacks had their own worship services, generally twice a week; on Sunday morning and on some other midweek evening. "At these meetings, they sing and pray, read the scriptures, and exhort each other to the faithful discharge of their Christian duties."[31] (2) Blacks had their own leaders in the church who were both slave and free. This was a specially recognized position for which there was designated training. (3) Blacks had their own Sunday school and their own Sunday school staff. (4) Black leaders were usually expected to settle the disciplinary problems that arose among the black communicants. (5) Black teams visited the sick. (6) Blacks conducted their own burial services. (7) Blacks had their own societies within the church. One such society was a burial society that had its own cemetery on the northeast side of Charleston, separate from the white cemetery, which was located in back of the church. The black Lutheran cemetery, located on Columbus near Hanover street, is said to have existed at least from 1840 to 1860, and at least 150 bodies were interred there.[32] Another black organization at St. John's was a missionary society, which at times contributed to the Synodical Missionary Society.[33]

The urban strategy conducted at St. John's progressed so well that the president of the South Carolina Synod, the Rev. Stephen A. Mealy, at the 1837 meeting of the Ministerium, held it up as a model to be emulated elsewhere:

> In the Lutheran congregation in this city [Charleston] the instruction of the colored people long since received the attention which its importance demands, and perhaps in no other congregation in our country do the colored members possess greater advantages for obtaining the essential elements of religious knowledge.[34]

As part of that same address, president Mealy added: "It is my deliberate impression that if rightly approached [hundreds of Negroes] would become worthy members of our communion."

What was happening at St. John's was unusual. In 1820, while still a member of the North Carolina Synod, the Rev. Mitze

> ... complained in an address to [the] synod, that he is prevented

from administering the Lord's Supper because he admits Negroes thereto, and baptizes them; he prays for a resolution to be made which is to be read in all our churches. But as the rule respecting Negroes admission to our church as contained in the book called Luther from page 167 appear plain, they can be read in the churches where necessary.[35]

With the exception of St. John's in Charleston, most of the Lutheran churches in the lower South were a bit slow to work with blacks until the early part of the 1840s. Twenty-nine blacks were baptized at St. John's in 1829, whereas only nine blacks were baptized in all the other congregations of the South Carolina Synod. In 1830, 40 blacks were baptized at St. John's Church, whereas only six blacks were baptized in the other Lutheran churches of the lower South. Again, 44 blacks were baptized at St. John's in 1835, while only 19 blacks were baptized in the rest of the synod.

In 1845, the Lutheran Church at Sandy Run, South Carolina with 20 black members is referred to as typical of the number of blacks belonging to the Lutheran churches in the South Carolina Synod.[36] By 1849, the Rev. P. A. Strobel reported that all but six of the South Carolina Synod's 43 congregations contained Negro as well as white members.[37] Strobel's report is inconsistent with the summary of the parochial reports of the South Carolina Synod for 1849. Of the 47 congregations submitting a report that year, less than one-third report either baptizing or having blacks as communicant members.

If 1816–1825 were years of rapid growth in the number of black members at St. John's, then the years 1832–1845 are of monumental significance in the history of North American Lutheranism. During that period, the black Lutherans at St. John's Church made two attempts to send a missionary to Africa. Although the first attempt failed, they succeeded on the second attempt—and thus became the first group of Lutherans (black or white) to send an American missionary to Africa.

What undoubtedly stirred the hearts of black people about mission work in Africa were the increasingly harsh conditions in the South following the Denmark Vessy and Nat Turner rebellions, together with the growing colonization movement. One source indicates that in 1832, 146 blacks left the city of Charleston for Liberia.[38] Strobel puts the figure at about 250.[39]

The first attempt to send a missionary to Africa (which failed) took place in 1832. The prospective candidate was Mr. Jehu Jones, a black tailor who had been a member of St. John's, Charleston, since at least 1823. Jones went to New York City where he was ordained by those members of the Lutheran Ministerium still in the city after the adjournment of their regular meeting. Thus, Jehu Jones has the distinction of being the first black man to be ordained as a Lutheran minister in the U.S. After ordination, Jones returned to Charleston to gather up his family. Upon returning, he ran afoul of the Negro Seaman's Act, which mandated that any free black could be sold into slavery if he entered or re-entered Charleston once he had departed.[40]

Jones managed to make a hasty departure back to New York, leaving his family behind. While there, he attempted to enlist the aid of the American Board of Commissioners for Foreign Missions for his Africa mission.[41] They referred him elsewhere. In September 1833, Jones met with the Lutheran Ministerium of New York, seeking their aid. Their inaction brought to an end the first attempt at sending a missionary to Africa. (However, we shall hear more about Jehu Jones in chapter 7.)

Between the first and second effort to send a missionary to Africa, Daniel Alexander Payne became the first black to enroll in a Lutheran seminary and the second black person to be ordained by Lutherans (though it should be noted that Payne was never a Lutheran and initially did not want to become a minister, least of all a Lutheran minister).

Payne's first love was teaching. In 1829, at the age of 18, he organized what eventually became the largest school for blacks in the city of Charleston. In 1834, his school closed because of the newly enacted laws which would not permit black people to operate or teach in their own schools. Through Payne's contacts with the Rev. J. Bachman (in Charleston) and the Rev. Strobel (in New York), he enrolled at Gettysburg Seminary in 1835. Payne made it clear to everyone, including president Schmucker at Gettysburg, that he would enter the seminary on two conditions: first, that he would not have to embrace the teachings of the Lutheran Church (Payne was a Methodist from his youth), and second, that he would not be trained for African colonization.[42] His conditions were acceptable to everyone.

During his second year at Gettysburg, Payne "got the call" to enter the ministry. However, illness prevented him from completing his seminary training. In June 1837, he was licensed to preach by the Franckean Synod and ordained by that group in 1839. The Franckean Synod was a small Lutheran group in New York that had taken a strong antislavery stand.

The Franckean Synod wanted to send Payne to the West Indies, but nothing ever came of those plans. Though Payne was licensed and ordained by Lutherans, he never served a Lutheran congregation and hence should not be considered a Lutheran. Instead, in 1841, he became a member of the African Methodist Episcopal Church and went on to become (1) one of that church's outstanding bishops, (2) that church's leading advocate of a well-trained clergy, and (3) the founder and president of Wilberforce University in Ohio. While not claiming Payne as one of its own, the Lutheran Church did play an important role in helping him discover his call into the ministry as well as training him for that work.

The black members of St. John's in Charleston did not give up their dream of sending a missionary to Africa. In 1845, they found another candidate in Boston J. Drayton, a black man who had served in a leadership position at the church for several years. The president of the South Carolina Synod reported that Drayton had sought and received permission to go to Africa as a missionary of the Lutheran Church. Drayton received his credentials and thus became the third black man to be ordained by the Lutheran Church in the U.S. and the second hope for a black missionary to Africa.

The pastor of St. John's acknowledges that the mission to Africa was supported almost exclusively by blacks. What is strange is the pastor's apparent coolness toward the whole project; he neither supported nor opposed it. Even though the South Carolina Synod had a flourishing foreign mission society, nowhere in its minutes does it acknowledge or indicate support for the Africa mission.[43]

In November 1845, Drayton set sail for the colony of Maryland, located immediately southeast of Liberia. He wrote back to the states,

> I have been blessed by the Lord to find a field of labor not in competition with any others, that the Lord has reserved for us. The governor has told me that I can have as much land as I want to build on in the name of the Lutheran Church of America. I will begin a school. . . . I will build it large enough that it may be used

as a church. We shall call it the Lutheran Missionary School.[44]

Drayton did not fare well as a missionary, partly because of the hostility of the indigenous peoples. Very shortly, he gave up his work as a missionary to become governor of the colony, which eventually was annexed by Liberia in 1857. After annexation, Drayton became the Chief Justice of the Liberian Supreme Court. He died in 1866 in a drowning accident. Although his career as a missionary was short-lived, Drayton has the distinction of being the first colored missionary sent to Africa by the Lutheran Church in North America.

Notwithstanding the major role it had in shaping the 1817 Five Point Plan and the efforts at St. John's Church in Charleston, Lutherans in the lower South initially were not very aggressive in reaching out to black people. Except for the work being done at St. John's, by 1835 less than one black convert a year on the average was being taken into each of the Lutheran congregations in the lower South. Strobel, writing in the mid–1840s says that except for St. John's, few congregations in the South Carolina Synod took much interest in blacks.

The major event that pushed the lower South away from its policy of benign neglect regarding blacks to a more active stance was the growing abolitionist movement. Lutherans—North and South—had officially taken the position that the institution of slavery was a political, not an ecclesiastical, issue. However, abolitionist rhetoric grew so heated that the South Carolina Synod finally spoke out at its 1835 convention:

> Whereas individuals and Societies of the North, calling themselves abolitionists, under the pretence of ameliorating the conditions of our servants, have created an excitement deeply affecting our interests, and calculated to sever the bonds of attachment which exist between master and slave; and whereas this unjustifiable interference with our domestic institution is opposed to the Constitution of our common country, is subversive of our liberties as men and contrary to the precepts of our blessed saviour, who commanded servants to be obedient to their masters, and the example of the holy Apostle Paul, who restored to his lawful owner a runaway slave; therefore:
>
> 1. *Resolved,* unanimously, that this Synod express their strongest disapprobation of the conduct of the Northern Abolitionists— and that we look upon them as the enemies of our beloved

country; whose mistaken zeal is calculated to injure the cause of morals and religion.

2. *Resolved,* that we will hold no correspondence with the Northern Abolitionists, and that should they send to us any of their incendiary publications, we will immediately return them.

A third resolution expressed appreciation for the fact that no Lutheran ministers were associated with abolitionism, and warned that South Carolina Lutherans would never "countenance such doctrines."[45]

On the other hand, two years later, in 1837, the Franckean Synod spoke out vigorously against slavery on moral grounds and took the position that they would not have fellowship with any Lutheran who favored slavery.

Following its proslavery pronouncement of 1835, the South Carolina Synod recognized that resolutions were not enough. They joined with other southerners and adopted the position that the best way to refute the abolitionists was to evangelize the slaves aggressively. The question was how to do it.

Although Lutherans spoke glowingly for over two decades of the urban strategy at Charleston, they did not duplicate it elsewhere. Rather, Lutherans in the lower South settled on a two-pronged approach to blacks.

The Master-Slave Strategy. The adoption of this strategy meant that they were going to work seriously at the Five Point Plan (at that point 20 years old). The best way to work with blacks (as they saw it) was through Lutheran slave owners. Slaves would be included in the same congregation as their masters because the establishment of separate all-black congregations was seen as a threat to "domestic tranquility." One Lutheran minister in the lower South took a contrary position. The Rev. Jacob Crim suggested that "his experience led him to believe that a ministry among the slaves could probably be carried out more effectively by Baptists than by Lutherans."[46]

The Plantation Missionary Strategy. The third approach to evangelizing blacks was to implement a strategy used by other denominations in South Carolina, that is, the so-called plantation mission or chapel, where plantation slaves would assemble under the supervision of a special missionary (actually, an itinerant preacher). This was a departure from the Five Point Plan in that the plantation missionary would not direct his efforts towards the slaves of Lutheran masters. Rather, his efforts would be directed towards very rural areas where there were large plantations with no local Lutheran congregation.

The plantation missionary strategy was implemented immediately. A missionary was first hired in 1837 on an experimental basis for one month. The record indicates that he was still at work the following year. He continued to report to the South Carolina Synod until 1859. In that year, the synod's secretary reported that the plantation missionary's work was so blessed "that the field is too large for a single laborer to occupy to advantage and [he] urges us to send at least one more laborer into this inviting field."[47] His work, however, was not limited to blacks. He was equally involved with whites.

The master-slave strategy was implemented slowly. It did not produce noticeable results until the late 1840s. By 1849, one third of the South Carolina Synod's growth came from black accessions, and blacks constituted one-sixth of the synod's total membership.[48]

In 1852, the president of the South Carolina Synod, while exhorting the church to further work among the slaves, said,

> In many churches, the room designed for the accommodation of our colored population is not sufficiently large, that when they come to church they can gain a place within to hear the word.[49]

While blacks were initially included in the same congregation with whites, there appeared to be a need to modify this approach. In the same address cited above, the speaker advised pastors to

> ... meet [the slaves] occasionally apart from the whites, with only the elders or a few citizens present, and preach to, or exhort them, in a plain and simple manner ... [and] give oral catechetical instruction to all, both old and young.[50]

At the 1858 convention of the South Carolina Synod, the president suggested that pastors go somewhat further in special efforts to work with blacks:

> While the colored population in our community enjoy the privilege of attending upon the means of grace in connection with their owners, would it not be more encouraging to them, if their respective pastors would, as often as time and other circumstances

would admit, hold special services for them, and adapt their language and discourses to their capacities; and in addition thereto, give oral catechetical instruction to their children? In my opinion, such a course would be attended with the most happy results.[51]

As a result, the convention passed a resolution making it the duty of pastors to hold special services for blacks. At the following year's meeting of the synod, there was a roll call during which each pastor gave a brief report on what he had done.

It was gratifying to learn that nearly all had given the subject proper attention, and that our colored brethren had every necessary attention and instruction.[52]

Notwithstanding increased efforts to work with blacks, Lutherans in the lower South had some difficulty concealing their ambivalence and defensiveness about the church's work with black people. The repeated reference to "oral instruction" (maintaining the prohibition against teaching blacks to read and write) underscored their fear that religion might weaken the ability of whites to control the slave population and might even upset what they referred to as "domestic tranquility."

This policy, however, was not consistently applied. For example, the Rev. J. Bachman, chief Lutheran defender of slavery in the South, wrote a letter to *The Missionary* in which he stated that even though some of the states had passed laws to prohibit teaching slaves to read, nevertheless,

These laws soon became a dead letter. Many servants [slaves] are taught to read by the younger portion of the white members of the family, and the Bible is found in thousands of families of the colored.[53]

For almost fifty years, from 1816–1865, black Lutheranism in the lower South extended from Georgia on the east to Mississippi on the west, with its geographic center in the state of South Carolina.

After the demise of the Salzburger experiment in the early 1780s, the next we hear of blacks in the Lutheran Church in Georgia is in 1838. Zion Lutheran Church, the first Lutheran Church in Macon County, was a large wooden structure with three doors: one for men, one for women, and a back door for slaves. The slaves were reported to have attended services regularly and partook of Holy Communion at a separate table.[54]

L. Bendenbough of Haralson, Georgia, in a letter to *The Lutheran Observer* for October 1854 indicates that

> ... a portion of the members received into the church during our meeting were from the colored population ... [and that] a portion of the church is assigned to them.[55]

In 1859, there were 8 Lutheran churches in Georgia with a communicant strength of 655 whites and 61 blacks.[56] At the service celebrating the formation of the Georgia Synod on Sunday July 29, 1860, there were three services: one at 10:00 a.m. for whites, another at 4:00 p.m. for blacks, and later, a candlelight service for whites.[57] In 1855, the little Mississippi Synod reported 289 white and 53 colored communicants. Approximately 16 percent of the communicant members of that synod were black.

Numerically, black Lutheranism reached its peak in the lower South in 1859 with at least a total of 1,030 communicant members (see Table 11). A decline in black Lutheranism became most noticeable in 1862. The black communicant membership of the South Carolina Synod had gone from a high of 969 in 1859 to a low of 365 in 1865. During the thirty-five year period 1830–1865, however, the South Carolina Synod reported a total of 7,120 baptisms of black adults and infants.

Summary and Conclusions

The first organized, systematic effort by Lutherans to evangelize black people in North America (the Salzburgers in the 1750s) was unquestionably part of a political process to introduce slavery into Georgia. The second organized, systematic effort by Lutherans to evangelize black people got underway just as the antislavery movement in American society was developing a healthy head of steam. This second organized effort at evangelizing U.S. blacks was also launched in the South, lasting from 1816 to 1865.

Despite the near unanimous adoption of the Five Point Plan to work with black people (slave and free) in 1817, there was never any such thing as "the solid South" in the Lutheran outreach program towards black people.

Table 11: Black Accessions in the South Carolina Synod 1830–1865

| Year | No. of Congregations | Baptisms | | Confirmed This Year | Members Received | Communicants | No. of Congregations Reporting Blacks |
		Infants	Adults				
1830	26		46	18			3
1831	27		50	21			5
1832							
1833	30		91	35			5
1834	28		61	23			3
1835							
1836	28		49	17			7
1837	24		49	22			4
1838	27		27	3			1
1839	32		72		22		5
1840	34		70		21		6
1841			53		20		
1842							
1843							
1844	36		152		115	348	12
1845	39		184		96	429	10
1846	46		149	57	442	9	
1847	47		123		44	439	13
1848	39		126		65	394	14
1849	47		111		56	402	16
1850	46		103		61	424	14
1851	44		136		90	432	13
1852	46	209	68		233	635	16
1853	50	175	76		160	683	17
1854	52	165	64		117	789	20
1855	47	134	33		138	815	20
1856	52	151	33		103	764	20
1857	51	181	112		249	851	18
1858	43	176	63		150	832	16
1859	49	129	73		189	969	19
1860	48	146	52		118	952	19
1861							
1862-a	44	160	52		131	954	18
1862-b	40	105	16		44	845	15
1863	36	91	35	75		740	13
1864	45	75		110		825	15
1865	30			35		365	11

127

1862-a. From the January 1862 minutes of the South Carolina Synod.

1862-b. From the October 1862 minutes of the South Carolina Synod which are described as the Parochial Report for 1861 and 1862.

1830–1851: Infant and adult baptisms are combined.

Lutherans in the upper South went to work immediately. The largest number of black accessions to the Lutheran Church in the upper South took place between 1817 and 1830. Two-thirds of the recorded black accessions in the upper South occurred between 1817 and 1840. Even though Lutherans in the lower South succeeded in bringing more blacks into the Lutheran Church than did their counterparts in the upper South, black Lutheranism in the upper South was more enduring than that in the lower South. After the Civil War, when the Synodical Conference began working in the South, the results of the work of upper South Lutherans were still evident in the faithfulness of such persons as Sophronia Hull and the old black Lutherans at Conover, North Carolina. It would appear that the master-slave strategy worked differently in the upper South than it did in the lower South.

The single most successful endeavor launched by Lutherans during this period was the urban strategy at St. John's Lutheran Church in Charleston. With the exception of the work done at St. John's in Charleston, the organized Lutheran outreach program in the lower South did not really get under way until a quarter century after the adoption of the Five Point Plan. The effort to evangelize blacks in the lower South was, in fact, rather brief. Seventy percent of the black accessions to the Lutheran Church in the lower South took place in the 15-year period 1850–1865.

In the fifty-year period during which southern Lutherans attempted to work with black people (1817–1865), an estimated eight to ten thousand blacks (at a minimum) were brought into the Lutheran Church in the South. The vast majority of these (over seven thousand) were in the lower South. By the beginning of the Civil War, black people constituted a significant proportion of the communicant membership in at least three of the southern synods and in all likelihood in at least two others. Twenty percent of the communicant members of the South Carolina Synod in 1859 were black. Eighteen percent of the communicant members of the Mississippi

Synod in 1855 were black. Ten percent of the communicant members of the Georgia Synod in 1859 were black. Given the fact that more blacks were taken into the North Carolina and Tennessee Synods than were admitted to the Georgia and Mississippi Synods, blacks were in all probability a significant part of the communicant membership of the former two synods.

Lutherans utilized three different strategies in their efforts to win black people: (1) a master-slave approach, the most widely used; (2) an urban strategy, the least widely used; and (3) a plantation-missionary strategy. The most successful of the three (the urban strategy) was implemented at the request of black people before the adoption of the Five Point Plan.

Several significant firsts occurred during this period.

At no other time have black people constituted so large a proportion of the membership of American Lutheranism.

The first American black men (specifically, three) were ordained by Lutherans between 1832 and 1845.

The first black to attend a Lutheran seminary entered Gettysburg in 1835.

The first black male to serve as a foreign missionary of U.S. Lutheranism was sent abroad in 1845.

What is unusual about this period of American Lutheran history is that Lutherans in the North, who were much better organized, more numerous, and with more resources than those in the South, exerted so little effort to reach out to the black community.

Jehu Jones and the First All-Black Lutheran Church 1832–1849

Unquestionably, the most successful effort in the U.S. to build black Lutheranism during the first half of the 19th century took place at St. John's Lutheran Church in Charleston, SC. The effort was so successful that the black members of St. John's resolved to send a missionary to Africa. The person selected to serve as missionary was a black man, Jehu (John) Jones. Jones (introduced in the previous chapter) was a free black man who had been a member of St. John's, Charleston, since the early 1820s and who also had served as one of the "leaders" of the black group there.[1]

Jones' efforts to go to Africa, begun in 1832, were beset with one difficulty after another. In order to be ordained, Jones had to leave Charleston and go to New York. At that time, black men were not ordained for the Lutheran ministry in South Carolina. His request for assistance for the Africa mission was turned down, first by the American Board of Commissioners for Foreign Missions and then by the Lutheran Ministerium of New York. He returned to Charleston to get his family and tie up affairs. The law prohibited free Negroes from returning to Charleston once they left. Tradition has it that when Jones returned to Charleston, he was threatened with jail. Pastor Bachman of Charleston told city authorities that if they put Jones in jail, they would have to put Bachman in jail.[2] The city authorities backed down. Jones was quickly spirited out of town, barely escaping being enslaved.

Jones never got to Africa. It would be an understatement to say that Jones' plans changed. He and his family were uprooted from their home and business and spent the next two and a half years wandering up North. There is no detailed account of where he went. It is known that between 1832 and 1839 he was in New York, Philadelphia, and Boston. This wandering, coupled with his prior experience at St. John's, may account for his efforts to establish an all-black independent Lutheran congregation, first in Philadelphia, and later in New York.

Jones spent some time in at least three of the four northern urban centers where he saw that black Christianity had taken two decisive steps.

First, he saw independent black congregations in operation:

—The First African Baptist Church in Boston (organized in 1805)

—The First African Presbyterian Church in Philadelphia (organized in 1807)

—The Abyssinian Baptist church of New York city (also organized in 1807) and

—St. Philip's Episcopal Church (black) of New York City (organized in 1818).

The all-black church was not limited to the major urban centers of the North. Independent black churches

> ... also appeared in the smaller cities and towns of the Northeast. In both Providence and Newport, Rhode Island, black churches emerged during the first quarter of the nineteenth century. The earliest churches in both cities developed out of self-help organizations known as African Union Societies that have been in existence since the 1780s.[3]

The second thing Jones saw as he wandered up North was the emergence of the independent black denomination:

—The African Union Methodist Church (A.U.M.C.), organized 1813.

—The African Methodist Episcopal Church (A.M.E.), formed by five independent black churches in 1816.

—The African Methodist Episcopal Zion Church (A.M.E. Zion), organized in 1821

—The American Baptist Missionary Convention (black), organized in 1840.

Jehu Jones quickly learned that, despite the growing interest in abolition, northern Christians had not totally disengaged themselves from the racism that permeated American society. If there were differences in the North, they were that (1) among northern Christians there was less fear concerning the evangelization of blacks, and (2) there was much greater willingness to let blacks organize separate churches. In fact, northern Christians saw the formation of separate churches as an opportunity to rid themselves of what they perceived to be the black nuisance.

The formation of black denominations was something else. Even though whites took a permissive attitude towards the formation of separate black congregations, they still wanted to exercise control over them. The desire to control black Christians, even when organized in separate congregations, finally led to the formation of the all-black denomination.

There were other issues as well behind this development. First, blacks needed to look at the Scriptures in terms of their particular circumstances. When whites looked at the Word of God, they saw themselves as the New Israel in the promised land. When blacks looked at themselves in the light of God's Word, they saw themselves as the Old Israel enslaved in Egypt. Second, tied to these differing views of self and the world was the black man's search for community in an environment that persistently sought to exclude him, even in his own community. Third, while whites were going about the business of trying to separate the spiritual from the social, blacks took the position that the social, the economic, and the political were inseparable from the spiritual.

Choosing Philadelphia

Given these realities, Jones decided to organize an all-black Lutheran congregation in the city of Philadelphia. His choice of that city as the place to begin deserves examination.

In the small towns of Pennsylvania (and elsewhere in the North), blacks attended the churches of white folk much as they did in Charleston, segregated seating and all.[4] Philadelphia was quite different. A report from as early as 1813 shows that there were six all-black churches in Philadelphia: one Episcopal (the largest, with 560 members), three Methodist (with a combined membership of 1,426), one Presbyterian (with 300 members), and one Baptist (with 80 members).[5]

In 1838, four years after Jones organized St. Paul's, there were 16 all-black churches in Philadelphia: eight Methodist (with 2,860 members), four Baptist (with 700 members) two Presbyterian (with 325 members), one Episcopal (with 100 members), and one Lutheran church (St. Paul's, with 10 members). One thing that made the growth of the all-black church possible is that Philadelphia had the second largest free black population of any city in the U.S., and it was growing rapidly (see Table 12).

Table 12: Free Black, Slave, and White Population of Philadelphia 1790–1860

Year	Free Negroes	Slaves	Whites
1790	2,102	387	51,902
1800	6,795	85	74,129
1810	10,514	8	100,688
1820	11,884	7	123,746
1830	15,004	20	173,173
1840	19,831	2	238,204
1850	19,761		389,001
1860	22,185		543,344

Source: Edward Raymond Turner, *The Negro in Pennsylvania 1639–1860* (New York: Arno Press & The New York Times, 1969)

Philadelphia also was host to popular black, beneficial societies, growing from 15 in 1815 to 50 in 1830, four years before Jones began his work there. The beneficial societies functioned, among other things, as a kind of social insurance group for black people, and they were almost always affiliated directly with one of the all-black churches. One writer summarized the development of the all-black church with the associated beneficial society as follows:

> [The church was vital to blacks in 19th century Philadelphia] because [blacks] were so closed off from the benefits of white society. The church became a fundamental prerequisite to a decent life and, indeed, bearable existence.[6]

In 1838, of the 3,300 black households in Philadelphia, 2,776 were affiliated with some church, that is, approximately 84 percent of the black households of Philadelphia were church going. Only 5 percent of the black households in Philadelphia were affiliated with a white church. "... nonchurch affiliation was the distinguishing characteristic of the most disadvantaged group [blacks] in the community."[7]

Given the above, Jones' chances of drawing blacks into a predominantly white congregation as had been done in Charleston were slim. For blacks, to join a white church in Philadelphia in the 1830s would have been to cut themselves off from major sources of support and assistance.

St. Paul's Colored Lutheran Church

Jehu Jones was not a timid man, nor without faith, vision, or self-confidence. Given his work at St. John's in Charleston, he knew what black people could do. He was also aware of some of the limitations of the Charleston strategy. In Philadelphia, Jones saw the possibility of the full expression of what was foreshadowed in Charleston. Without the support or backing of any board or agency, Jones began working to establish a black Lutheran church in 1834, supporting himself and his family through his trade as a tailor.

St. Paul's building was dedicated on May 1, 1836.[8] It was located at 130 South Quince Street and consisted only of a basement. He intended to equip the basement as a school. Jones was personally responsible for $2,000 that went into the erection of the basement. Before the dedication of the building, he had traveled to Boston and other eastern cities to raise funds.[9]

One reason for organizing St. Paul's and assuming such indebtedness was the sense of homelessness Jones and his family had experienced since leaving Charleston. As he wrote in a letter to the *Lutheran Observer,* for three years he had "strayed from church," separated from the public worship he had come to love.[10]

Six months after the dedication service, St. Paul's was in serious financial difficulties. With only a basement and a temporary roof and with winter coming, Jones appealed in a letter to St. Michael and Zion Lutheran Churches in Philadelphia for assistance.

By January 1837, creditors were pressing for payment. The largest creditor, to whom they owed $824, agreed to withhold foreclosure if they could raise $500. The congregation resolved that the Lutheran Church at large should be informed of their predicament.

If unsuccessful in raising money from that source, the pastor should travel to Europe and seek aid there.[11]

By 1838, St. Paul's had only ten members. In April of that year, the church property was conveyed to three gentlemen in trust, pending a meeting of the East Pennsylvania Synod. In the meantime, a fund-raising fair had been planned under the direction of Mrs. M. Rex, a member of St. Michael's Lutheran Church in Philadelphia.[12]

The last we hear of St. Paul's Lutheran Church in Philadelphia is in a letter Jones wrote to Rev. John Bachman in Charleston, dated August 10, 1839, in which Jones informed Bachman that the second story (the ground floor) of the church building was near completion. In spite of Jones' hopes, with only 10 members and no ongoing financial support, they could not survive.

Jehu Jones did not give up. In 1849, he was in New York City trying to start another all-black Lutheran church. He appealed to the Lutheran ministerium. A study committee of that body brought in a report that Jones had misrepresented himself and misappropriated funds. His character and integrity, as they saw it, were questionable, and their support should not be forthcoming. This is the last we hear of Jones and his efforts to organize an all-black Lutheran congregation.

Summary

Following the adoption of the Five Point Plan in 1817, the events that took place between 1832 and 1849 (chapters 6 and 7) appear to mark an important turning point in U.S. black Lutheranism. During this period, the Lutheran Church ordained its first black ministers (Jehu Jones, Daniel Alexander Payne, and Boston J. Drayton). A black man (Payne) enrolled in the seminary at Gettysburg. A black preacher (Drayton) went to Africa as a missionary of the Lutheran Church. The first all-black independent Lutheran congregation was organized in the U.S. For the first time, there was an organized effort to work with free blacks in the North.

Of the three black men Lutherans ordained, the most visionary (insofar as black Lutheranism is concerned) was Jehu Jones. True, in adopting the Five Point Plan, Lutherans finally committed themselves to work with black people. Lutherans, however, had not decided to *enter* the black community with the Gospel. Lutherans did not attempt to plant Lutheranism *within* the black community. Lutherans did not attempt to make Lutheranism an *integral* part of the life of the black community and therefore an integral part of the life of black people. Rather, it attempted to make black people an appendage of white congregations, just as slaves were an appendage of their slave owners. In a word, Lutherans were not ready to hand the Gospel over to black people. The one person who saw this most clearly and sought to change the strategy of black Lutheranism was Jehu Jones.

In the half century before the organization of St. Paul's Colored Lutheran Church in Philadelphia, it had become clear that if black people had a choice about joining a Christian church in the U.S., the overwhelming probability was that the congregation of their choice was going to be black.

With Jones we get a glimpse of the difference between the response of black people to Christianity in the North as contrasted with that response in the South. When Jones was working in Philadelphia, 84 percent of the black households of that city held membership in a Christian church. At the same time, only 30 percent of Charleston's black population held membership in a Christian church. While there were a number of reasons for this difference, it seems the pre-Civil War Lutheran Church in the U.S. centered its efforts in the wrong place when reaching out to blacks. The Lutheran Church concentrated its main efforts in the South where the largest number of blacks were to be found. The Lutheran Church itself, however, was strongest in the North. And it was in the North that the Christian Church was most accessible to blacks, and a larger proportion of the black population held membership in the Christian Church there.

At first glance, Philadelphia seems to have been the ideal place to attempt to change the strategy for black Lutheranism, that is, by organizing a black Lutheran congregation. At the time, it was a center of Lutheranism in the nation. It had a large and growing free black population that overwhelmingly demonstrated its willingness and ability to support the church. However, there was at least one important drawback: the black community in Philadelphia was already over-churched. The establishment of any new church in Philadelphia's black community in the mid-1830s had to be undertaken, if at all, as a long-term project.

Insofar as the record goes, the establishment of St. Paul's Colored Lutheran Church in Philadelphia was essentially a one-man project. While Jones had been ordained by the New York Ministerium, he was never a formal member of any synod or ministerium and, therefore, did not work within the framework of the institutional church. One cannot say whether Jones was a loner by chance, by choice, or of necessity. On several occasions he did seek financial assistance from his fellow Lutherans and apparently was even willing to go to Europe for assistance. He was a committed and persistent man. He was willing to give up everything to go to Africa. When that failed, he was willing and did in fact support himself and his family for 17 years while attempting to establish a church in Philadelphia and later in New York.

The Old Lutherans in the South, 1865–1891

Following the Civil War, what remained of black Lutheranism was still located in the South, principally in the Carolinas and Tennessee and to a lesser degree in Virginia, Georgia, and Mississippi.

The quarter century immediately following the Civil War can be described as a time of testing and growing crisis for black Lutheranism. The foundation on which black Lutheranism had been built was being tested. The critical question was, Could black Lutheranism survive?

The Lower South

The South Carolina Synod spent twenty years (1866–1887) trying to decide how it should respond to the new relationship between blacks and whites. At the 1866 meeting of the South Carolina Synod, president Boinest candidly admitted that many of the pastors just did not know what to do and were waiting to see how other denominations would work in this new situation. Since others (e.g., the Tennessee Synod) had suggested the formation of a separate black ecclesiastical organization, Boinest recommended that the South Carolina Synod follow suit. The convention rejected the proposal and passed a motion to "retain the same relation to the freedmen as we have heretofore done."[1]

A committee at the 1867 synodical convention reported that "in some localities [the freedmen] seem inclined to keep up a friendly Christian relation with those at whose altars they formerly worshiped." The vestry at St. John's Church in Charleston, however, was clearly irritated that some of the freedmen were now sitting in the same pews with whites. In 1869, the constitution of St. John's Church was changed so that only white males could hold membership in the congregation.

Black membership in the South Carolina Synod began to drop precipitously. In 1866, the South Carolina Synod reported 388 black communicants. In 1867, the synod reported 212. Finally, in 1868, the last year that the South Carolina Synod reported the number of black communicants, there were only 144.

At the end of the Reconstruction, the South Carolina Synod again took up the question of what to do about the freedmen. One pastor took the position that the ten-year period of the synod's sitting on its hands was probably for the best. "The clouds of war and prejudice have hitherto involved the matter in difficulties and doubts which would have vitiated our efforts."[2]

A number of suggestions were made by pastoral conferences, synodical conventions, and even at the General Synod South with regard to systematic work among blacks. These included such projects as (1) a training school for blacks, (2) an orphanage, (3) a system of university scholarships, and (4) the training of black ministers. There was so much talk and so little action that a correspondent for *The Lutheran Visitor* finally wrote:

> Years have been spent in the endeavor to determine how to go about the work, to excogitate and perfect the best means of making a beginning. Let all this be stopped, and let's go to work and do it.[3]

Some action was finally taken. Two young black Methodists were found who wanted to become Lutheran ministers. On October 7, 1883, they were confirmed and accepted as candidates for the Lutheran ministry. Shortly thereafter, they began studying theology at Howard University in Washington, D.C. One of the candidates dropped out of the program a year later because of financial problems and homesickness. In 1887, the other student, Frank Jones, came close to completing his studies. Nothing more, however, was heard of him. With these events the South Carolina Synod formally ended its involvement in black ministry.

The relationship of individual congregations and pastors with blacks did not necessarily end. One investigator reported,

> Only in the area of pastoral acts did the old relationship continue for a longer period. In one parish, over a third of the weddings

performed between 1867 and 1883 were for Negro couples.[4]

However, a situation at St. John's, Charleston, is more indicative of the times. A year after the blacks were effectively removed from that congregation, they petitioned to have the church's black cemetery, established in 1840, transferred to them. St. John's committee reported to the vestry at its April 8, 1870 meeting:

> Gentlemen: The committee to whom was referred the petition of Ann Skirving, Phillis Ling, Francis West, Wm. Cole, and others, free persons of color, asking to have the Burial Ground held by us turned over to them, would beg leave to say, We have given the matter due consideration and have come to the conclusion that the Vestry have no power or authority to do so in as much as the Vestry of this Church were appointed by the Trustees [?], and nothing save an order from that Source would relieve them from any future responsibility. All of which is respectfully submitted and the Committee would ask to be discharged.[5]

The request of the former black members of St. John's was turned down. The matter came to the vestry's attention again on April 21, 1911:

> The President (of the congregation) stated that the title to the Lutheran Graveyard on Columbus Street was in our Church, and it was referred to the Graveyard Committee to examine into same so that it should not lapse.[6]

At the October 13, 1911 meeting of St. John's vestry

> Mr. Lanneau reported that the fences around the Colored Lutheran Cemetery on Columbus Street were down and needed repairs. That he had collected $40.00 from the Sexton in Charge for burial fees and paid same to Treasurer. The first money that had been received from this service in a great many years.
>
> The Committee on Graveyards was asked to take charge of the matter and report what arrangements for fences could be made.[7]

By 1957, St. John's had lost title to this little graveyard surrounded by a brightly colored wooden fence.[8] In 1983, the Charleston Housing Authority had gained title to the property and was in the process of building on the land when it was discovered to be a cemetery. Research revealed that the graveyard had been used between 1840 and 1860, with at least 150 people buried at the site.[9]

The Upper South

Concurrently with the earlier events, the Tennessee Synod was trying to determine the status of black Lutherans in its midst. At its 1866 convention, it issued the following resolution:

> *Whereas,* the colored people among us no longer sustain the same relation to the white man that they did, formerly, and that change has transferred the individual obligations and responsibilities of owners to the whole church; and
>
> *Whereas,* some of them were formerly members of our congregations and still claim membership in them, but owing to the plainly marked distinctions which God has made between us and them, giving different colors, and so forth, it is felt by us and them also, that there ought to be separate places of worship, and also separate ecclesiastical organizations, so that everyone could worship God with the least possible embarrassment; and
>
> *Whereas,* colored people are considered firm adherents of our church, we feel it is our imperative duty to assist them in adopting such measures as will best meet the necessities of their present condition; be it therefore,
>
> *Resolved,* that whenever any of our colored brethren desire to preach, that they make application to some one of the ministers of our Synod, who shall inform the president; when it shall be the president's duty to appoint two ordained ministers, who, in connection with two laymen, whom they may choose, shall constitute a committee to examine the candidate, whereupon ... if satisfied to license them to preach, catechize, baptize and celebrate the rites of matrimony among them of his own race ... until the next session of the Synod. This license does not authorize them to preach in our churches, or to take part in our ecclesiastical meetings; nevertheless, they are permitted to worship with us as heretofore, yet we advise them to erect houses for themselves in which they may worship.[10]

The Tennessee Synod's attempt to spell out the future of black Lutheranism was a mix of some old things and some that were new. The new in the Tennessee proposal was (1) the black lay preacher

141

would now perform all the same duties as the white pastor, (2) those duties could only be performed in a black congregation, and (3) the black pastor would have to be re-licensed every year.

The more unusual suggestions in the Tennessee proposal were that (1) blacks put up their own church buildings and (2) form their own ecclesiastical organization. Inasmuch as blacks had not yet received their "forty acres and a mule," that first item was quite impractical. The second was quite inconsistent with the generally held conception of the unity of the church. Lutherans are not comfortable with the splintering of the church. Apparently the Tennessee Synod was driven to these proposals by the embarrassment they felt with the new relationship between blacks and whites. In spite of that, the Tennessee and North Carolina Synods moved from resolutions to action. Both synods began by licensing black lay preachers.

Thomas Fry applied to the Tennessee Synod for licensure in 1865. Fry was born on George Washington's plantation at Mt. Vernon and later taken to North Carolina. There, he is reported to have studied the Lutheran Confessions while tending his master's whiskey still—, however, when he was examined by a committee of the Tennessee Synod, the committee concluded that he could neither read nor write. Some say he had a ministry in both Lincoln and Catawba counties and that he organized St. Peter's Lutheran Church in Catawba county. Other reports indicate that Fry lived less than a year after he was first licensed.

Michael M. Coble (Cobb), born in Guilford County, was licensed in 1868 to preach by the North Carolina Synod. Dickinson contends that Coble did not have a church, but preached mostly in the homes of his people in and around Concord, NC.[11] The following report on Coble's work was presented to the 1870 convention of the North Carolina Synod:

> Your Committee, under whose care this colored licentiate has been placed would submit the following:
>
> He believes that this Ministerium has adopted the right course, in presenting to the colored population the offers of the Gospel, by preachers of their own color.
>
> The report of Michael Coble for the last year, which is herewith submitted, shows an increase of his labors, as compared with the

year previous. Your Committee is convinced that he is accomplishing much good amongst his class.

No. Congregations, 2; Communicants, 124; Infants Baptized, 10; Adults bap., 46; Expul., 8; Confirmations, 46; Admissions, 3; Restorations, 1; Funerals, 3; S. School, 1; Teachers, 2; Scholars, 29; Prayer Meeting, 2.[12]

Coble was a free spirit and is said to have preached for the Lutherans one Sunday and the Methodists the next. He ultimately joined the Methodist Church and was removed from the rolls of the North Carolina Synod in 1880.[13]

Thomas Sutherland is referred to on two different occasions in the North Carolina Synod minutes. First, in 1873, the minutes note that "Rev. J. G. Neiffer presented the report from Thomas Sutherland—colored man of Salisbury—in reference to the performance of his duties."[14] The following year, the synodical minutes reveal that "The Committee to whom was referred the licensure of Thomas Sutherland (colored), reported that they had performed that duty."[15] After 1874, Thomas Sutherland disappeared from the synodical record.

David J. Koontz was born in Davidson County, North Carolina, in 1846. After serving as a licensurate, he was ordained by the North Carolina Synod in 1880. He was the pastor of Pleasant Grove Church, which is said to have been one of the first colored Lutheran churches organized and received into the North Carolina Synod.[16] He baptized, instructed, and confirmed W. Philo Phifer.

When Koontz was ordained at the 1880 meeting of the North Carolina Synod, he was also commissioned to engage in "missionary operations among the colored people within our bounds, or at least devise some plan by which the colored people may have preaching."[17] That same year, Koontz reported to the North Carolina Synod that he had 14 communicant members, 20 Sunday school pupils, and three Sunday school teachers. At that same meeting, he contributed $1.20 to the synodical treasury.[18] The North Carolina Synod in turn provided some financial support for Koontz's work. In 1880, they gave him a stipend of $40. In 1881–1882, it was raised to $160. In 1883, it was reduced to $55, but in 1884 it was raised to $210. In 1884, Koontz submitted his resignation to the North Carolina

Synod because he felt that he was not getting adequate support. His resignation was not accepted.

Samuel Holt was the fifth black man to enter the ministry of the Lutheran Church during this period. Holt was born in Alamance County, first licensed in 1872, and ordained by the North Carolina Synod in 1884.

Nathan Clapp, also born in Alamance County, was the sixth black man to be ordained by the Lutheran Church. He was ordained in 1884 by the North Carolina Synod and served two churches: Samuel Holt Chapel and Elon College School House.

It may be of interest to digress for a moment to explain that as early as 1882, the Maryland Synod made the first effort at providing prospective black candidates for the Lutheran ministry with formal training. They proposed sending black candidates to Howard University in Washington, D.C. The Maryland Synod asked Lutherans in Virginia to assist them in this project. The Virginians thought it was a good idea but did very little to help out.[19] In 1884, the Maryland Synod reported that five black men were studying for the ministry at Howard University: Daniel Wiseman, A. M. Park, W. Philo Phifer, Frank B. Jones, and John Schumpter.[20] All of these men, with the exception of Wiseman, were from North Carolina. Of the five, only Wiseman and Phifer succeeded in serving in the Lutheran ministry. The Maryland Synod project lasted five years (1883–1888) and cost $1,300.[21]

In North Carolina, the work among black people had been placed directly under the supervision of the president of the Synod. However, because they were having increasing difficulty supporting that work, the North Carolina Synod offered the whole project of black ministry to the General Synod South in 1883. The General Synod South declined the offer. The North Carolina Synod then offered the project to the General Synod North, with the proviso that it remain under the supervision of the North Carolina Synod. The General Synod North also declined the offer. The message was clear: The North Carolina Synod wanted out of its involvement with black Lutherans.

The Alpha Synod. The work among black Lutherans was in such precarious financial shape that the North Carolina Synod finally suggested that the black preachers support themselves by taking secular jobs. The black brothers took matters into their own hands and, at the 1889 meeting of the North Carolina Synod, submitted the following resolution:

> We, the colored ministers and delegates, members of the North Carolina Synod, petition your honorable body to appoint a committee composed of three white ministers, with instructions, at as early a day as practical, to organize the colored brethren and congregations now belonging to our Synod, into a colored Evangelical Lutheran Synod, to be based upon the doctrinal basis of the United Synod and to be governed by the Constitution of the North Carolina Synod until such time as it shall be in condition to formulate and adopt a constitution of its own; and that this committee report to the next convention of this body.[22]

They did not wait until the next convention of that body. At that same convention, on May 8, 1889, the Alpha Evangelical Lutheran Synod of Freedmen in America was organized at St. John's Ev. Lutheran Church in Cabarrus County, North Carolina. The founding members were David J. Koontz, president; Philo W. Phifer, recording/corresponding secretary; Samuel Holt, treasurer; and Nathan Clapp. At its founding, this first and only black Lutheran synod within the continental United States consisted of five congregations (located in Concord, Charlotte, Elon College, Gibsonville, and Lexington, NC), with a total membership of 180 baptized souls. Only two of the four pastors (Koontz and Phifer) could read and write, and only three of the congregations had a building of its own.

The formation of the Alpha Synod was neither a bold declaration of independence, nor was it a daring act of faith. It was precipitated by a crisis. Before the meeting of the North Carolina Synod in 1889, the matter of an all-black synod had received little thought and absolutely no preparation. Black Lutheranism, to put the matter bluntly, was faced with bankruptcy. This fragile group was about to lose one of its three church buildings. (The North Carolina Synod, in a show of support for the fledgling Alpha Synod did vote to give them $25 so that they could hold on to the church property at Concord.) All efforts by the North Carolina Synod to provide some kind of support had proven fruitless. Simply put, the issue facing black Lutheranism in North Carolina was survival. So the black brothers decided to take matters into their own hands. However, in 1891, the Alpha Synod effectively went out of existence, barely two years after its formation (see Chapter 9 for more about the Alpha Synod).

Summary

The second organized effort by North American Lutherans to evangelize black people began in earnest in 1817. That effort was preceded by eight years of synodical resolutions which indicated that political issues were not an inconsiderable sticking point, especially for Lutherans in the lower South. In this instance, the political issue was the maintenance of the institution of slavery.

This second effort by the Old Lutherans in the South to evangelize blacks lasted 75 years, from 1817 to 1891. During the first 50 years of that effort (1817–1865), eight to ten thousand blacks were brought into the Lutheran Church. The last 25 years of that effort (1865–1891, the focus of this chapter) was a period of growing crisis in black Lutheranism. In 1870, approximately 125 blacks could be identified as communicant members of the Old Lutheran Church in the South. By 1891, (excluding the Synodical Conference), only 180 blacks were communicant members of the Lutheran Church in the South, principally in North Carolina. One writer concludes that the decline in the number of black Lutherans following the Civil War can be explained by the fact that before the Civil War black people became Lutheran by chance, not by choice. Following the Civil War, when they had a real choice in the matter, they left the Lutheran Church.

This conclusion is drawn from the old master-slave theory of black church affiliation. Broadly stated, that theory holds that Euro-American Christians should take credit for bringing Christianity to black people. Additionally, the theory holds that black people, especially slaves, did not have much choice in the matter of joining a Christian church. They were either sent or brought to church by their masters. An unstated but important element was the coercive power of the slave master. Therefore, as the master-slave theory would have it, slaves became Lutheran (and members of other church bodies) more by chance than as a matter of personal choice and conviction.

How and why blacks joined the Christian Church and what they sought is a critical issue not satisfactorily dealt with by the master-slave theory of church affiliation. One needs to remember that slave masters were usually skeptical about and opposed to introducing slaves to Christianity. And Lutherans did so primarily when abolitionism became a serious issue undoubtedly as a way to rationalize the continuation of slavery. As you recall, Lutherans in the lower South became serious about evangelizing blacks barely fifteen years before the issuance of the Emancipation Proclamation.

Even though slavery imposed many limitations, it is important to understand that blacks had at least three choices when it came to affiliating with a church. First, they could choose not to join any church. Second, they could join the church of their master. Third, they could join any one of a number of "invisible" (underground) churches.

We have an opportunity to weigh the merits of the master-slave theory of church affiliation by comparing the behavior of blacks in Philadelphia (where that theory was not operative because all blacks were free) to the behavior of blacks in Charleston, South Carolina (where the majority of blacks were slaves). Just before the outbreak of the Civil War, approximately 84 percent of the black households in Philadelphia held formal membership in one of the publicly established churches of that community. At the same time, only 30 percent of the black population of Charleston was formally affiliated with a church. In addition it should be pointed out that a number of those in Charleston who chose not to hold membership in a church still attended the Sunday school of various churches; these and a growing number of blacks were affiliated with one of the "invisible" (underground) black churches in the community. One investigator reports than when the Civil War ended, 2,000 blacks (almost 10 percent of the black population) in Charleston who had been members of the "invisible" AME Church came out of the closet.[23]

With regard to the disappearance of large numbers of black Lutherans immediately following the Civil War, a number of factors seem pertinent. So the theory that slavery encouraged church membership does not hold.

First, joining the Lutheran Church was sociologically quite different from joining many of the other Christian churches. When one joined either the Methodist or the Baptist church, one was almost immediately a fully accepted member of that body. By contrast (and still today), when blacks join a white Lutheran congregation, it takes on the average two to three generations to become a fully accepted member of that group. The vast majority of blacks (70 percent, as previously noted) joined the Lutheran Church in the 15-year period just before the end of the Civil War. Many of them were children who spent little time in the Lutheran Church before being invited to leave.

Second, to say that black Lutherans "disappeared" after the Civil War is not correct. They were either asked to leave Lutheran congregations or were summarily put out.

Third, when blacks were "invited" to leave those Lutheran congregations in the South, there was no place (i.e., no Lutheran congregation) to which they might go. This was in sharp contrast to conditions that other black Christians faced. The Methodists and Baptists had worked with blacks from the middle of 18th century, almost three quarters of a century before Lutherans even began discussing the possibility of working with blacks. The vast majority of blacks who did join the Lutheran Church did so barely ten years before the beginning of the Civil War. By contrast, the Methodists and Baptists had not only trained a considerable number of blacks leaders before the Civil War, their churches had become indigenous to the black community by that time. The Lutheran Church can hardly be said to have become an indigenous part of the black community even today in the last quarter of the 20th century.

The formation of the Alpha Synod in 1889, the culminating event of that era in black Lutheranism, was in no way comparable to the formation of the African Methodist Episcopal Church or any of the other black denominations. The formation of those black denominations was a genuine protest movement. Like most protest movements, one has to reject the lie (in those instances, the lie of racism within the Christian Church) in order to embrace the truth. The Alpha Synod was not a protest movement. It was an act of desperation whose central objective was the survival of black Lutheranism in much the same form and on much the same basis as it had always existed. The important accomplishment of the Alpha Synod was to bring together finally the Old and New Lutherans in North Carolina. We shall have an opportunity to examine the consequences of this meeting in the following chapter and also to take another look at the question, Did blacks become Lutheran by choice or by chance?

III

NEW DIRECTIONS

9

The Rebirth of Black Lutheranism, 1877–1950

Any perceptive student of church growth who examines black Lutheranism among the Old Lutherans in the South between 1866 and 1891 would most likely conclude that he is watching the death process slowly unfold before his eyes. There seem to be only two questions to ask: How long will it last? and, When will they hold the funeral?

Those questions are premature. Several groups led to a new development: the New Lutherans (the Synodical Conference), the Other Lutherans (the Joint Synod of Ohio), black Lutherans (the Alpha Synod), and even some non-Lutherans. Cumulatively, these led to what can rightly be called *The Rebirth of Black Lutheranism*. This era consists of a number of new beginnings by a number of different participants. We have chosen to examine the era in stages of an ongoing process because the efforts were continuous, overlapping, and at many points they re-enforced each other.

Stage one consists of efforts to reach what the New Lutherans called "the heathens." In large measure, stage two involves the revival of black Lutheranism in North Carolina. In stage three, non-Lutherans invited the Lutheran Church into Alabama. In stage four, black Lutheranism become a national urban phenomenon.

Stage One: Mission to the Heathen

The initial phase of the rebirth of black Lutheranism was launched from a totally unexpected quarter—the New Lutherans who had only recently settled in the Midwest. They were so new to the American scene that few of them spoke English. Nevertheless, the Evangelical Lutheran Synodical Conference of North America

151

(an 1872 loose federation of several Lutheran synods), in a flurry of action, suddenly became "the new boy on the block" for black Lutheranism.[1] Within three months, from mid-July to October 1877, they went from the initial discussion about entering the arena of black missions to actually placing their first missionary in the field. Their entry into black missions, like the formation of the Alpha Synod, was fueled by a sense of crisis. Because of increasingly hostile relations between the Synodical Conference and the Leipzig and Hermannsburg Mission Societies in Germany, the Synodical Conference terminated its participation in those societies' foreign mission programs. The crisis was that the Synodical Conference was suddenly without any foreign mission program. From their perspective, any Christian body without a foreign mission program was like a house of worship without a steeple. It just wouldn't be a complete church. As the mission committee of the Synodical Conference saw it,

> If we make no use of the desire of our Lutheran Christians to do something for heathen missions, they will surely apply their money where we would not like to see it go.[2]

In 1877, when the convention of the Synodical Conference heard the resolution to enter black missions, the delegates saw a need, they were enthusiastic, and there was money in the bank ($3,188.71) to get started. What was to hinder them? The mission board urged its newly installed missionary (a white) to make a tour of the field immediately. Twice, between October 1877 and July 1878, he crisscrossed parts of the South: Georgia, Mississippi, Louisiana, Alabama, Florida, and Tennessee. Sending a white man into the rural South on that kind of mission was most unwise and could only fail. It was 1877. The Reconstruction had just ended; the carpetbaggers had done their damage; and Southern whites, especially in rural areas, were not about to have some strange white man "foolin' with their niggers."

The itinerary and the results of the tour are quite revealing. The mission board obviously had not bothered to do its homework before sending that missionary. The tour itself was not at all informative. Had the Synodical Conference or the man they sent done a minimum of research, the tour would have revealed exactly where to begin: the Carolinas, Virginia, and Tennessee. As recently as 17 years before, blacks constituted a very significant part of the Lutheran Church in those states. At the very moment that the Synodical Conference was looking for blacks, the North Carolina Synod was trying to give their blacks away. The second place to begin would have been the port cities of the eastern and gulf coasts. Migrant Lutherans from the Virgin Islands (such as Daniel Wiseman) had already begun to arrive.

There was yet another difficulty. The Synodical Conference was blinded by its own conception of the task, viewing it as a mission "to the heathen." That perception precluded the possibility that some blacks were indeed Christian, and of those, some might even have been Lutheran. With that view of the world, there was no need to ask, Do we have a constituency among black people? and no need even to do homework.

As a result, the New Lutherans (the Synodical Conference) did not get off to a promising start. Its first missionary, Pastor Doescher, was almost immediately in theological difficulty with the Synodical Conference. The problem was that Doescher was willing to preach the Gospel anywhere, also in non-Lutheran churches. In the eyes of the mission board, this constituted the most blatant kind of unionism. Another example of his unionistic spirit was his willingness to bring into his work at New Orleans a promising young black Presbyterian (Willis Polk) as an assistant pastor. By 1879, Doescher was no longer working for the Synodical Conference. However, to his credit, it should be noted that while in New Orleans he opened a Sunday school in Old Sailor's Home, a most disreputable building. This was, in fact, the beginning of Mt. Zion Lutheran Church. In January 1879, a Christian day school was opened with 26 pupils. By the end of the month, there were 120 pupils.

Before leaving the Synodical Conference, Doescher did succeed in opening the Synodical Conference's first black mission, namely, in Little Rock, Arkansas. He began with a Sunday school in December 1877. The following year, a congregation was organized and took the name St. Paul's Colored Lutheran Church. That same year (1878), a church building was erected, and the first black Lutheran Christian day school was established with 46 pupils.

In 1878, the mission board commissioned its second missionary, Rev. Frederick Berg, fresh out of Concordia Seminary, St. Louis, sending him to take Doescher's place in Little Rock. While Berg found that three-fifths of the black population of Little Rock was affiliated with some Christian church, he could find no sign of "serious Christian belief and life among the 6,000 Negroes [there]."[3] Even though he repudiated Doescher's willingness to preach the Gospel anywhere, he did consent (under pressure) to preach in the local black Methodist church on condition that many of the other black preachers in town would be present. As Berg saw it, this would be a grand opportunity to present the *complete* understanding and truths of Scripture, which these conservative Lutherans of the Synodical Conference believed they alone believed. He was quite crestfallen to find that of all those present "... only two preachers confessed their ignorance and expressed the wish to learn from me."[4] (In the ghetto, we call that last statement evidence of "arrogance on wheels.")

When Berg first came to Little Rock, he found himself being warmly welcomed when he identified himself as a missionary. To his chagrin, he later learned that, to the members of the black community, "missionary" meant Missionary Baptist, a label no good Synodical Conference Lutheran would be caught dead with. His use of the term "sinner" also carried a totally different connotation in the black community. To them, a sinner meant someone who was unchurched.

Since the majority of the black population at Little Rock was already Christian (or at least affiliated with some church) and Berg had few accessions to report, his account of the average day at school was enough to legitimize (in his and the mission board's view) what he was doing as "true mission work among the heathen."

> At 8:30 the first bell rings and a troop of darkies storms in and begins to make the most scandalous racket. One or the other immediately comes with a complaint about clothing torn either in play or as the result of a thrashing. They often crowd around my desk by the dozen to tell me something trifling and pull at my books. Then at 9 o'clock school begins. All make a lunge, not for their seats, but for the water bucket. After 10 minutes all are finally seated but not until I have roared at them like a lion, thundered out threats at them and soundly thrashed a few. Finally they are still as mice. The command—Rise! The Our Father follows. Again, a hideous noise as they sit down. I spring into their midst, pleading, screaming, stamping, to obtain quiet. The class

must hear Bible history now and answer questions. . . . But they chatter even when one stands right next to them and make impertinent noises with their feet, tablets, and books, and often halt me for five minutes. Then comes the ABC lesson, but instead of looking at the alphabet chart they look elsewhere. Meanwhile the other classes should prepare their lessons. . . . Pictorial Primer Reader class: no preparation, no attention during recitation. Third Reader class: worse yet! Fourth Reader—wretched! The cane must be raised high. It whistles through the air, landing on the lazy, stupid churl.[5]

Berg left Little Rock after three years, exhausted and frustrated.

The third missionary sent into the fray was Rev. Lorenz Wahl. At first glance, he seemed a more likely candidate, since he had spent eleven years as a missionary in India. If there was any drawback, it was the problem of language. Wahl was born in Germany, and his English was not calculated to make him a winner in his new field: Mobile, Alabama. He served there only about two years, 1880–1881. Since most of the black population, as in Little Rock, was already affiliated with some Christian church, the chapel that Wahl opened quickly turned into a school. Disavowing the black heritage altogether, he set about teaching his black students how to sing German chorales and nothing else. He, too, did not last long.

For the moment, we shall skip the fourth missionary (N. J. Bakke) and go to the fifth one sent by the mission board. He was Rev. W. R. Buehler, born in Germany, who had spent some time in Africa as a missionary. Buehler's field was Prince Edward County, Virginia, where he established St. Matthew's Lutheran congregation. Buehler lasted longer than the previous three missionaries. He left his charge in 1886 when he received a call to teach in Germany. The mission was closed that same year. Reportedly, it was closed because the work was begun without the mission board's knowing that the overwhelming black population of Prince Edward County was already churched, though non-Lutheran. Lueking contends that the mission board

... blamed [the Negroes] for giving a false report of the real situation, even though the Mission Board had access to Buehler's personal reports each year from 1881 [to 1886] and had sent no fewer than three officials from the Board to inspect the field.[6]

Two years later, the mission board reopened that field at the request of the black people in Prince Edward County.

Lueking summarizes the initial efforts of the mission board of the Synodical Conference as follows:

> This survey of the records of the early [Synodical Conference] missionaries to Negroes during the 1880s reveals the remarkable consistency in outlook and practice which prevailed among the [missionaries]. Their letters and articles supply cogent proof of the almost insurmountable difficulties encountered by the consistent maintenance of the goal to remake Negroes in the Lutheran image. Berg and Wahl held out for two years at their respective posts. Buehler stood fast for six years. All left the work because they requested to be released, and the reports about their leaving were always candid enough to state that the missionary left "because he had lost enthusiasm for the work and wished to return to the parish ministry" or, as in the case of Berg, "he became sad and discouraged."[7]

There were other difficulties. Two German language periodicals widely circulated in the Missouri Synod, *Der Lutheraner* and *Die Missionstaube,* reported with some regularity on the progress of the new mission to the black community. The language of both journals was condescending, referring to the prospective converts as "the children of Ham," or "the perishing darkie heathen," and depicting blacks in highly negative racial terms.[8] In addition, just seven years after the Synodical Conference began its work, there arose a series of debates within the Synodical Conference about whether to continue the mission and how much should be expended on it. One missionary in the field, in a carefully worded rebuttal, accused the Synodical Conference of looking upon its work in the black community as an experiment, not a genuine commitment.

Not all the news was bad. In 1879, the first English language publication in the Missouri Synod appeared. It was called *The Pioneer.* Its original purpose was to deal with global missionary issues. In reality, it dealt almost exclusively with the Synodical Conference work among blacks in the South. Unlike *Der Lutheraner* and *Die Missionstaube, The Pioneer* regularly depicted the Negro as the hero of its stories and referred to him as "the freedman of the South."

The Synodical Conference did find in Rev. N. J. Bakke a missionary who would stay the course. He was ordained and commissioned in 1880 and sent to work in New Orleans. It was there that the Synodical Conference finally succeeded in establishing a bridgehead in the black community.

Although Bakke replaced Doescher in New Orleans, he built on the latter's base. In 1881, a second Christian day school was opened in New Orleans, which served as the starting point for St. Paul's Lutheran Church. However, its chapel, built at the cost of $300, was so rudely constructed that the residents of the community quickly named it "The Chicken Coop." In 1883, St. Paul's dedicated a new chapel and in 1891 a new two-story school building was dedicated. In 1888, a third Christian day school was opened in New Orleans. This was the beginning of Bethlehem Lutheran Church. By 1891, Bakke's own parish, Mt. Zion, had 240 baptized members and St. Paul's had 136 baptized members. Whether by chance or by choice, much of the work in New Orleans was with the Creole population.

Another "success story" in the annals of black Lutheranism comes out of Mensura, LA. Henry Thomas, a member of St. Paul's in New Orleans, moved to Mansura in the late 1890s. After several months in the community, he met three gentlemen—Pete Batiest, Scott Normand, and P. M. Lehman—all of whom were quite upset about their treatment at the hands of the local Roman Catholic priest. The three gentlemen were craftsmen and, as members of the local Roman Catholic parish, had recently worked hard at the construction of a new church building. After the new building was completed, they found themselves as blacks more rigidly segregated at church than before. Not only did they feel personally mistreated in the church which they had helped build, their children were badly neglected.

After Thomas told them about the work of the Lutheran Church in New Orleans, they asked him to invite his pastor to come to Mansura. The outgrowth of that meeting was the establishment of St. Paul's Lutheran Church (in 1898) at Cocoville, now called Lutherville, about two miles from Mansura. What is so special about St. Paul's is the number of pastors it has given to the Lutheran Church. Those 12 are Rev. P. D. Lehman; his brother, Rev. Dr. Harvey Lehman; their nephew, Rev. Gulfrey Laurent; Rev. John Thompson; Rev. E. B. Berger; Rev. Dr. Joseph Lavalais; Rev. Othniel Thompson; Rev. Luther Robinson; Rev. Edgar Robinson; Rev. Dewitt Robinson;

Rev. Edwin Thompson; and Rev. Felton Vorice.[9] The Lehmans, Thompsons, Robinsons, and Laurents are all related to each other.

Even though St. Paul's in Lutherville has never become large or self-supporting, few congregations can match the record it established. Many in the church affectionately refer to the pastors who came out of St. Paul's as "The Mansura Mafia."

Stage Two: The Resurrection of the Old Black Lutherans

This phase of the rebirth process is called a resurrection because it was begun in a number of different places by blacks who had been Lutheran before the Civil War.

This stage began, prematurely it would seem, in 1880, when two black churches, Reformation Church at Hartford, CT, and Trinity Church in Greenport, Long Island, were accepted as members of the New York Ministerium. No one seems to know who the members were or how they came into the Lutheran Church. As congregations, they did not last long. After 1885, nothing is known of these two churches. One commentator suggests that their demise was due to the lack of consistent leadership.[10]

A more lasting resurrection took place in Washington, DC, where the principal player was a young man who had grown up in the Danish West Indies and was one of the early black Lutherans to migrate to the U.S. His name was Daniel Wiseman. One of Wiseman's biographers says that he did not know that he was black until he came to the United States.

Wiseman was one of the participants in the program of Lutheran theological education at Howard University sponsored by the Maryland Synod in the 1880s. He was the only one in that group to complete his theological studies at Howard. Wiseman came under the tutelage of the pastor of Luther Place Memorial Church in Washington, DC. The church had a number of black members. With Wiseman ready to enter the ministry, what better opportunity was there than to follow the fashion of the day, i.e., put blacks and whites in separate congregations? In fact, Luther Place Memorial Church contributed to the purchase of the land on which the new black church, Redeemer, was to be built.

Wiseman graduated from Howard University in 1884, was licensed, and began building a Sunday school. He was ordained as pastor of Redeemer Lutheran Church, in 1886 and served that congregation for 58 years.

The next evidence of rebirth took place in and around the city of Baltimore. There is reason to believe that some work had been done by the Lutheran Church with black people in Baltimore as early as 1878. The Synodical Conference missionary at Little Rock, Arkansas, reported that C. B. Lewis of Baltimore

> . . . who was received into the Lutheran Church by confirmation . . . was sent hither to receive preparatory instruction before entering upon his collegiate studies for the ministry at Columbus, Ohio.[11]

Elsewhere in Baltimore, a dedicated layman remodeled an old gristmill in the suburbs and started a Sunday school for black youngsters in 1890.[12] Shortly thereafter, he established an orphanage and started worship services in conjunction with the Sunday school. This new venture in the suburbs was called Our Savior Lutheran Church. It was generally under the sponsorship of members of the Joint Synod of Ohio. It grew so rapidly that the local sponsoring group asked for assistance from the synod. Rev. Taylor Johnson (black), who had been trained by some of the Lutheran pastors of Baltimore, served as the first pastor of Our Savior. Shortly after he began his work in the suburbs, he established a Sunday school in the heart of Baltimore's black community. That was the beginning of St. Philip's Lutheran Church. Its first house of worship was dedicated in 1896.

Work among blacks took on a somewhat more official status in Baltimore when, in 1897, the Lutheran Board for Colored Missions of Baltimore was incorporated. This was the official vehicle through which black mission work was conducted in the Joint Synod of Ohio for the next 40 years. In 1904, P. W. Phifer, after falling out with the Synodical Conference, became pastor of St. Philip's.

The fourth place where rebirth took place was in North Carolina when the Synodical Conference finally realized that there were already black Lutherans in the land. A year after the Alpha Synod was organized, it lost its real leader with the death of David Koontz from food poisoning. As their situation deteriorated, P. W. Phifer, at the behest of the Alpha Synod, appealed to the Synodical Conference for assistance. (That is how the Synodical Conference "discovered" the black Lutherans in North Carolina.) Phifer first wrote to the Synodical Conference in January 1891. Within three months, the Synodical Conference sent a committee of three to confer with the pastors of the Alpha Synod—Phifer, Holt, and Clapp. They met

> . . . in a negro cabin in Burlington [North Carolina], the proprietor of the only hotel in the place having turned them [the Synodical Conference committee] out because they were Negro missionaries.[13]

Bakke, one of the members of the Synodical Conference's committee of three, came up with an interesting assessment of these black Lutherans in North Carolina. He saw them

> . . . posing as Lutheran, but who, as most of the colored preachers of the time, were illiterate and possessed no knowledge of true Christianity nor of confessional Lutheranism.[14]

The committee reported to the mission board,

> Only the simplest catechism questions were addressed to these men, yet one named Brother Holt sometimes shook his head and commented that the question was too deep for him. We all agreed in the fundamental doctrines, but when we came to altar and pulpit fellowship, Brother Holt had some definite objections and indeed not ungrounded ones. For how had he conducted his ministry for years? Not only in the same church with Methodists, but both pastors regularly changed off in preaching to one another's congregations. . . . Brother Holt did not want to give up this cordial exchange. He stubbornly defended this syncretism to the last; finally, however, when he was driven into a corner and could no longer defend himself he dropped his hands and said, "I'm beaten." Though it was painful for him, he promised no more pulpit and altar fellowship with these errorists. The others, likewise, though unknowingly caught in the same sin, promised the same. They were all overjoyed over the unity of faith which had been brought about by this meeting. They thanked us for the instruction they had enjoyed and gave their pledge that this conference would be of great blessing for them and their congregations.[15]

The committee "advised the [Mission] Board to take charge of the field, provided a man could be found who would instruct the preachers and superintend the mission."[16] The man sent to take charge was Bakke himself. He was introduced to Lutherans in Concord, NC, at a service conducted by Pastor Phifer. Phifer's text was Acts 20:29, "For I know this, that after my departing shall grievous wolves enter in among you, not sparing the flock."[17]

Phifer's text was prophetic so far as the Alpha Synod was concerned. The Synodical Conference representative, Bakke, called the first conference of workers in November 1891. As Bakke put it, the new conference was "composed of survivors of the defunct Alpha Synod," (Clapp, Holt, Phifer) and himself.[18] The status of being "defunct" was conferred on the Alpha Synod, not by the members themselves but by Bakke, and indicates what he had in mind. At one point, Bakke says that Holt and Clapp retired from the ministry in 1892. But in another place, Bakke explains in detail that, since he was "convinced of [their] deficiencies . . . to administer the means of grace to their hearers, [he] persuaded them to resign."[19]

Phifer was not so easily dealt with. Although Phifer had been working with Bakke in Concord, NC, the Board (in 1900) "requested" Phifer to serve some country congregations in Cabarrus County since Phifer was "the only available man."[20] Phifer's removal was not a request, it was an order. Nor was he the only "available man." As Phifer saw it, this was a blatant disregard of the doctrine of the call. A mission board could not nullify a call properly extended by a congregation.

Bakke, as the mission board's representative, held the purse strings. Phifer, in effect, told Bakke that he could keep his money. Phifer took most of the members and formed a splinter church. Bakke's report to the mission board describes the incident as follows:

> Some [of the Negroes] did not like the new order of things; others, the better class, stood by me. . . . Had I been alone in the field I could have gained their confidence as I have done elsewhere. . . . He [Phifer] no doubt has the confidence of the members. He is of their race, and the race question which has always been troublesome has now reached the boiling point in North Carolina.[21]

Phifer left the Synodical Conference, briefly served a church in the Concord area, and then started a church in Charlotte which was affiliated with the Joint Synod of Ohio. From Charlotte, Phifer went to Baltimore where he served as the pastor of St. Philip's church until his death in 1911.[22] One writer refers to the Phifer-Bakke episode as the "atrophy of Bakke's evangelical spirit."[23] It is with this incident that we see the demise of what was left of the Alpha Synod.

Expansion by Request. The North Carolina field into which the Synodical Conference had been invited (and subsequently known as the Immanuel Conference and/or the Eastern Field) quickly became the mission board's largest and most stable area of work. There was a significant change in the manner in which new areas of work were identified as well as the manner in which churches were started. The new method was that blacks themselves requested assistance rather than "waiting to be found." The following are some examples:

—In the winter of 1893, the black members of the Lutheran Church at Concord requested worship services at Mount Pleasant.[24] This became Mount Calvary Lutheran Church in Mount Pleasant, NC. In 1897,

> ... a delegation from a colored settlement in the neighborhood of Dry's Schoolhouse, Cabarrus Co., seven miles south of Concord, came to attend the Lutheran services at Grace Church. On the previous Sunday the same delegation had paid a similar visit to the Presbyterian church of the city. They were in search of a pastor.... Shortly afterwards the delegation returned and requested [that the Lutherans come] and preach to them.[25]

—That request led to the formation of St. Peter's Lutheran Church at Dry's Schoolhouse.

—Mount Calvary Lutheran Church at Sandy Ridge, NC, was started at the request of a Lutheran family.[26] It is known today as Mount Calvary at Kannapolis.

—In 1893, "Twenty-four men and women signed a petition for Lutheran services. This resulted in the organization of Concordia Lutheran Church at Rockwell, NC."[27]

—In the summer of 1893, a delegation from Gold Hill "presented ... a petition signed by 50 men and women to come and preach there."[28] This was the beginning of Zion Lutheran Church.

> A woman residing in Salisbury, who on her visits to relatives at Gold Hill attended the Lutheran services there, requested the

writer to give her catechetical instruction, which he occasionally did. This was the beginning of the Salisbury mission.[29]

—"A petition, signed by thirty men and women was received in 1894."[30] Five of these had been members of the Lutheran Church since before the Civil War and had been worshipping with whites. This was the beginning of the work at Conover and Catawba, NC.

—In 1898, two Lutheran families in Southern Pines, NC, requested that a representative of the Lutheran Church come and preach to them. This was the beginning of St. James Lutheran Church.[31]

—A minister (not Lutheran) by the name of Samuel W. Hampton asked that the Lutheran Church begin work in Monroe, NC. He donated the land for Bethlehem Lutheran Church that was built there.[32]

The many requests from black people in North Carolina bring to mind other requests that had come to the Synodical Conference at an earlier date. In 1881, black people in Meherrin, VA, asked a Lutheran pastor to start a church and school in their community. That led to the formation of St. Matthew's Lutheran Church. In 1882, black people living in Springfield, IL, asked that a Lutheran church be started in their community. That led to the formation of Holy Trinity Lutheran Church.

When the Alpha Synod invited the Synodical Conference into North Carolina, the Conference found itself playing in an entirely new ball game. The Conference missionary no longer asked, Where do I go next? Black people, many of whom had been Lutheran since before the Civil War, pointed the way for the Synodical Conference.

Training Black Church Professionals. A development of equal importance was the training of black professionals for the work of the church. A tentative effort was made at St. Paul's Colored Lutheran Church in Little Rock with the establishment of St. Paul's Lutheran Academy. The Academy was a part of the Christian day school, "formed [for] the most advanced pupils of the school [and] designed to furnish—at some future time—the teachers and preachers of our mission-work in the South."[33] Berg wrote,

> We are pleased to have with us Mr. C. B. Lewis of Baltimore, who was received into the Lutheran Church by confirmation, and was sent hither to receive preparatory instruction before entering

upon his collegiate studies for the ministry at Columbus, Ohio. He is already actively engaged at work under five tutors.[34]

The establishment of that academy was a bit premature. Its location and the absence of a resident pastor ultimately contributed to its failure.

The first successful attempt to train blacks for the Lutheran ministry began with Nathaniel Burkhalter, who entered Concordia Seminary at Springfield, IL, in 1882. Between 1882 and 1903, other young black men such as John McDavid, Lucius Thalley, Thompson, and Wiley Lash attended the Springfield seminary.

Between 1890 and 1915, 19 males studied for the ministry of the Synodical Conference. An additional 22 male and female teachers served in the Christian day schools maintained by the Synodical Conference (see Appendices A and B for their names and a brief biography).

Immanuel Seminary and College. Immanuel was established specifically to train black professional church workers. The college, opened in 1903 with five young black men, was located in two rooms on the second floor of Grace Lutheran school in Concord, NC. The larger room served as a classroom by day and a dormitory for male students at night. An old house in the rear of the church was the kitchen/dining room. One of the students, F. Foard, was the cook.[35]

Immanuel consisted of three departments: a theological seminary, a two-year normal department (for teacher training), and a high school. That same year (1903), Luther College, modeled on the same pattern as Immanuel, was opened at St. Paul's Lutheran Church in New Orleans. After the first year, both schools were coeducational.

Immanuel was moved to Greensboro, NC, in 1905 and continued to operate for the next 56 years. John F. Nau, son of Immanuel's second president, pictured the main building at Greensboro:

Immanuel's administration building was a monstrosity. A government survey of the original administration building at Immanuel Lutheran College described it in the following words: "The building is a two-story granite structure of an inconsistent, mixed, and wasteful type of architecture. It is heated by stoves. The interior shows bad workmanship, inexperienced planning, and poor material." It had numberless small towers gracing the roof, with an enormous tower in the center. It was a very ornate and picturesque building; but, as stated in the documents of the school systems of North Carolina, a building which was an excellent example of how *not* to build a school. In the basement were the commissary and the boiler room. On the second floor, which was also the ground floor, were the offices of the faculty members, a large hall for devotional services, several classrooms, and a small library. On the second floor were more classrooms, and the third floor was finished on the inside with beaverboard, which was in terrible condition. The Naus referred to the monstrosity as "the castle on the Rhine."[36]

In 1904 the Synodical Conference passed a resolution that all blacks who sought to become pastors or teachers should be educated at Immanuel or Luther College. In the 1920s, Eugene Stoll (a young black man who could easily pass for white) completed the first year of his theological education at Concordia Seminary in St. Louis. After that, he was sent to Immanuel to complete his preparation for the ministry.[37] The effort to send all black students to Immanuel was effective until 1942, when a prospective black candidate for the ministry entered Concordia College in Oakland, California. Ultimately, he completed his preparation for the ministry at Concordia Seminary in St. Louis.

Stage Three: Alabama

Within a twelve month period, 1915–1916, two Lutheran groups began working in the black communities of Alabama. The first was the Joint Synod of Ohio; the other was the Synodical Conference. Their work went in different directions, and each group seemed to ignore the other. They have to be examined separately.

The Joint Synod of Ohio. This synod began its outreach program in 1915 in Prattville, AL. By 1917, the Joint Synod of Ohio had 100 confirmed black members, three Christian day schools with 200 pupils, one black pastor, and three black day school teachers.[38] Between 1915 and 1924, seven stations were opened in Alabama and one in Jackson, MS. No other new beginnings were made in Alabama until the mid–1940s.

On entering Alabama, the major project of the Joint Synod of

Ohio's strategy was the opening of a Christian day school. The largest of these schools was in Tuscaloosa in connection with Christ Lutheran Church. That institution ultimately consisted of an elementary and high school, which through the years operated under four different names: St. Paul's School, the Dobbler Institute, St. Paul's Academy, and the Martin Luther Institute.

In some instances, for example at Wetumpka, the people of the community petitioned the Lutheran Church to start a school rather than a church. The school was so popular that some of the students walked three miles a day to attend classes. At St. Paul's in Clanton, the school was equally popular, so much so that, when the school's subsidy was discontinued, the members of the congregation determined to continue the school on their own. When the first resident pastor was assigned to St. Paul's, the congregation "concluded that only two services a month were necessary. They encouraged [the new pastor] to take up public school work and serve the church on a part-time basis."[39]

The Joint Synod of Ohio made extensive use of lay workers, hoping these lay workers would be a recruiting source for professional black pastors. In principle, using lay workers was commendable; in practice, there were two difficulties. First, many of the lay workers were not well-grounded in Lutheranism. Second, they tended to work most effectively with a seasoned and committed pastor—a condition that rarely existed (see Appendices C, D, and E).

The Synodical Conference in Alabama. The Conference came to Alabama as a result of the following letter written in late 1915 by a young black Methodist school teacher, Miss Rosa Young.

Neenah, Alabama
October 27, 1915

Rev. C. F. Drewes
St. Louis, Missouri

Dear Friend:

I am writing you concerning a school I have organized. I began teaching here in 1912 with seven pupils in an old hall, where the cattle went for shelter. Since then I have bought (with money collected in the community) five acres of land and erected a four-room schoolhouse thereon, beside our chapel, which we are working on now, bought 45 seats, 5 heaters, 1 school bell, 1 sewing machine, 1 piano, a nice collection of useful books, and 150 New Testaments for our Bible-training Department.

I am writing to see if your Conference will take our school under its auspices. If you will take our school under your auspices, we will give you the land, the school building, and all its contents to start with. If you cannot take our school, I beg the privilege to appeal to you to give us a donation to help us finish our new chapel. No matter how little, any amount will be cheerfully and thankfully received.

This school is located near the center of Wilcox County, 12 miles from the county seat, 54 miles from Selma, Alabama, two miles from the L and N Railroad, amid 1,500 colored people. The region is very friendly; both white and colored are interested in this school. I hope you will see your way clear to aid us.

Yours humbly,
Rosa J. Young[40]

Miss Young was determined, patient, persistent, and pushy in that uniquely southern manner that was always cloaked in polite, good manners. She was committed to one thing throughout her life: lifting up black people in rural Alabama.

Already in 1912, at the age of 22, Miss Young had organized the Rosebud Literary and Industrial School at Rosebud, Alabama. By 1914, a boll weevil infestation had brought her school, not to mention the whole county, to the brink of bankruptcy. The above letter, which she wrote to the Synodical Conference, was one of the last in a series of efforts to save her school from going under. The Synodical Conference responded affirmatively.

Within a twelve-month period the Synodical Conference became the second group of Lutherans to begin mission work among blacks in Alabama. The Joint Synod of Ohio opened its first mission at Prattville in 1915. The Synodical Conference opened its first mission at Rosebud in 1916. Had the Synodical Conference planned its strategy according to generally accepted standards of mission outreach, Wilcox County (the site of Rosebud) would have been one of the least likely places to begin. Few places in the United States were more poverty stricken, more rampant with ignorance and superstition, or more ingrained with hopelessness than Wilcox County.[41]

In less than 12 months, Wilcox County became the most rapidly growing mission field ever entered by the Lutheran Church in U.S. history. Christ Lutheran Church, the first, was organized on Easter Sunday at Rosebud in 1916. It began with 100 baptized souls, 70 communicant members, and 22 voting members. Table 13 shows the growth of the Alabama field to the year 1948.

Table 13: Statistical Report of the Alabama Field for the Years 1927, 1931, 1946, and 1948

	1927	1931	1946	1948
Congregations and Preaching Stations	29		32	
Day School Teachers			29	
Day Schools	27		30	
Day School Pupils	1,466	1,182	1,227	1,265
Sunday School Pupils		1,558	1,657	
Communicant Members	996	1,464		1,702
Baptized Members	1,789			3,648

Source: Statistics compiled by the author from the official reports of the Alabama congregations to The Lutheran Church—Missouri Synod.

Miss Young was one of the key persons. When the doors of the church were opened at Rosebud, she was the first to answer the "altar call." she demonstrated that there are two kinds of Christians: believers and disciples. The first center everything on what they believe; the second are acutely aware not only of what they believe, they also know that they have been called to a specific ministry. Miss Young was a disciple with a ministry. Hers was a teaching ministry within the church.

She named some of the reasons why she was interested in a teaching ministry:

As a general [rule], there were no schoolhouses [in rural Alabama]; for the most part the public schools were taught in the churches. Most of the churches were dilapidated and so exposed to the elements that one might as well teach outdoors under an oak tree. There were big holes in the roofs and in the floors. Many a time during a heavy shower of rain the large children would have to hold an umbrella over me while I heard a class recite.

In some of those churches there were small heaters, but no flues; so we had to take out a window pane and run the stovepipe out through the side of the wall. When the wind was high on a cold day, the smoke would turn us all away from the fire. In churches where there were no heaters we were obliged to build big fires outdoors. Then I would have to watch the little fellows to prevent their clothes from catching fire.

The educational advantages offered these children by the state were entirely inadequate. The school terms lasted only three or four months a year. Before the children could get a good start in school, the term was over. During the long vacation of eight or nine months the children would forget most, if not all, of what they had learned during the previous year.[42]

Rosa Young lit a fire. Two of her students at the Rosebud school, Sara and Mary McCants, were also confirmed on Palm Sunday 1916. After school was out in May, they went home to Vredenburg and started a Sunday school in an old log cabin. Miss Young walked 15 miles from Rosebud to Vredenburg to lend her support. That Sunday school was the beginning of St. Andrew's Church in 1916.

The news of what was happening at Rosebud soon spread throughout the county. James McBride came to see for himself. He went home to Oak Hill, and through his efforts St. Paul's mission at Oak Hill was started in 1916.

In August 1916, Rosa Young and Luella McCants traveled from Rosebud to Buena Vista by ox cart; there Miss Young organized the Sunday school that was the beginning of St. James Church.

Miss Young was instrumental also in establishing Mt. Carmel Church at Midway in 1917. She helped start Bethany at Nyland in 1918, Mt. Olive at Tinela in 1918, and Zion at Tait's Place in 1919.

Rosa Young touched others who in turn went out and planted the seeds of Lutheranism. Her brother Sam Young started the work at Mount Calvary in Tilden, Dallas County, in 1916. Sam also started Grace Church at Ingomar in 1919. From Rosa's work at Midway, Mrs. Viola Williams and her daughter Elizabeth started Faith Church in Mobile; the C. P. Smith family started Pilgrim in Birmingham; and Mr. and Mrs. James Scott started St. Philip's at Catherine.

It didn't stop there. Two of the McCants brothers began Ebenezer in Atmore, and the Durden and Smith families started Bethlehem at Holy Ark. Even elderly ex-slaves got into the act. An elderly lady locally known as Aunt Rosa started Hope Church at King's

Landing. Mrs. Fanny Steele began St. Luke's at Lamison and St. Matthew Church at Arlington.

Lutheranism in Alabama grew from the grass roots, not the result of a church planner or administrator sitting in his office deciding where and when a church was to be planted. Lutheranism in Alabama's black belt was carried from community to community by simple, committed lay people.

In those early years, each church usually had its own Christian day school. A church/school was usually built on the so-called "T" plan and consisted of a sanctuary and two classrooms and could be constructed for approximately $3,000.

Ordinarily the pastor taught in the Christian day school Monday through Friday and performed his other pastoral duties after school and on the weekend.

Alabama Lutheran Academy. The Alabama field grew so rapidly that it was not possible to staff the growing number of day schools with pastors and teachers trained at Immanuel and Luther Colleges. In November 1922, Alabama Lutheran College was established. Its primary purpose was to prepare young women for the church's mission schools. If there was room, young men might attend, provided they intended to prepare themselves for the ministry. The school was located in Selma, AL, and consisted of a high school and normal department. The school was initially housed in a rented cottage. In 1925, the college moved to a 13-acre site in the northeastern part of the city of Selma. That same year, an elementary school was introduced on the campus.

Alabama Lutheran College was the first Lutheran institution of higher education to be staffed solely by blacks. The faculty consisted of the Rev. R. O. Lynn, president; the Rev. Paul D. Lehman and the Rev. Isaac Holness, professors; Miss Anna J. Hudson, instructor; and Mrs. Lou Jenkins, matron. Subsequently, Alabama Lutheran College became a preparatory school in the Missouri Synod's system of higher education, and its name was changed to Concordia College.

When the Synodical Conference began working in Alabama, its efforts were centered in Wilcox County and was the most rural field in which the Synodical Conference had ever worked (see Table 14).

A population decline in rural Alabama, which began with the onset of the boll weevil infestation, was accelerated by the draft during World War I (see Table 15). The depopulation of rural Ala-

Table 14: Percent of Population of Wilcox County That Was Rural in 1910, 1940, and 1950

1910—82.7% Rural
1940—69.0% Rural
1950—56.2% Rural

Source: United States Census for 1910, 1940, 1950

Table 15: Black Population of Wilcox County in 1910, 1930, and 1980

1910: 27,602
1930: 19,319
1980: 10,151

Source: United States Census for 1910, 1940, 1950

bama did not stop church growth, but in the mid–1930s did slow it down.

School enrollment was most immediately affected as depopulation set in. In the long run, that decline in the rural populaton had serious consequences for the congregations. Too few people were left to maintain the many congregations that had been established. By the time blacks were accepted into the Southern District of the Missouri Synod in 1961, many of the congregations had to be consolidated (see Table 16).

Early on, the growth of black Lutheranism in Alabama led to the organization of the third regional association within the Synodical Conference. The association, known as the Alabama Luther Conference, met annually and included pastors, teachers, and congregations. In order to facilitate the fellowship and work in that region, the conference published a newsletter, *The Alabama Lutheran.* Shortly after its initial appearance, it was asked to change both its name and the scope of its coverage so that it could serve the entire black constituency of the Synodical Conference. The newsletter appeared in January 1923 under the new title *The Colored Lutheran.*

The other noteworthy development on the Alabama field was the annual Sunday school convention. In addition to its emphasis on mutual edification and fellowship, the members of the convention developed a lively interest in bringing the Gospel to Africa. By 1930, the young black Lutherans in Alabama had collected $6,000 to assist the church in beginning mission outreach in Africa. Another

Table 16: Black Lutheran Congregations Consolidated in Alabama by 1961

1. Immanuel, Vredenburg
   a. Buena Vista
   b. Tenile
2. St. Paul, Oak Hill
   a. Rosebud
   b. Ackerville
   c. Hamburg
   d. Ingomar
3. Holy Cross, Camden
   a. Rock West
   b. Possum Bend
   c. Longmile
   d. Taits Place
4. Epiphany, Arlington
   a. Catherine
   b. Midway
   c. Lamison
   d. Myland
   e. Pinehill
   f. Vineland
   g. Thomasville

Source: Richard C. Dickinson, *Roses and Thorns* (St. Louis: Concordia Publishing House, 1977), 71

important function of the Sunday school convention was to give young black Lutherans the opportunity to meet and begin the mate-selection process (see Appendix F).

Stage Four: Becoming a National Urban Phenomenon

The growth of the Alabama field between 1916–1930 was so rapid and organizationally demanding that the new direction black Lutheranism took in the 1920s almost went unnoticed. Beginning with the first systematic efforts to work with black people in 1750, black Lutheranism was located almost exclusively in the South. Between 1920 and 1950, there was a rapid change in the geographic location of black Lutheranism. With the 1920s, black Lutheranism began spreading to the North, Midwest, and far western regions of the continental U.S. Between 1920 and 1950, 34 black Lutheran congregations were established in those parts of the country.

The roots of this new movement go back to the 1870s when black Lutherans began migrating from the Danish West Indies, settling in New York City.[43] By the 1890s, it is estimated that each year at least a hundred black Lutherans from the Danish West Indies were coming to New York City.[44] The impetus for that migration was the economic depression that gripped the Danish West Indies. In 1917, when the United States purchased the islands from Denmark, several thousand black Lutherans were already in the city of New York.

Within the continental U.S., blacks started moving out of the South in significant numbers just before the turn of the present century. The contributing factors were economic stagnation, racial oppression, and new job opportunities that came with World War I. Some of the members of St. Matthew's in Meherrin, VA, began moving to Yonkers, NY, in the 1890s. By 1907, there were 40 black Lutherans from Meherrin living in Yonkers.[45]

The growth and development of black Lutheranism in the North and West came in two waves: the first was from 1923 to 1939, the second from 1940 to 1950.

The first wave led to the establishment of the following congregations:

1909: Yonkers, NY—Bethany Lutheran Church; Synodical Conference.

1913: Bronx, NY—The Danish West Indian Lutheran Church.

1923: New York, NY—Transfiguration Lutheran Church; ULCA.

1924: Chicago, IL—St. Philip Lutheran Church; Synodical Conference.

1925: Los Angeles, CA—St. Paul Lutheran Church; Synodical Conference.

Philadelphia, PA—St. Philip Lutheran Church; Synodical Conference.

1926: Cincinnati, OH—Immanuel Lutheran Church; Synodical Conference.

Oakland, CA—Bethlehem Lutheran Church; Synodical Conference.

St. Louis, MO—St. Philip Lutheran Church; Synodical Conference.

1927: Baltimore, MD—St. Philip Lutheran Church; Synodical Conference.

1932: Philadelphia, PA—Christ Lutheran Church; ULCA.

Washington, DC—Mt. Olivet Lutheran Church; Synodical Conference.

1934: New York, NY—Holy Trinity Lutheran Church; ULCA.

Evansville, IN—Grace Lutheran Church; Synodical Conference.

1937: Detroit, MI—St. Philip Lutheran Church; Synodical Conference.

1938: Cleveland, OH—St. Philip Lutheran Church; Synodical Conference.

Pittsburgh, PA—Faith Lutheran Church; Synodical Conference.

1940: Houston, TX—Holy Cross Lutheran Church; Synodical Conference.

The initial growth of black Lutheranism in the North and West was quite different from that which occurred in Louisiana and Alabama from 1877 to 1930, which began as an effort to reach the unchurched. Black Lutheranism in the North and West began as an effort by black Lutherans themselves to maintain and preserve their Lutheranism. When blacks migrated from the South, they did so, not as individuals but as kinship groups, so that black Lutheranism was brought to the North and West by families. In some instances, those families were fairly large kinship groups that formed the core of the new congregations.

Black Lutheranism was brought to Oakland, CA, by three sisters who had been members of the Lutheran Church in New Orleans: Mrs. Bessie Wilcox, Mrs. Adelia Pollard, and Mrs. M. Golphin. It was brought to Harlem by many families—hundreds of blacks who had been members of the Lutheran Church on St. Thomas and St. Croix. It was brought to Philadelphia by the De Loach family who had been members of Bethlehem Church in New Orleans.[46] It came to Los Angeles through two large families from New Orleans: Mrs. Josephine Walters and her eight adult children and through Mr. and Mrs. William Johnson and their seven adult children.

At first the establishment of black Lutheran congregations in the North and West was much slower than it had been in Alabama. Black

Lutherans were in New York City for 50 years before Transfiguration Lutheran Church was organized. Members from St. Matthew's (Virginia) had been in Yonkers for over 20 years before Bethany Lutheran Church was organized.

The first wave of black Lutheranism in the North and West differed from that in Alabama and Louisiana in other ways. In Alabama and Louisiana, basic to the church's strategy was the establishment of Christian day schools, sometimes before a congregation was organized. By contrast, not one of the first wave black Lutheran congregations in the North and West began with a Christian day school. They usually began by organizing a worshiping group in someone's home, a rented hall, or, as in New York, at the YWCA.[47]

The second wave of the North/West movement of black Lutheranism established the following congregations:

1942: Indianapolis, IN—Our Savior Lutheran Church; Synodical Conference.

New York, NY—St. Paul Lutheran Church; ULCA.

1944: Columbus, OH—St. Philip Lutheran Church.

St. Louis, MO—Holy Sacrament Lutheran Church; Synodical Conference.

Memphis, TN—Calvary Lutheran Church; Synodical Conference.

1945: Gary, IN—Good Shepherd Lutheran Church; Synodical Conference.

Dayton, OH—Redeemer Lutheran Church

Philadelphia, PA—Annunciation Lutheran Church.

Detroit, MI—St. Titus Lutheran Church.

1946: Portland, OR—Bethesda Lutheran Church.

Detroit, MI—Berea Lutheran Church; Synodical Conference.

St. Louis, MO—St. Michael Lutheran Church; Synodical Conference.

Kansas City, MO—St. John Lutheran Church; Synodical Conference.

1947: Los Angeles, CA—Community Lutheran Church; ALC.

New York, NY—Mt. Zion Lutheran Church; Synodical Conference.

1949: Toledo, OH—St. Philip Lutheran Church; Synodical Conference.

1949: Alton, IL—Berea Lutheran Church; Synodical Conference.
      Philadelphia, PA—Christ Lutheran Church; ULCA.
1950: San Diego, CA—Messiah Lutheran Church; Synodical Conference.
      Oakland, CA—Harbor Homes Lutheran Church.

Much of the second wave of black Lutheranism in the North and West came immediately following World War II. The pace with which black Lutheran congregations were established was faster during the second wave than in the first wave. During the 17-year period of the first wave, 1923–1940, 18 congregations were organized. During the 9-year period of the second wave, 1942–1950, 20 congregations were established.

Some of this North/West growth took place at the expense of southern congregations, so that the late 1930s and 1940s began a period of retrenchment and consolidation for many southern congregations, especially those in rural areas.

During the second wave, mission boards and local mission committees showed more initiative in helping to establish new congregations. In fact, some new Lutheran denominations entered the arena—for example, the Augustana Synod, the Evangelical Lutheran Church, and the National Lutheran Council.

During this second wave, the Christian day school began to re-emerge as an important component of the black church. Christian day schools were established at St. Titus and St. Philip's in Detroit. At Mt. Zion in New York, Dr. Clemence Sabourin used the Christian day school in a particularly effective manner to stabilize the newly organized congregation and to reach out to the community in innovative ways. The Christian day school during this period, however, never occupied the same position of importance in the strategy of North/West black churches as it had in southern black Lutheran congregations.

The changes in black Lutheranism, nevertheless, were dramatic. By 1936, one fourth of the black baptized members of the Synodical Conference were in the North and West. In the five-year period before 1936, the black membership of the Synodical Conference as a whole grew by 26 percent. During that same period, however, the black membership in the North and West grew by 92 percent.[48]

By 1950 there were 10,881 confirmed black Lutherans in 130

congregations in the ULCA, the ALC, and the Synodical Conference (see Table 17):

Table 17: Black Lutheran Congregations and Preaching Stations in the U.S. in Rank Order of the Number of Confirmed Members by State, 1948–1950

State	Number of Congregations	Number of Confirmed members
1. New York	4	2,237
2. Alabama	42	1,298
3. Louisiana	10	1,192
4. North Carolina	14	937
5. Missouri	8	784
6. Michigan	5	648
7. Illinois	6	641
8. Ohio	5	530
9. Pennsylvania	4	419
10. Washington, D.C.	2	409
11. California	5	338
12. Maryland	2	329
13. Indiana	4	325
14. Mississippi	2	192
15. Florida	2	123
16. Virginia	1	83
17. Texas	3	78
18. Nebraska	1	55
19. Oklahoma	1	51
20. Oregon	1	41
21. Tennessee	3	40
22. South Carolina	1	22
23. Georgia	1	20
24. Kentucky	1	9
25. Kansas	1	–
26. Minnesota	1	–
Total	130	10,881

Source: Constructed from information in Ervin E. Krebs, *The Lutheran Church and the American Negro* (Columbus, Ohio: Board of American Missions, American Lutheran Church, 1950), 28–30, 85.

—The southern states, where U. S. black Lutheranism began, included a little more than a third of the members in well more than half of the congregations; while

—The North/West had grown to 45 percent of the membership in less than a fourth of the congregations. Not only were the North/West black congregations significantly larger than their southern counterparts, they were all urban. By 1950, black Lutheranism was more highly urbanized than the constituency of the Missouri Synod (see Table 18).

Table 18: Number of Black Lutherans in 1950 by Region

Region	State	Number of Confirmed Members
North/West		
	New York	2,237
	Michigan	648
	Illinois	641
	Ohio	530
	Pennsylvania	419
	California	338
	Nebraska	55
	Oregon	41
Border States		
	Missouri	784
	Washington, DC	409
	Maryland	329
	Indiana	325
	Texas	78
	Oklahoma	51
Southern States		
	Alabama	1,298
	Louisiana	1,192
	North Carolina	937
	Mississippi	192
	Florida	123
	Virginia	83
	Tennessee	40
	South Carolina	22
	Kentucky	9

Source: Constructed from information in Ervin E. Krebs, *The Lutheran Church and the American Negro* (Columbus, Ohio: Board of American Missions, American Lutheran Church, 1950), 28–30, 85.

There were other developments during the northern and western movement of black Lutherans that are of special importance: (1) For the first time, black Lutheran congregations became self-supporting. The first to do so were St. Philip's, Chicago, and St. Philip's, St. Louis. (2) For the first time, black Lutherans became members of the Missouri Synod and the American Lutheran Church. (3) For the first time since the establishment of Immanuel Lutheran College, blacks were admitted to institutions of higher education in the Missouri Synod. (4) For the first time, with the formation of the Lutheran Human Relations Association of America, racism in the Lutheran Church was openly attacked by black pastors and congregations.[49] (5) For the first time, racially inclusive Sunday schools were established.

The Vision of Africa

Just as it moved towards a national presence, black Lutheranism "accidentally" became involved in the spread of Lutheranism to Africa.

The General Conference, assembled in convention in August 1925, at Concord, NC, by resolution asked the Synodical Conference to send missionaries to Africa. To show their good faith in this matter, the General Conference immediately began gathering offerings to support that endeavor. The Alabama field (of the General Conference) was especially enthusiastic in its support of the impending work in Africa.

At almost the precise moment that the General Conference was sending its resolution to the Synodical Conference, sixteen Christian congregations in northern Nigeria formed the Ibesikpo United Church. A primary objective of the new church organization was to send one of its members to the United States to train for the ministry. The person chosen was Senior Evangelist Jonathan Udo Ekong, the son of Chief N. E. Udo.

Jonathan Ekong arrived in the U.S. in May 1928 and headed for Howard University to begin ministerial studies. Upon arriving at Howard, administrators discovered that he had not yet completed high school. He was, therefore, sent to Livingston College in Salisbury, NC, which had a high school as well as a bachelor of arts program on its campus.

While enrolled at Livingston College, two incidents changed Mr. Ekong's course of action. He learned from an African American periodical that the Synodical Conference was interested in doing mission work in Africa. Second, he attended St. John's Lutheran Church (African American), located near the Livingston campus. After observing the services and talking with the pastor, the Rev. Felton Vorice (one of the "Mansura Mafia"), Ekong enrolled at Im-

179

manuel Lutheran College and Seminary in Greensboro, N.C.

During Ekong's matriculation at Immanuel in 1934, the Synodical Conference decided to begin mission work among the Ibedio people of Nigeria. As a student, Ekong assisted in translating Luther's Catechism into the Ibedio language.

After completing theological studies at Immanuel, Ekong enrolled at A and T College in Greensboro for additional training. He was awarded his theological diploma in 1938 and returned to Nigeria that same year. Ekong served the church in a number of capacities until his death in 1982 at the age of 101.

Summary

The rebirth of black Lutheranism in the last quarter of the 19th century was produced as much by crises in the black community as it was by crises within the Lutheran Church. It was a crisis in the Synodical Conference which led that body to open its mission to the "black heathens," as they were called. It was a crisis in the Alpha Synod which led that group to invite the Synodical Conference into North Carolina. It was a crisis in Wilcox County that brought the Lutheran Church into rural Alabama.

For 200 years before the rebirth of black Lutheranism, the base from which the Lutheran Church reached out to black people was the local white congregation and its pastor. With the possible exception of the Plantation Missionary in South Carolina, Lutherans did not genuinely enter the black community or the life of the black people they sought to work with. When a black person joined the Lutheran Church, he/she had to leave the black community. As noted in chapter 7, the Lutheran Church was minimally aware of the ramifications of this mode of operation. The church saw this as a problem of simpleminded people and suggested that pastors speak to blacks accordingly. With the organizing of separate black congregations, the 200-year tradition of avoiding the black community seemed to change.

Another significant change came with the rebirth of black Lutheranism. For 200 years (1669–1866), reaching out to black people had always been a matter of "local option." Even after the adoption of the Five Point Plan in 1817, it was at least thirty years before many local congregations in the South decided to exercise their option. In the North, there appears to have been little awareness that an option existed. With the creation of the Board for Colored Missions by the Synodical Conference, not only was there a new policy mandating work with blacks, that policy was put into action.

Once it was reborn, black Lutheranism spread in diametrically opposite directions, almost at the same time. In 1915, there was an almost explosive growth of black Lutheranism in the most rural parts of Alabama. In the 1920s, black Lutheranism was carried to the most urban sections of the North and West. In 1950, after almost 300 years, black Lutheranism was predominantly urban and northern.

Black people suggested that a reborn black Lutheranism might differ from its ante-bellum counterpart. Pre-Civil War black Lutherans emerged after the Reconstruction calling for the establishment of congregations in North Carolina. Even some non-Lutherans got into the act. Blacks (primarily lay people, not a few of whom were women) not only invited the Lutheran Church into Alabama, they also carried Lutheranism from hamlet to hamlet. A growing number of blacks entered full-time service in the work of the church as pastors and teachers. Black laity also brought Lutheranism to the large urban communities of the North and West. Finally, in the middle of the severest depression the nation has known, black Lutherans began assuming full financial responsibility for the support of their own congregations.

IV

WHERE DO WE
GO FROM HERE?

10

The Great Debates
1930–1964

No serious observer of the church could possibly question that some kind of rebirth of black Lutheranism was taking place. Black Lutheranism had broken out of its regional (southern) confinement. It was clearly moving towards becoming the most urbanized part of Lutheranism, the same direction in which American society itself was headed. By 1930, there were more black Lutheran congregations in the U.S. than there were congregations in either the Slovak or Norwegian Synods. There were almost as many black Lutherans in the U.S. as there were members in the whole Norwegian Synod. Had all the black Lutheran congregations in the U.S. been members of the Synodical Conference, they easily could have outvoted either the Slovak or the Norwegian Synods. Why, then, this protracted debate about "Where do we go from here?" (To call it protracted is an understatement, considering that it lasted from 1932 to 1964.) Why did all the major Lutheran bodies in the U.S. find themselves dealing with the same issue at the same time? What was the debate really about?

The problem existed because, in part, the issue was not always raised in a straightforward manner. In 1932, it appeared as part of an evaluation of what the American Lutheran Church (formerly the Joint Synod of Ohio) had been doing in the black community during the previous 46 years. In 1936, it surfaced as a proposal in the United Lutheran Church to create an all-black synod. In 1938, it appeared as a proposal of the General Conference (black ministry pastors of the Synodical Conference) to form either an all-black synod or an all-black district within one of the synods of the Synodical Conference. The issue was not clearly resolved even after 30 years of debate. Since these three groups saw the issue from different perspectives and with different concerns, we shall deal separately with them as well as with the National Lutheran Council.

The American Lutheran Church

Dr. Hein, president of the newly organized American Lutheran Church of 1930, first raised the issue publicly after he made a survey and evaluation of the ALC's various ministries in 1932.[1]

> During the past winter, your president visited the most important of our Colored Mission stations in Alabama. While the schools seem to be progressing satisfactorily, there is evidently a lack of white and colored leadership in the churches, and the colored congregations are not supplied with pastors or the administration of the means of grace as the needs of the new converts require. Since 1886 the Joint Synod of Ohio has spent $340,000 for colored mission work. Yet, after 46 years of labor, we have but 797 communicant members. . . . This is evidently due to the fact that the Board has not been able to secure competent men who would devote their lives to the cause of colored missions. Unless the Church supplies men and means, this work will always be done in a haphazard way. If we are not able to do the work, it seems to the writer that, rather than pursue such a policy in the future, we should inquire whether there are other Lutheran bodies who are able and willing to carry on the work as it should be done. There is undoubtedly a large mission field for the Lutheran Church among the colored population of the South. To enter this field and to do the work halfheartedly is a sin against these people and against the Lord. Our Church must decide whether it wants to continue the work. If so, she is duty bound to furnish both men and means to the Board entrusted with the administration.[2]

Dr. Hein's report was somewhat misleading both by what he said as well as by what he did not make clear. First, while the Joint Synod of Ohio had been working in the black community for 46 years, the truth of the matter is that for the first 30 years (1886–1915), the Joint Synod of Ohio had worked with blacks principally only in Washington, DC, and in Baltimore. Not until after 1915 did the Joint Synod of Ohio begin work in Alabama and Mississippi. And in those 30 years, the average expenditure per year for colored missions came to less than $1,500 (see Table 19). It was misleading

Table 19: Total Disbursements for Negro Missions by the American Lutheran Church, 1886–1949

Year	Amount
1886–1888	$100.00
1888–1890	
1890–1892	507.40
1892–1894	4,147.08
1894–1896	1,496.76
1896–1898	4,191.21
1898–1900	1,952.20
1900–1902	1,904.06
1902–1904	2,766.54
1904–1906	1,469.14
1906–1908	1,595.64
1908–1910	2,614.58
1910–1912	2,600.45
1912–1914	4,225.93
1914–1916	6,265.20
1916–1918	15,562.21
1918–1920	23,344.90
1920–1922	33,036.20
1922–1924	35,446.81
7/1/24–10/1/24	3,170.47
10/1/24–1/1/26	26,116.29
1/1/26–12/13/27	56,219.91
1928	24,564.67
1929	39,256.77
1930	23,575.92
1931	22,000.00
1932	19,950.00
1933	9,126.31
1934	10,166.54
1935	10,624.74
1936	11,436.61
1937	16,104.68
1938	14,983.48
1939	18,500.00
1940	20,350.00
1941	24,376.04
1942	20,620.89
1943	25,523.02
1944	28,667.42
1945	49,076.67
1946	54,130.83
1947	52,256.91
1948	90,411.45
1949	73,885.04

Source: Ervin E. Krebs, *The Lutheran Church and the American Negro* (Columbus, Ohio: Board of American Missions—American Lutheran Church, 1950), 50–51.

to suggest that the Ohio Synod had been seriously involved in black mission work for 46 years.

Second, Dr. Hein did not make clear that black missions had never really enjoyed the commitment of the church at large.

Third, Hein did touch on a serious problem when he referred to the difficulty of getting personnel to work in black missions. But that, in part, would appear to be the result of a lack of the denomination's own serious commitment to the project. In addition, Hein seems not to have clearly identified the problem they were having with the Christian day schools. While he took the position that the schools were "progressing satisfactorily," the truth is that the schools had become an end in themselves and were not geared either to build worshipping communities of believers or to equip the new converts to engage in ministry. The message conveyed to the local black community was that the Lutheran Church was a benevolent society interested in secular education.

Hein's report did accomplish three things. First, it brought the issue of black Lutheranism to the attention of the entire American Lutheran Church. Second, he clearly stated that the ALC had not carried out its mission in the black community as it should have. Third, the ALC would have to either change its policy or look to some other Lutheran body to evangelize the black community.[3]

There was an implicit comparison in Hein's report, as well as a suggestion as to what the ALC should do if it did not change its policy of working in the black community—the comparison to the Synodical Conference (which, during approximately the same number of years, had won six times the number of accessions to the ALC).[4] In addition, the Synodical Conference had succeeded in attracting a number of blacks to the pastoral and teaching ministry. There was no doubt who that "other Lutheran body" was, if the ALC decided to get out of black missions.

The United Lutheran Church in America

The 1936 proposal to the ULCA to create an all-black synod came from the Georgia-Alabama Synod. This call for a new synodical structure seemed to imply that the ULCA was doing nothing with regard to black missions and that the time had come to make a fresh start—

and that is the way the ULCA understood it. However, the denomination seems to have ignored several facts.

First of all, the ULCA had more black members in 1936 than the Synodical Conference. True, the majority (though not all) of their black members were in the Virgin Islands; but they were, nevertheless, members of an American Lutheran body, not part of a foreign mission field. "Making a new beginning in black missions" was somewhat inappropriate. Second, the Georgia-Alabama Synod proposal seemed to ignore the shift already taking place in the black population generally, as well as among their own black members, namely, away from the South and away from the Virgin Islands to the northern part of the U.S.

The 1936 ULCA convention turned the Georgia-Alabama Synod proposal over to its Committee on Boards and Committees. From the outset, the committee took the position that any approach to the black community by the Lutheran Church should be a cooperative endeavor. It therefore recommended two seemingly contradictory proposals: (1) that the ULCA make an outright annual grant of $2,000 to the Synodical Conference for its work in the black community; (2) that the best way to proceed with black missions was through the established work of the ALC's Board for Colored Missions.[5] Contradictory they were not. Both proposals reinforced the ULCA's underlying commitment to make black missions a cooperative effort. A joint commission of eight was formed in 1940— four from the ALC and four from the ULCA. The joint commission immediately committed itself to cooperation in its policy statement:

> Controversial differences of viewpoint and opinion between Lutheran synodical bodies now extant shall not be permitted to disturb such ministering to the colored race.[6]

In 1940, the executive committee of the ULCA recommended that the joint commission be expanded to include other Lutheran bodies, and, as evidence of the ULCA's good faith in this cooperative effort, that an annual appropriation of $2,000 be given to the ALC's Board for Colored Missions.

Noteworthy here was that, with the formation of the joint commission and the annual contribution of $2,000 to the ALC, there was a merging of the issues raised by the ALC in 1932 and those raised by the Georgia-Alabama Synod in 1936. Thereby the ALC's Board for Colored Missions became the vehicle for the ULCA's entrance into black mission work in the South. By 1948, the Evangelical Lutheran Church (the Norwegian Lutherans) and the Augustana Lutheran Church (the Swedish Lutherans) had joined the joint commission in this attempt at intersynodical approach to the black community.

The National Lutheran Council

The National Lutheran Council (which at this time included the ULCA, the ALC, and several other Lutheran synods, but not the Missouri Synod) got into black ministry as a result of the exigencies of World War II. Through their efforts to serve Lutherans living in the temporary communities that sprang up around defense plants in such places as San Diego and Vallejo, CA, and Vanport, OR, the Council found itself ministering to interracial Sunday schools and worshipping communities. In some instances, the Sunday schools were 50 percent black. The National Lutheran Council had not planned this kind of interracial activity; it just happened.

In 1947, after the war, five member denominations of the National Lutheran Council approved "in principle" setting up a Department of Special Missions within the Council to handle black missions.[7] The five member-churches were the Augustana Lutheran Church, the United Evangelical Lutheran Church, the ULCA, the Suomi Synod, and the Lutheran Free Church. Approval "in principle" did not mean that all of the groups were ready to participate in such a joint venture.

In 1949, at an informal meeting of the National Lutheran Council on black missions, a number of important issues finally came into the open. Many of the member-churches of the Council indicated that, while they were interested in working in the black community, they did not accept that as their responsibility. Rather, they felt black missions was the responsibility of the ALC. Still professing no obligation for black outreach, many of them acknowledged that they were facing a problem: an increasing number of their northern urban congregations were being surrounded by blacks. Again, assuming no responsibility for black outreach, they felt that if the Lutheran Church were to work with blacks, that effort should be concentrated in the North, not in the South as the 1936 Georgia-Alabama Synod had proposed.

The participants in this informal meeting concluded that there would be advantages if the National Lutheran Council were to take charge of black missions. It would help the individual Lutheran church bodies recognize their responsibility to work in the black community. Second, the pool for recruiting workers would be much larger. However, there was an organizational problem: As long as the ALC was in charge of black missions, pastors from the other Lutheran bodies would have to join the ALC in order to enter black missions. Many were reluctant to do that.

That same year, 1949, the Program and Policy Council of the American Lutheran Church passed the following resolution:

> *Whereas,* Jesus Christ came into the world to seek and to save all men, and
>
> *Whereas,* He is no respector of persons or classes as defined by men, and
>
> *Whereas,* His church through its responsible leadership must admit to limitations of workers and resources which necessarily restrict the scope of its operations, therefore be it
>
> *Resolved,* That the Program and Policy Council concur with the resolution of the Board of American Missions in offering our Negro work to the National Lutheran Council and pray God's blessing upon this action.[8]

By 1950, all necessary plans had been completed to transfer this inter-synodical program of black missions to the National Lutheran Council's Division of American Missions.

The 1954 Supreme Court Brown Vs School Board decision brought about an abrupt change in this cooperative venture under the National Lutheran Council. Again, the ALC took the lead in urging change. Since, in the view of the ALC, the Supreme Court had outlawed segregation, the ALC closed the Alabama Lutheran Bible Institute, its secretary for black missions resigned, and the ALC reassigned the money it contributed to the NLC's black mission project to its own Board of American Missions. The ALC also recommended that the NLC terminate its Committee on Church Work in the Negro Community and create a subcommittee on intercultural outreach.

The following year, 1955, the National Lutheran Council established ICOR (Intercultural Outreach) with the following mandate:

1. To study pertinent facts about cultural groups in America not now normally reached by the Gospel.

2. To ascertain barriers in the point of view of the church and the factors in the cultural social experience and religious background of these people which hinder the church's ministry to them.

3. To discover successful experiences of the church in reaching them.

4. To relay this information to boards and congregations in order to assist and promote the cause of bringing the Gospel to these groups.[9]

ICOR did not work because it emphasized integration and inclusiveness. In the late 1950s the Lutheran Church simply was not ready for that. The field services program of ICOR was terminated in 1961, leaving unanswered the question, "Where do we go from here?"

The General Conference

The General Conference, established in 1920, was an organization of pastors (black and white), teachers, and congregations involved in black ministry within the Synodical Conference. It was formed when the three black conferences of Louisiana, Alabama, and North Carolina recognized the need for fellowship, mutual edification, and a mechanism through which all blacks in the Synodical Conference could tackle issues of mutual concern. This was the most important black Lutheran group to be organized since the Alpha Synod was established forty years earlier in North Carolina. However, it had no formal status or power within the Synodical Conference.

The issue raised by the General Conference in 1938 appeared to be identical with the issue that had been raised by the Georgia-Alabama Synod two years earlier, but that was not the case. The two proposals sprang from very different concerns and sought to address very different problems.

To understand what the General Conference was trying to do,

one first has to understand the Synodical Conference itself—how it was organized and how it functioned—because that was what the General Conference was trying to get at.

In 1938, the Synodical Conference consisted of four autonomous synods—Missouri, Wisconsin, Norwegian, and Slovak. Only synods, not congregations or individuals, held membership in it and were entitled to participate in its deliberations. While the motivation for forming the Synodical Conference was the maintenance of a Lutheran theological tradition (as the founders understood that tradition) the primary practical task undertaken by the Synodical Conference was mission work in the black community of the United States.

Organizationally, the Synodical Conference carried out mission work in the black community through its Missionary Board, headquartered in St. Louis. The missionary board formulated, supervised, and carried out policy. The Synodical Conference at biennial meetings approved policy and budget.

The missionary board carried out policy through a full-time executive secretary, who in turn worked through three full-time field superintendents, one each for the three major mission fields. If an issue concerning black ministry arose in any one of the mission fields, it was decided by the field superintendent. If the field superintendent did not have the authority to decide the issue, it was sent to the executive secretary. If the executive secretary did not have the authority to decide the issue, it went to the full missionary board. If the missionary board did not have the authority to decide the matter, it went to the Synodical Conference.

In 1927, at the fiftieth anniversary of the Synodical Conference's work in the black community, the General Conference all but submitted a proposal to form a black synod. The General Conference didn't really want a separate black synod but rather some kind of official recognition and status within the Synodical Conference.

Five years later, the General Conference did submit a petition requesting "formal status" within the Synodical Conference, continuing the hope for recognition—but the Synodical Conference turned down that request on the grounds that almost all of the black congregations were on some kind of subsidy.

Finally, in 1938, the General Conference did request the formation of an all-black synod. The 1938 petition sprang from the frustrations and mounting problems facing the General Conference. While white pastors serving the Synodical Conference held membership in one of the constituent synods of that body, black pastors were consistently excluded from such membership, leaving them completely disenfranchised within the church at large. Black people had no voice whatsoever in the church at large to decide their destiny.

The position of black pastors was further undermined, especially on the Alabama field, because most of them did not have a "call" to the congregation they served. (In a few moments, we shall see how the missionary board maneuvered this.) Lacking a call, any pastor could be moved about arbitrarily by the field superintendent. (This was the problem Phifer had with Bakke in 1900.) This led to uncertainty, unrest, and no small amount of distrust on the part of black pastors. The issue had been simmering for almost 40 years and had reached the boiling point.

Third was the issue of salaries, which for black pastors was determined by the field superintendent. In a number of instances, that decision was based on the personal relationship between the superintendent and a given pastor. The issue was compounded by the depression of the 1930s. Between 1931 and 1935, the Synodical Conference budget for black ministry was cut almost in half (see Table 20). Some pastors found their own remedy. Pastor Lash opened a very successful grocery store. The Rev. Fred Foard operated his own farm. The Rev. John McDavid was a contractor. Pastor Thompson operated a very successful dry cleaning business. The Rev. P. D. Lehman made parish calls on the street car and later took

Table 20: Expenditures for Black Missions by the Synodical Conference, 1930–1938

Year	Amount
1930–1931	$158,545.38
1931–1932	142,328.75
1932–1933	109,587.76
1933–1934	87,143.80
1934–1935	81,898.98
1935–1936	83,174.26
1936–1937	82,690.46
1937–1938	89,012.14

Source: The Missionary Board of the Lutheran Synodical Conference, Treasurer's Report, June 30, 1949. p. 7.

a job at night in a factory.

Perhaps the most alarming evidence of problems within Synodical Conference black Lutheranism was the loss of over 50 percent of its black pastors during the ten-year period 1928–1938. Some of that loss can be attributed to the depression. And it should be added that some of those who left the ministry eventually returned. However, the reasons black pastors cited for leaving the ministry were the lack of fairness accorded them as blacks, the arrogance and arbitrariness of some superintendents and the missionary board, and the virtual exclusion of blacks from any recognized place in the life of the church.

The problems faced by pastors had their counterpart on the level of the black congregation. While many pastors were not given a call to a specific congregation, black congregations were not permitted to issue a call to a pastor. The missionary board accomplished this by insisting that mission congregations receiving a subsidy delegate certain congregational rights to the board. Dickinson cites the following clause from the constitution of Bethany Lutheran Church, Nyland, AL.

> While according to God's Word the congregation has the right and power to choose and call its own ministers and teachers, but being dependent on the missionary board of the Synodical Conference for the support of pastor and teacher, the congregation waives this right at present, and until the time the congregation becomes self-supporting, delegates this right to the missionary board. The minister which the missionary board calls and sends shall be the pastor of the congregation.[10]

The constitutions of mission congregations contained other prohibitions. Black Lutheran congregations could not sing hymns not found in *The Lutheran Hymnal*. There were prohibitions on the amount of money a mission congregation could spend without the approval of the missionary board. Black Lutheran congregations, like black pastors, could not join any of the constituent synods of the Synodical Conference. These were not just organizational problems, they were theological problems concerning the doctrine of the "call" as well as the doctrine of the church.

The underlying issue was one of power and control. The foregoing practices had the effect of rendering both black pastors and congregations powerless. If one could not join any of the judicatories of the Synodical Conference, then one did not have a voice in the church; one did not have a vote in the church; nor did one have the opportunity to appeal anything to an impartial group within the church.

There was yet another problem, not clearly articulated by the General Conference, but nevertheless felt by many. The Synodical Conference had, perhaps unwittingly, confused the Gospel with human culture. To put the matter differently, in its work in the black community, the Synodical Conference had attempted to convert black people to German culture under the guise of bringing them the Gospel. Black congregations had to be organized like German Lutheran congregations. Black congregations had to sing German hymns as German Lutheran congregations sang them. Black Lutherans had to think in German theological categories as German Lutherans thought. All issues of church life had to be defined and thought through as German Lutherans defined them and thought about them. In order to be a "good black Lutheran," one had to become a "good black German." One could not be authentically Lutheran unless he/she was authentically German.

Summary and Conclusions

For the third time within 123 years, the fate of black Lutheranism became a major topic of discussion within U.S. Lutheranism. The first such discussion (1809–1817) led to the adoption of the Five Point Plan, i.e., the decision to extend the Gospel to black people. The second major discussion began in 1866, immediately following the Civil War. The issue then was, how shall the Lutheran Church work with the freedmen?

The third major discussion began in 1932 from essentially two different perspectives and involved a concern for rather different issues. The one perspective was that of the representatives of national Lutheran denominations such as the ALC, the ULCA, the National Lutheran Council—those who essentially stood *outside* black Lutheranism. The issues were (1) whether the church had a responsibility to bring the Gospel to the black community, and (2) if so, how? Ironically, they raised these questions just as black Lutheranism was becoming a national phenomenon, entering a period of unusual growth. These discussions continued for over thirty years without a definitive answer.

The other perspective was that of the General Conference, essentially those who stood *inside* black Lutheranism. The issue was the status of black Lutheranism within the church. The General Conference sought to resolve this issue as the Alpha Synod had done, i.e., they asked someone else to give them what they sought— a black synod. Some contend that the manner in which the General Conference pursued this issue is indicative of the brainwashing to which they were subjected within the Synodical Conference.

11

Integration, Inclusiveness, or What? 1947–1990

The "Great Debates," begun in the early 1930s, only seemed to come to an end when the three largest Lutheran bodies drew up significant policy decisions against the backdrop of major upheavals within American society as well as changes within these denominations themselves. In 1947, the Missouri Synod formally decided to begin the process of integrating black pastors and their congregations into its various geographic districts. The American Lutheran Church pulled out of the cooperative effort of the National Lutheran Council and adopted another form of integration following the 1954 Supreme Court Brown vs Board of Education decision. The Lutheran Church in America adopted a policy of inclusiveness at almost precisely the same moment that the United States Congress passed the 1964 Civil Rights Act.

The Synodical Conference (Missouri Synod)

In 1946, the Synodical Conference proposed a rather different plan, one that ultimately brought the debate within the Synodical Conference to an end. It suggested that all subsidized black congregations and future plans for black ministry be administered by the various district home mission committees of the Missouri Synod. (The Missouri Synod was by far the largest synod in the Synodical Conference.) Funds would be provided by the Synodical Conference. It was implicitly recognized that the Synodical Conference was turning over its administration of black ministry to the Missouri Synod and that those in black ministry would ultimately hold formal membership in Missouri.

In 1947, the Missouri Synod accepted this proposal and made

it official policy. Before its adoption, however, many blacks within Missouri were skeptical about the new policy and voiced serious reservations. When the proposal to integrate the Synodical Conference work into the districts of the Missouri Synod was brought before the General Conference, that proposal was adopted by the smallest possible margin: one vote. Blacks noted the fragmentation of black leadership and the isolation that might occur.

The Lutheran Human Relations Association of America

The fears that many blacks had about integration were allayed by the promise that the Lutheran Human Relations Association of America would perform those functions heretofore performed by the General Conference. The LHRAA had been the most outspoken group in the Lutheran Church on matters of race and integration. However, the LHRAA had no formal ties with any Lutheran body. This free association of concerned individuals began in 1945 as a series of local institutes on race relations held in St. Louis and Chicago under the direction of the Rev. Andrew Schulze. In 1950, these institutes became national events held annually on the campus of Valparaiso University in northern Indiana. The institutes ultimately led to the formation of the national LHRAA whose objectives were

A. To emphasize the commission of our Lord Jesus Christ to preach the Gospel to every creature without respect of persons.

B. To deepen the realization within the Christian Church that God has made of one blood all nations and people.

C. To assist congregations in their outreach to all people living in their communities.

D. To promote the practice of Christian love toward all people through education and communication within the Evangelical Lutheran Synodical Conference of North America.[1]

The LHRAA's thrust was both the reduction of prejudice and discrimination as well as the integration of blacks into existing white congregations. The LHRAA was responsible for the many resolutions concerning integration that came before the Missouri Synod in the 1950s. In time, it also attempted to become a pan-Lutheran organization, including in its membership Lutherans from all the Lutheran bodies in the U.S.

Notwithstanding its many worthwhile efforts, LHRAA had its limitations. Despite its interest and consistent efforts to bring about integration, it never integrated its own paid staff. When this fact was brought up (as it was on a number of occasions), the white leadership of LHRAA always gave the same answer: "We can't find any qualified blacks for the job." No black person ever served as a staff member of LHRAA. It was not until 1958 that a black person, Dr. Clemence Sabourin, was elected president of the Association. The foregoing issue pinpoints a more profound problem that served to limit the effectiveness of LHRAA. Frequently, in integrated groups such as LHRAA, blacks tend not to push black issues as vigorously as they would in an all-black organization. Blacks themselves, in integrated groups, tend to compromise black issues in order to maintain peace, hoping that something will get done. Consequently, more assertive and impatient blacks tend to avoid joining groups such as LHRAA. Finally, LHRAA was in some ways co-opted by Valparaiso University so that, ultimately, stifled by the relationship with the university, LHRAA was forced to relocate.

Integration: A Two Stage Process

The integration of African-Americans within the Missouri Synod was a two stage process. The first stage (initiated in 1947) consisted of granting black pastors and their congregations formal membership in the Synod, a process that took 14 years to complete. It began in the Southeastern District when black pastors were admitted as advisory members. Next, black congregations were admitted as advisory members. Finally both pastors and congregations were accepted into full membership in the district, thus becoming members of the Missouri Synod. In 1961, the Southern District was the last to accept blacks into full membership.

Between 1947 and 1961, all but one of the separate structures that had been created to handle black ministry were dismantled. The General Conference was disbanded. The regional black conferences were disbanded. Immanuel College and Seminary were closed. The one institution for black ministry that remained was the Alabama Lutheran College and Academy. The missionary board of the Synodical Conference slowly became an anachronism. Just before it died, however, the Rev. Joseph Lavalais became its first black member. Even though the Synodical Conference itself was not created solely for the purpose of conducting work in the black community, it too was dismantled in the early 1960s.

The 1954 Supreme Court Brown vs Board of Education decision was the most immediate encouragement for the Missouri Synod to begin the second stage of its policy of integration—integration *within* the local congregation. At its 1956 national convention, the Synod passed two resolutions. The first, entitled "Race Relations As Such," was quite lengthy and concluded as follows:

> That we acknowledge a fourfold responsibility of the Church in the area of race relations:
>
> a. To teach and to practice the unity of faith which transcends the barriers of race and ethnic origin;
>
> b. To condition its members to work in the capacity of Christian citizens for the elimination of discrimination based on race or ethnic origin, in the home community, the city, state, and nation;
>
> c. To teach the Word of God so that specific application is made to what is God-pleasing in the Christian's relation to his fellow man of a different racial or ethnic origin, so that in these modern times, when the whole world has become one neighborhood, Christian people may be found establishing a pattern of social living in keeping with justice and equity according to the Second Table of the Law;
>
> d. To make such application of Christian teaching to life (in keeping with the foregoing) not only to help men in their temporal needs, but primarily for the sake of the kingdom of God, so that man may, as our Lord has taught, "see your good works and glorify your Father which is in heaven."[2]

At the same convention, the Missouri Synod passed something that was potentially a bit more substantial:

> Memorial 409—Re: Establishment of Congregations on a Non-Segregated basis:
>
> *Resolved,* That the Lutheran Church—Missouri Synod in convention assembled in St. Paul, Minnesota, June 20–30, 1956, be petitioned to declare as its policy

1. That all congregations of its constituency include in their missionary outreach all persons within their geographic area, without discrimination based on racial or ethnic grouping;

2. That no mission shall be established with the express purpose of serving only one racial or ethnic group on a segregated basis (at the same time, not overlooking the fact that there may still be certain communities where, because of the absence of members of other racial or ethnic groups, the constituency of a congregation may be of one racial or ethnic group);

3. That congregations operating in so-called "blighted areas" or changing communities be encouraged to continue operations in those areas rather than relinquish their properties through sale to other denominations, and that the various District Mission Boards be encouraged to subsidize these congregations when this becomes necessary, so that the souls in these communities, regardless of race or ethnic group, may be won and served.[3]

At the time that these resolutions were adopted, the Missouri Synod appeared to be best positioned (of all Lutheran bodies) to move forward in black ministry. It was well on its way to completing the integration of black ministry on the level of its districts. It had more black pastors, congregations, and black members than all the other Lutheran bodies combined. Its black congregations were more widely dispersed and were more stable than those of any other Lutheran body.

Missouri's method of integration had its drawbacks. First, the new policy of integration meant that the administration of black ministry was fragmented. There was no structure or effort for national planning, coordination, or evaluaton. It was assumed that each district mission board was composed of leaders who possessed the knowledge, skill, and will to carry out this complex task. To compound these shortcomings, this second stage of the integration process was launched at precisely that moment in history (1956) when American society and its black population were undergoing monumental change.

Second, there was unbelievable confusion and naivete concerning the policy itself. Out of hand, it was assumed that integration and black ministry were one and the same thing: If one were pursuing a policy of integration, one was doing black ministry. Adding to the confusion, this policy of integration/black ministry was pursued under the most extraordinary circumstances—primarily in dying, inner city, white congregations. In reality, many instances of integration/black ministry were an attempt to save dying, white congregations. Memorial 409 (above) tacitly admits that. One could hardly have chosen a more difficult way of going about integration/black ministry.

Finally, in adopting the 1956 policy decision concerning integration, the Missouri Synod went back to the principle of local option, which was an integral part of the 1817 Five Point Plan of the North Carolina Synod's proposal to work with blacks. Integration within a given congregation was left to the discretion of the local congregation. No guidelines or support staff were provided to help congregations move into these troubled waters.

The Black Lutheran Caucuses

The 1968 urban riots following the assassination of Dr. Martin Luther King, Jr. underscored some of the inadequacies of Missouri's policy of integration. With impetus from Dr. Albert Pero, an urgent meeting of black Lutheran pastors was called to begin the process of taking their lives and destiny within the church into their own hands. For the first time in history, blacks did not ask for the church's permission, official status, or recognition.

When the black pastors in the ALC and LCA heard about Pero's proposed meeting, they wanted to join the brothers in Missouri. Together, in 1968, black pastors from all three Lutheran groups formed the Association of Black Lutheran Clergymen. This was the first all-black group of Lutherans to organize since the demise of the Alpha Synod in 1891.

This joint effort was beset with discord from the very beginning. At its second meeting, the difficulties surfaced around such issues as (1) a power struggle between the younger and older pastors, especially within the Missouri Synod, (2) a communion service which posed doctrinal problems for the men from Missouri, and (3) the question of whether Caucasians should be included in the ABLC. At its third meeting in 1969, the power struggle continued. In an effort to dilute the power of the older pastors, the name of the organization was changed to the Association of Black Lutheran

Churchmen, instead of Clergy. This gave all black Lutherans, clergy and laity, the right to vote. By this means the older pastors were ousted from all elected offices.

The older pastors of the LCMS called a protest meeting in Atlanta. From that Atlanta meeting the present Black Clergy Caucus of the LCMS emerged. The BCC did not sever its relations with the ABLC. Rather, it succeeded in restructuring the ABLC so that each group of pastors (ALC, LCA, and LCMS) would function as an autonomous group within the ABLC, coming together on those tasks which were mutually acceptable. The ABLC held a total of seven meetings and eventually died in 1972.

As black Lutherans were trying to work out their various organizational problems, a political/theological storm was brewing within the Missouri Synod. Despite the conviction of many black Lutherans within the Missouri Synod that this was not their battle, the storm led to a reshuffling of the denominational affiliation of some black Lutherans.

In 1976 the difficulties within the Missouri Synod finally led a number of pastors and congregations to leave that body and to form a new Lutheran church organization: the Association of Evangelical Lutheran Churches. The Missouri Synod lost approximately 10 percent of its black clergymen but only one of its black congregations. A few of those black pastors ultimately returned to the Missouri Synod.

That split opened up opportunities for blacks that apparently were not open in Missouri. At the formation of the AELC, Dr. Will Herzfeld became the vice president of that group. In 1984 he became bishop of the AELC, the highest ranking position held by any black person in American Lutheranism during the 20th century. Dr. Albert Pero became a tenured member of the faculty at the Lutheran School of Theology in Chicago, a position still not accorded a black person within any of Missouri's theological seminaries.

The Commission on Black Ministry

The Black Clergy Caucus was increasingly concerned that Missouri's policy of integration had left outreach to the black community fragmented and without direction. In 1975, after persistent urging, the LCMS formed the Black Mission Models Task Force to deal with

Missouri's floundering outreach to the black community. The mind-set of the LCMS towards black ministry was revealed in the proposed composition of the Task Force. Synodical officials suggested that the Task Force be composed of six whites and three blacks. The Black Clergy Caucus objected strenuously. They finally agreed on eight blacks and three whites, with an additional black serving as the director of the Task Force: Dr. Richard Dickinson.

One of the important outcomes of the Task Force was the recommendation to form a Commission on Black Ministry. That recommendation was brought to the 1977 synodical convention but was not adopted. By the 1979 convention, however, the commission had been established and the following bylaws were adopted for the commission's task:

Function. The commission shall do the following:

1. Plan, coordinate, and expand black ministry in the Synod in cooperation with the convention of black Lutheran congregations, the appropriate division chairman, and the President of the Synod.

2. Represent the concerns of black ministry before the boards, commissions, committees, and judicatories of the Synod.

3. *Staff.* The commission shall engage an executive staff in accordance with the applicable bylaws pertaining to personnel. Duties of the executive secretary shall be established by the commission in consultation with the synodical President and the appropriate division; whereupon the position description shall be submitted according to the bylaws to the Board of Directors for approval.[4]

One of the early tasks undertaken by the Commission on Black Ministry was the convention of black Lutheran congregations referred to above in item #1. That took the form of biennial Black Ministry Convocations. At its 1988 meeting in Memphis, the Convocation decided to hold its meetings annually.

There were now three black groups within Missouri concerned with black ministry: (1) the Black Clergy Caucus, (composed of black Lutheran clergymen, (2) the Commission on Black Ministry (composed of 4 clergymen, 4 laypersons, 1 parochial school teacher), and (3) the Convocation (a plenary group composed of black Lutheran congregations). None of these three groups has any formal authority to implement anything regarding black ministry in the Missouri Synod. The BCC is, in fact, an extra-synodical organization. The three groups do, however, coordinate their efforts closely and provide black Lutherans in the Missouri Synod with an opportunity for fellowship and mutual edification, while also serving to push a black agenda within the denominations.

The Failure of Integration/Black Ministry

On paper, the Missouri Synod appeared to have a very positive record when it came to integration and black ministry. In addition to the many resolutions it had passed beginning in 1947, during the twelve-year period from 1975 to 1986 the Missouri Synod debated 33 resolutions that dealt directly with integration/black ministry. (This does not include a number of rather complex resolutions concerning the maintenance of the college at Selma, AL.) Those resolutions dealt with (1) the production of educational material, (2) the administration and functioning of the Commission on Black Ministry, (3) the recruitment of black professional church workers, (4) evangelism and the opening of new black congregations, (5) training for ethnic ministry, (6) the elimination of racism, (7) youth ministry, (8) the equal deployment of professional church workers, and (9) publicity and public relations concerning black ministry. Twenty-six of the thirty-three resolutions were adopted.

For an understanding of what in fact was going on in the synod, one only need examine a few of those resolutions. Resolution 10–07, adopted at the 1977 Dallas convention, reads,

> *Resolved,* that the Synod encourage Districts to fund, develop, and/ or utilize evangelism programs, efforts, resources, and personnel for congregations that either anticipate or are involved in racial transition in their communities.[5]

At the 1979 St. Louis convention, Resolution 1–23A "To Recruit Workers for Ethnic and Special Ministries," which was adopted, speaks of setting up both recruitment and training programs:

> *Resolved,* That the Districts of the Lutheran Church—Missouri Synod be encouraged through their respective mission committees and boards to consult with the synodical Commission on Black Ministry when prioritizing new mission starts in areas which

are black, with the synodwide goal of establishing at least one new mission station each year in a predominantly black area.[6]

One more example: Resolution 6–10A, entitled "To Consider Employment of Black Faculty and Professional Staff" (which was adopted) stated,

> *Resolved,* That each college and seminary be encouraged to continue considering employment of at least one black faculty or professional staff member.[7]

No good bureaucrat could miss the key words in those resolutions: *encourage* or *urge*. Nothing is mandated or required. The resolutions typically omit reference to any timetable for accomplishing the objectives, nor is there reference to any means for implementation, whether it be structural, monetary, or personnel.

The inaction of Missouri, despite its many fine-sounding resolutions, led to growing frustration for the black constituency. Frustration finally erupted in calls for the formation of a black district or synod. After the events surrounding Seminex and the AELC, the prospect of another split in the synod led Dr. Bohlmann to call an urgent summit conference for January 1986. In preparation for that, the synodical president ordered the research department to conduct a survey of black ministry. The conference sought to address these among other important survey findings: (1) Between 1974 and 1984, there was a 14-percent decline in the number of black Lutherans in the Missouri Synod, despite a 21-percent increase in the number of congregations supposedly involved in black ministry; (2) in the synodical (national) office of the church, there was only one black person who occupied an executive/managerial position; (3) only 19 of the 37 geographical districts of the Synod reported any involvement in black ministry; (4) only one district employed a black person in an executive/ managerial position, whereas no district employed a black person in a professional/technical position, and only one black was employed in a district clerical/service position; (5) nine districts reported the existence of some kind of coordinating body for black ministry; (6) six districts gave budget figures for the above committees which ranged from $1,500 to $28,000; (7) only five districts held regular conferences for those involved in black ministry, with another six districts indicating that there was no need for such conferences; (8) in the 1984–1985 academic year, while blacks accounted for nearly 10 percent of the total enrollment in synodical colleges and seminaries, they constituted only 2 percent of those students preparing for the pastoral ministry and 1.7 percent of those preparing to enter the teaching ministry of the church. Stated differently, nearly 90 percent of the black students enrolled in synodical schools were enrolled in general education as non-church-work majors, compared to 45 percent of the white students who were enrolled as general education majors; (9) in the 13 synodical colleges and seminaries, 8 blacks held executive/ managerial positions, 9 blacks held technical/professional positions, 50 percent of which were employed at one school (Concordia College in Alabama), with the seminaries employing only one black instructor; (10) by contrast, in the 57 service agencies affiliated with the synod, 18 blacks held executive/managerial positions, and 598 held clerical/service positions.[8] It would appear from the survey data that as of 1985, integration tends to become a reality in the Missouri Synod the further removed one is from the officialdom of the church.

As of December 31, 1988, there were 83,985 baptized African-Americans who held membership in the Lutheran Church—Missouri Synod, and 88 black pastors were on the synod's clergy roster. In that same year, African-American Lutherans in that church body raised over $22 million to support the work of the church.

The American Lutheran Church: Instant Integration by Administrative Fiat

The Great Debate concerning black ministry for the American Lutheran Church came to an abrupt end in 1954 when the Supreme Court ruled that separate but equal facilities were inherently unequal and therefore unconstitutional. The National Lutheran Council's cooperative effort at black ministry (in which the ALC participated) constituted a "separate structure," in the ALC's view, and therefore was deemed unequal and unconstitutional. The ALC immediately pulled out of that cooperative black ministry effort; it closed the Alabama Lutheran Bible Institute; its secretary for black missions resigned; and it reassigned the money it contributed to the NLC's black mission project to its own Board of American Missions. Black ministry was now under the joint supervision of the ALC's various district mission committees and the Board of American Missions. In theory, black ministry was now integrated into the mainstream of the ALC. In practice, this integration had more to do with who was to administer black ministry and the removal of the appearance of segregation than with anything else.

When the American Lutheran Church initially adopted its policy of integration (1954), the majority of its black congregations were in Alabama. Within two years (October 1956) a deputy executive secretary of the Board of American Missions reported to the Board that (1) he found the work in Alabama among blacks to be frustrating, (2) that the rural areas of Alabama were losing population, and (3) that their urban black Lutheran congregations were not making any progress with regard to evangelism or stewdarship.[9] In a word, Alabama black Lutheranism was in a no-growth phase.

At that same meeting, the Board made two decisions. No further capital investments were to be made in the Alabama field until there was some progress in evangelism and stewardship. Second, the current subsidies were to be continued for another year, with special efforts to improve the field's evangelism and stewardship performance. The message was clear: The Board was not going to make any long-term commitment concerning its black work in Alabama unless there some evidence of progress.

At the February 1957 meeting of the Board of American Missions, its deputy executive secretary reported that (1) since 1916, the ALC had spent at least one and a half million dollars on black mission work in the South with very meager returns, and (2) that as of February 1957, there were only five black congregations left in Alabama, none of which was very promising (see Table 21). Including such a gloomy, superficial report in the Board's official minutes strongly suggested that an important decision was in the making (if not already in place).

There was indeed an important decision in the making. A special committee presented the following resolution to the Board of American Missions in its October 1957 meeting (based on a visitation by the deputy executive secretary of the Board together with the officials of the Ohio District to the Alabama Black Conference congregations):

Whereas, Repeated attempts to conform the congregations of the Alabama Conference with the natural and normal growth and development patterns of the Home Mission program have not been successful; and

Whereas, The congregations of the Alabama Conference are socially and emotionally unlike the majority of other congregations under the guidance of the district Home Mission Committee;

Be It Resolved

1. That the Ohio District Home Mission Committee petition the Board of American Missions to release the Ohio District Home Mission Committee from the responsibility of supervision of the Alabama Conference.

2. That we recommend to the Board of American Missions that the work in the Alabama Conference be terminated since the door to our effective witness has apparently been closed; and we further recommend that the Board of American Missions discontinue the work where there has been an apparent lack of response to the Gospel Witness, and that the available resources of men and funds be applied where a more effective witness in Negro communities can be made.

OR

3. We recommend to the Board of American Missions that the Alabama Conference be considered as a distinct mission of the Church at large and that it be supervised and financed as such, and not be identified with the Ohio District, or any other district, but with the American Lutheran Church alone.[10]

The recommendations of the Ohio District Mission Committee were discussed with the president of the American Lutheran Church and, reportedly, they did not meet with his disfavor. The minutes of that same Board meeting included a report

... on the work of the Missouri Synod which indicated that in spite of constant pointing to the Missouri Synod's work as a successful venture into this type of mission work, the advances are extremely small, with large sums of money being poured into the program.

Six months later, at the April 1958 meeting of the Board of American Missions, its deputy executive secretary reported, "The year 1957 has seen the Alabama Conference disintegrate more than any other year in recent history." As part of that disintegration, he notified the Board that its St. Paul's congregation in Birmingham

Table 21: Congregations of the Alabama Lutheran Conference, 1954

Location, Church	Bapt. Mem.	Conf. Mem.	Com. Mem.	S.S. Pup.	Local Expend.
Anniston					
Faith					
Grace	253	135	115	57	2,322.92
Birmingham					
St. Paul	149	53	53	120	9,938.00
Booth					
St. Matthew					
Clanton					
St. Paul	40	22	20	13	267.15
Mobile					
Martin Luther	304	150	100	170	2,640.60
Montgomery					
Trinity	218	96	90	154	3,249.92
Tuscaloosa					
Christ	145	88	48	60	3,651.31
Wetumpka					
St. Mark					
Total	1,109	553	426	574	22,069.90

Source: *1956 Year Book of the American Lutheran Church*, 81.

had already been taken over by the Missouri Synod. After a lengthy discussion, the Board passed the following resolution:

> *Whereas,* Since the Synodical Conference (Missouri Synod) has 42 congregations located in Negro communities in the Deep South, and our additional 4 would find greater fellowship, more inspiration and better solidarity if attached synodically to that body; therefore be it
>
> *Resolved,* That the Executive Secretaries of the Board of American Missions be authorized to negotiate with the proper representative of the Missionary Board of the Synodical Conference for a procedure of transfer of these congregations to its jurisdiction where they may enjoy a greater fellowship; and be it further
>
> *Resolved,* That if the negotiations with the Synodical Conference prove fruitful that the Executive Secretaries of the Board of American Missions be authorized to execute the procedure with each congregation involved and that it be done in the same spirit

of love and concern as was the spirit that planted and nurtured these congregations even from the beginning.

Should any one of the targeted congregations not accept the above recommendations, the Board

> *Resolved,* That should a congregation not accept the proposal of the Board of American Missions in regard to synodical affiliation, that the table of expectancy for that congregation be carried through to completion and that the congregation will then be self-supporting with no further assistance from the Board of American Missions.[11]

Five congregations were potentially involved in the transfer. St. Paul's, Birmingham, had already made its decision to go into the Synodical Conference (Missouri Synod). That left Anniston, Mobile (Martin Luther Congregation), Christ congregation in Tuscaloosa, and Trinity congregation in Montgomery.

Given the reported transfer of St. Paul's Church (Birmingham) to the Synodical Conference at the April 1958 meeting of the Board of American Missions, the whole thing was a *fait accompli* before the Board took formal action.

The Synodical Conference Convention was notified that all the pastors serving in the ALC's Alabama Conference signed a petition to have their Conference transferred to the Synodical Conference.[12] They did so with a gun to their heads. The Board of American Missions (holding the gun, i.e., subsidy) gave them two choices: Sign the petition or go self-supporting. All but one of the Alabama Conference congregations (Martin Luther Church in Mobile) opted for the first choice.

The Synodical Conference formally agreed to the transfer of the ALC's Alabama Conference to its jurisdiction at its August 1958 convention. The most important condition of the transfer was that the Synodical Conference would pay $57,776 in mortgages which the ALC held on Alabama Conference church property.[13] Final details of the transfer were not completed until 1961.

The Synodical Conference's assessment of the Alabama Conference differed significantly from that of the Board of American Missions. While the ALC's mission board saw the Alabama Conference as a no-growth field, the Synodical Conference found that the Birmingham congregation "is exhibiting a steady growth and is proving itself to be a mission-minded church." Whereas the ALC's mission board estimated that it would cost at least $120,000 a year to bring the Alabama Conference to the point of self-support, the Synodical Conference reported that it was expending only $7,000 per annum in subsidies.[14]

Following the 1954 Supreme Court decision, the ALC approach to black ministry nationwide was similar to that of the Missouri Synod, i.e., centering their attention on blacks moving into urban areas where white congregations existed. The goal was to re-introduce a Lutheran identity into the heart of the city, given the exodus of whites. Those bearing this new Lutheran identity would supposedly be black. Most ALC congregations, however, were located in heavily rural, midwestern areas where there were relatively few black residents. Beginning in 1960, a special effort was made to recruit more black men for the ministry. This effort did not meet with great success. Somewhat indicative of the place of black ministry in the ALC at this time was that not until 1985 did the ALC hold its first conference "to which black Lutheran people came together to challenge the church and challenge themselves." In 1970, the ALC elected the first black person to its Board of American Missions and in 1983, its first black bishop, Dr. Nelson Trout of the Pacific District of the ALC.

By 1984, the ALC had approximately 66 congregations in which blacks made up 30 percent or more of the membership. On the average, these congregations had 265 baptized and 178 confirmed members.

The Lutheran Church in America: A Policy of Inclusiveness

Between 1940 and 1962, the predecessor of the LCA (the United Lutheran Church in America) had conducted black ministry largely through the ALC's Board for Colored Missions and then through the National Lutheran Council. Notwithstanding its work in the Virgin Islands and Guyana, the ULCA appeared to be unable to make a clear decision or commitment about its goals with regard to black ministry in the U.S.

That indecision changed abruptly shortly after the ULCA merged with several other Lutheran groups to form the Lutheran Church in America in 1962. This change with regard to black ministry was so abrupt that it might be compared to a radical conversion experience. For purposes of analysis, we shall look first at what occurred in the LCA on the national level and then examine those events that took place on the level of the local congregation.

The National Level. Three factors appear to be related to the LCA's new attitude towards black ministry, although the terms *black ministry* and *integration* rarely occur either in its literature or its discussion of these events.

The first factor related to the about-face in the LCA was the growing civil rights movement in the early 1960s, coupled with the social turmoil that it generated. The second factor was the desire to Americanize this new church body. The LCA was very interested in being identified with American society and the American social fabric; they no longer wanted to think of themselves or be thought of as an ethnic church. The third factor was the president of the LCA, the Rev. E. Franklin Fry, a forceful leader who was determined to push every area of the church into the main stream of American life. He was also deeply moved by the civil rights movement, especially the leadership of Dr. Martin Luther King, Jr. The impetus, however, was not theology but the pursuit of a social/political ideology.

The first major step in the LCA's new policy came at its second biennial convention in 1964, which began on the same day that Congress passed the 1964 Civil Rights Act. On that day, the LCA issued its "Social Statement on Race Relations," which held that "a racially segregated church is institutionalized disobedience."[15] That was more than just another pious platitude because, at that same meeting, the convention, following recommendations from its Board for Social Ministry, resolved to

1. authorize the establishment of an LCA coordinating committee on race relations:
   a. to consist of representatives or representation of each board, commission, auxiliary not excused from such representation by the Executive Council;
   b. To continue in existence until discharged by action of a convention or of the Executive Council;

c. to report to and through the Board of Social Ministry;
d. to explore ways of implementing the actions of the church on race relations;
e. to develop recommendations for constructive programs and projects to be carried on by the various program units of the church;
f. to request the president of the church to serve as chairman of the coordinating committee.[16]

Two items in the recommendation suggested that the newly proposed coordinating committee was more than just window dressing. First, a reporting mechanism was spelled out so that the committee would have to do more than just hold meetings. Second, the president of the church was to serve as the chairperson of the committee, meaning that the committee would not get lost in some kind of bureaucratic shuffle.

After three years of meetings, the coordinating committee concluded that (1) minorities should be involved in the committee itself, and (2) if the committee were to accomplish anything, it would have to develop a general plan or strategy of operation. A reconstituted committee (including minorities) then held a major consultation in 1967 concerning its work with blacks and concluded,

> Four years ago integration seemed to be the common goal of persons who were concerned about the improvement of race relations in the United States. Today integration is criticized as being a white man's goal and a white man's problem, while economic and political power seems to be the goal of leaders within the Negro community.[17]

The direction of the LCA was signaled by two events. In 1968, when Dr. King's father addressed the LCA convention, he was given $50,000 for the civil rights movement. Following the issuance of the Black Manifesto (drawn up by the National Economic Development Conference in 1969), the LCA asked its churchwide agencies to consider the formation of a financial program for minority group development. At the same time, a revolving fund of $130,000 was established which, in addition to church agency loans/grants, was to go for projects in the black community.

A subcommittee of the coordinating committee recommended the formation of a new structure to pursue the church's goals. Its recommendation was adopted at the 1972 LCA convention in the following bylaw:

> The Division (Division of Mission in North America, hereafter referred to as DMNA) shall work with other churchwide agencies toward achieving the church's mission and service goal. To this end it shall ... provide staff service for a committee on minority group interests that brings together minority group persons with representatives of churchwide agencies.[18]

The adoption of that bylaw led to the formation of the Consulting Committee on Minority Group Interests which consisted of three Latinos, two Native Americans, three Orientals, seven blacks, plus 15 staff persons.

Another important step was taken in 1970. The Board of Theological Education was asked to direct the seminaries of the LCA (1) to include in the seminary curriculum issues and questions of concern to black Christians, (2) to recruit black students more seriously, and (3) to be more serious in recruiting black faculty.

The adoption of a 1972 recommendation and the formation of the consulting Committee on Minority Group Interests shifted the work of black ministry from the Board for Social Ministry to the DMNA. In the following three years (1973–1975), the DMNA focused its attention on two kinds of congregations: (1) those with a membership of 50 or more blacks (there were 69 such congregations in the LCA), and (2) congregations in transitional communities (there were 75 such congregations in the LCA). The DMNA expended $3 million on the former and close to $23 million on the latter.

In 1974, the LCA tightened up its strategy by directing all churchwide agencies to confer with the Consulting Committee on Minority Group Interests in the development of programs and projects relating to minority persons and to secure minority staff persons to supervise programs related to minority group interests.

The next major step in the LCA's efforts in behalf of black ministry came with the adoption of the Consulting Committee's "Goals and Plans for Minority Ministry—LCA 1978–1984." The major goal was that "During the period 1978–1984, the LCA shall continue to become more inclusive in membership and expand its emphasis on justice in society."[19] Among the more important goals were (1) to have 100 minority group clergy and 10 minority group lay professionals by 1984, (2) that churchwide agencies should have 60 full-time executives or professional staff who are minority group persons by 1984, (3) that the LCA nominating committee should see to it that 10 percent of all nominees for churchwide offices for the 1980, 1982, and 1984 conventions should be minority group persons, and (4)

> That by 1984, synods will give counsel to congregations so that at least one-third of the minority group persons serving as pastors in the LCA will be serving congregations where the membership is a majority of white persons (suburban, town and country, and/ or city.[20]

Several items in the document were important. First, it explicitly points to the goal of inclusiveness as opposed to integration. Second, again and again, the document sets timetables for achieving the goals. Finally, the church directed itself to pursue inclusiveness on the level of the congregation, the district synod, as well as on the level of the national church bureaucracy.

The Congregational Level. A parallel and contemporaneous development in the LCA was the implementation of a so-called "area strategy" (sometimes called a "neighborhood strategy") in the conduct of ministry on the level of the local congregation. This was the grass-roots level where black ministry was to be pursued via the policy of inclusiveness.

The area strategy consisted of two emphases. The church ought to conceive of itself as a geographical parish which provides services to the people of that area, not just to the people who come to church on Sunday morning. Second, congregations in the same geographic area should be tied together organizationally and conceive of themselves as a team with a common focus.

The earliest and fullest development of the area strategy was the Central City Lutheran Parish in Philadelphia, frequently referred to simply as CCLP. Organized in the mid–1960s, this coalition of 27 congregations in Philadelphia sought to engage in ministry and mission cooperatively with the support of the Southeastern Pennsylvania Synod and the DMNA. To its credit, the DMNA's financial support was not used for operational costs of CCLP but went directly to the 27 congregations.

Geographically, CCLP included south, north, west, and central

Philadelphia, the same area that had been designated as Philadelphia's federal anti-poverty program area. At least 13 of the 27 congregations in CCLP were predominantly nonwhite. In 1970, consideration was given to expanding the boundaries of CCLP to include parishes in northwest Philadelphia. Ultimately, a new coalition was formed called the Northwest Philadelphia Lutheran Parish (NPLP). The area strategy spread across the country and was supported by the national church. In some instances, as in Philadelphia, a given city might have more than one coalition.

The characteristics of these coalitions were (1) sharing and mutual accountability in the "call process," so that every congregation participating in the coalition recognized that when there was a vacancy or some major decision to be made, they were a team in making that decision; (2) the pursuit of high liturgical style, so that rather than apologizing for the Lutheran liturgical tradition, that tradition was used with pride as the basis for community building; (3) the implementation of social action and social ministry programs; (4) a professional approach to the community, that is, making demographic and social analyses of a community and then designing a ministry around the findings of that analysis; and (5) the redevelopment of existing congregations.

After all the meetings, plans, and resolutions on the local and national level, there were some notable accomplishments. Two years after the formation of the LCA, there were 5,117 confirmed and an estimated 7,500 baptized blacks enrolled in that church body. In the ten-year period 1964–1974, the black membership of the LCA more than doubled. By 1982, there were 31,698 baptized blacks in the LCA, more than a 400 percent increase since 1964. In 1989, there were 48,868 baptized African-Americans in the LCA. The growth in black membership of the LCA came in the most highly urbanized centers of the U.S., specifically in three synods located in the northeast, three synods in the midwest, one synod in the west, and one synod in the border states (see Table 22).

The percentage of LCA congregations with minority membership rose from 13.9 percent in 1964 to 37.3 percent in 1974, almost tripling the number of congregations involved in black ministry within the LCA. During this period, however, blacks, still tended to be underrepresented in LCA congregations, except in those communities where the local population was 75 percent or more black.

Table 22: LCA Synods with the Largest Black Membership, 1980

Synod	Black Baptized Membership
Metro-New York	6,972
S.E. Pennsylvania	5,058
Illinois	4,044
Ohio	1,542
Pacific Southwest	1,314
Maryland	1,219
Michigan	1,203
New Jersey	868

Source: James Kenneth Echols, "Inclusiveness and Catholicity: Black Lutherans in the LCA," *Partners,* April/May 1984, 17.

In 1964, there were 13 black pastors serving in six district synods of the LCA. By 1974, there were 25 such pastors in 13 synods. In 1983, there were 55 black clergypersons in the LCA, seven of whom were women. In 1989, there were 111 African-American pastors listed on the clergy roster of the LCA. In 1979 Ms. Earlean Miller became the first black female to graduate from an LCA seminary. In the twenty-year period 1964–1983, black clergy in the LCA increased by 300 percent.

During the 1970s and 1980s, the largest number of blacks who entered the LCA ministry came from other communions. Some of them had experience in the ministry before entering the LCA. Those who adapted best were persons under 40 years of age and who had good educational backgrounds. Older black pastors who took over transitional churches in the inner city were not infrequently faced with unique personal financial problems. The Board of Missions would usually pay the pastor's salary, frequently below the minimum standard for the church, with nothing contributed to the pension fund.

Of the changes that took place in the LCA after 1964, one black LCA observer commented,

We sometimes facetiously say that during those days (from the mid–1960s on), the LCA had a lot of basketballs and a lot of basketball courts and engaged a lot of teenagers. Nobody ended up in the NBA, but we got a lot of Lutherans out of that. What basically happened is that LCA parishes that were receiving mission support were encouraged to develop social-action neighborhood-based programs. Most of them developed recreational programs for young people because most of the pastors were not very experienced at dealing with black adults. They had no background for that.[21]

Inclusiveness was not without its problems. Most of the congregations where the coalition plan was put into operation were transitional. Initially, some white members who did not live within the geographic boundary of the parish increased their time and monetary contributions to the new endeavor. However, once the congregation became 30 percent black, they would reduce their participation faster than new blacks came in. The whites who had been active then began to move out. The last to leave were white members of the church council. And the last member of the church council to leave would be the treasurer.

Many of the blacks who joined the LCA during this period did so in the hope of belonging to an integrated congregation. Some of the blacks who joined these inclusive congregations could deal with the obvious attempt at lingering control by whites. Others were frustrated because, while they felt that they were joining an integrated church, they discovered that as soon as they began to take responsibility, they were no longer in an integrated church. Those blacks who could not deal with the attempts at lingering control by whites became a part of the revolving door syndrome.

Another shortcoming of the LCA's work with blacks during this period was its weakness in teaching incoming blacks the faith of the Lutheran Church. Emphasizing liturgics and social action, it failed to help blacks form a distinctly Lutheran identity.

Much of the money spent on social action programs was not always expended for the sake of black ministry. In part, the effort to redevelop dying congregations was aimed at keeping open some of the old churches that grandma used to attend. Another motivation to do social ministry was the feeling that somehow this would magically become the church's evangelization tool.

As of December 31, 1989, following the merger of the LCA, the ALC, and the AELC, the combined ELCA denomination recorded 48,868 baptized African Americans and 111 African-Amercian pastors.

Summary

The Great Debates did not produce a resolution of the fundamental issues posed by black Lutheranism. Both the Missouri Synod and the LCA followed what was currently fashionable in the public arena—integration and inclusiveness. Missouri and the LCA differed in that Missouri's policy of integration was clearly a reaction, while the LCA's policy was in some measure more proactive.

Notwithstanding the many resolutions passed by both church bodies, there was not a clear understanding or awareness of the nature and depth of the institutional racism that afflicted the church. Missouri's two-stage strategy of integration ultimately led to a decrease in its African-American constituency. While the LCA's policy of inclusiveness brought about a sharp increase in its black constituency, inclusiveness took place within the context of white norms.

The American Lutheran Church, which began the Great Debates and which seemed to be most straightforward about its approach to blacks, was in fact the most confused of the three major Lutheran bodies. After declaring itself to be unreservedly committed to what was enunciated in the 1954 Supreme Court decision, it turned around in 1957 and proceeded to divest itself of the Alabama Conference, its largest field of black ministry. The reason was that the Alabama field did not conform to ALC standards of church growth; but it did not occur to the ALC that its assumptions applied to white congregations outside the South, not to church growth in black settings. This was one of the more blatant examples of cultural racism of that period.

Significantly, the changes that were taking place meant that, for the first time in 300 years, African-American Lutherans were now in a position to talk and act *on the inside* of the institutional church. It had taken a long time. Thereafter African-American Lutherans began the task of deciding the format and content for dialog. A number of organizations were developed, and a number of blacks were assigned positions in the church structure.

V

AFRO-AMERICANS INSIDE MAINLINE CHRISTIANITY: THE LUTHERAN EXPERIENCE

12

Summary

The purpose of this study has been to identify the major events of black Lutheranism in the New World. The study has identified the following as the major events:

1669: Black people, principally in what are now the states of New York and New Jersey, began coming to the Lutheran Church for the rite of Holy Baptism and/or marriage. They joined the Lutheran Church largely on their own initiative. They were both slave and free. Both slave and free blacks served on church councils. Blacks were also responsible for helping establish the Lutheran Church in the state of New Jersey. It was not until 1735 that the Lutheran Church formally spelled out the position of slaves in its midst.

1717: Black people first entered the Lutheran Church in the Danish West Indies via the route of baptism.

1735: The Lutheran Church formally spelled out the position of slaves in its midst in Berkenmeyer's constitution.

1735: Black people in the colonial South were baptized at Hebron Lutheran Church in Madison County, Virginia.

1740: Lutherans in the Danish West Indies conducted a school for slaves and began a systematic attempt to instruct slaves for church membership, using the Dutch language.

1753: The Salzburg Lutherans in Georgia launched the first organized/systematic effort in the continental U.S. to bring black people into the Lutheran Church.

1755: At the request of the king of Denmark, the State Church of Denmark began an organized/systematic effort to win black people for the Lutheran Church in the Danish West Indies. This effort was tied to the cultural conversion of black people.

1770: The State Church of Denmark initiated a new policy of working with black people in the Danish West Indies. That policy consisted of (1) the organization of separate congregations for blacks (the first such congregations in the New World); (2) creating a written alphabet and grammar for Dutch Creole, and the use of that language for the evangelization of black people; (3) modification of the liturgy; and (4) concentration on the urban black population.

1774: Lutherans in the deep South (initially, South Carolina) began baptizing black slaves. In some respects, church membership for black people was an extension of slavery.

1787: Lutherans in the Danish West Indies (1) initiated a program of free public education for urban slaves, and (2) began using lay workers in both their schools and churches. By 1800, black Lutherans outnumbered white Lutherans in the Danish West Indies.

1791: Black people were first permitted to join the Lutheran Church at Paramaribo, Dutch Guiana (Surinam). Within less than one century, black Lutherans, most of whom were free, outnumbered European Lutherans in the colony.

1803: Lutherans in the upper South, principally North Carolina, began baptizing the slaves of Lutheran masters.

1816: At the request of Charleston blacks, Lutherans in the lower South initiated an urban strategy for working with free and slave blacks. For the first time in the continental U.S., black lay leaders were an integral part of the church's work with the black community.

1817: Lutherans in the U.S. initiated the second organized/systematic approach to African-Americans with the adoption of the Five Point Plan by the North Carolina Synod. The Five Point Plan was initially operative in the upper South (North Carolina, eastern Tennessee, and Virginia).

1818: Free blacks were admitted to membership in the Lutheran congregation at New Amsterdam, British Guiana (Guyana).

1830: Lutherans in British Guiana began working with slaves. By the end of the decade, black Lutherans outnumbered European Lutherans in the colony.

1832: Lutherans began ordaining African-Americans for the ministry (Jehu Jones, Alexander Payne, B. J. Drayton).

1832: Jehu Jones, a black man, organized the first independent black Lutheran congregation (St. Paul's Colored Lutheran Church) in Philadelphia.

1835: Lutherans in the lower South (South Carolina) implemented the Five Point Plan, working with the slaves of Lutheran masters.

1837: Lutherans in the lower South commissioned a plantation missionary to work with blacks in those areas where there was no Lutheran congregation.

1839: Free public education for black people was extended to the rural areas of the Danish West Indies and was made compulsory.

1845: Black Lutherans in Charleston, SC, sent the first Lutheran missionary (Boston J. Drayton) to Africa.

1859: African-Americans in the U.S. constituted 10 to 25 percent of the membership of the Lutheran synods of the South. At no other times have black people made up so large a proportion of the membership of American Lutheranism.

1860: A precipitous decline in the number of African-Americans holding membership in U.S. Lutheranism began. By the end of the decade, less than 150 African-Americans were formally recognized as members of the Lutheran Church.

1866: Following the Civil War, the Lutheran synods of the South formally requested black members to form separate congregations and a separate black ecclesiastical organization, effectively putting many black people out of the Lutheran Church. This new policy also involved licensing and ordaining black pastors.

1877: The Synodical Conference undertook the rebirth of black Lutheranism in the South, in large measure following the policy advocated by the Tennessee and North Carolina Synods in 1866.

1878: The Lutheran Church in British Guiana was rebuilt by a Creole, the Rev. Mittelholzer. He created the first genuinely inclusive Lutheran Church in the New World. As part of his strategy to rebuild the Lutheran Church in British Guiana, Pastor Mittelholzer gained membership for himself and his congregation in the East Pennsylvania Synod in 1890.

1884: The first attempt by Lutherans to provide African-Americans with formal training for the ministry took place at Howard University in Washington, DC.

1886: Lutherans made their second attempt during the 19th century to work with black people outside the deep South. This effort was conducted under the leadership of the first formally trained black Lutheran pastor, the Rev. Daniel Wiseman. Wiseman had grown up as a member of the Lutheran Church in the Danish West Indies and was one of the early Lutheran immigrants from the islands to the U.S.

1889: Black Lutherans in North Carolina organized the Alpha Evangelical Lutheran Synod of Freedmen in America, the first and only separate black Lutheran ecclesiastical organization in U.S. history.

1890: The Joint Synod of Ohio established the third outreach effort of the 19th century towards black people outside the deep South, first in the suburbs of Baltimore, followed by the organization of St. Philip's Lutheran Church in the city of Baltimore.

1891: The Alpha Synod invited the Synodical Conference into North Carolina. This marks the beginning of the reclamation of old black Lutherans in the South. That invitation sounded the death knell of the Alpha Synod and the opening of the largest mission field administered by the Synodical Conference.

1901: Lutherans established the first seminary/college to train black pastors and Christian day school teachers at Concord, NC.

1908: Lutherans implemented an extensive social ministry program in the Danish West Indies, bringing the first black deaconess, Sr. Emma Francis, into the church.

1915: Lutherans, largely at the invitation of a non-Lutheran black woman, began work in the rural areas of the deep South, namely, in Alabama.

1916: American Lutherans took over the administration of the Lutheran Church in British Guiana after the death of Mittelholzer.

1917: With the purchase of the Danish West Indies by the United States, the Lutheran Church in the islands (now called the U.S. Virgin Islands) was transferred from the Danish State Church to the United Lutheran Church in the U.S. Separate Creole and white Lutheran congregations in the islands were formally abolished and replaced by fully integrated ones.

1920: Black Lutherans from the South began carrying black Lutheranism to the North, Midwest, and Far West. In the succeeding 30-year period, they turned black Lutheranism in the U.S. into a highly urban phenomenon.

1922: Lutherans established a second school at Selma, AL, to train full-time black church workers. This was the first Lutheran school of higher education to be staffed solely by blacks.

1947: Lutherans established a third training facility (the Alabama Lutheran Bible Institute at Montgomery, AL) for black full-time church workers.

1947: The Synodical Conference abandoned a separate structure for conducting work in the black community and began the process of integrating the administration of black ministry together with black pastors and congregations into the geographic districts of the Missouri Synod.

1950: After almost 20 years of discussion and debate, a number of Lutheran bodies (principally the American Lutheran Church and the United Lutheran Church) attempted to engage in a cooperative approach to work in the black community under the administration of the National Lutheran Council.

1956: The Missouri Synod adopted a policy of integrated congregations (principally in the inner city) and used this as its approach to black ministry.

1958: African-Americans began to assume positions of national visibility within the Lutheran Church. It began with the election of Dr. Joseph Lavalais to the Mission Board of the Synodical Conference, followed by Dr. Will Herzfeld's membership on the Board for Missions of the Missouri Synod, and the election of Dr. Nelson Trout as a bishop of the American Lutheran Church.

1964: The Lutheran Church in America adopted a policy of "inclusiveness" and launched an extensive program of outreach and social ministry in the black community.

1967: African-Americans inside the various Lutheran bodies began the process of organizing black caucuses. In the following quarter century, these organizations changed in form, but their objective remained that of articulating the concerns and objectives of black people within Lutheranism.

1967: For the first time, a major Lutheran body, the LCA, took the position that African-Americans *must* be involved in planning and supervising the church's work in the black community.

1977: The Commission on Black Ministry was organized to "plan, coordinate, and expand black ministry in the [Missouri] Synod."

13

Conclusions

At the beginning of this study, it was suggested that black Lutheranism has been surrounded by three myths: (1) the myth of No Contact (i.e., Lutherans have had little if any contact with black people), (2) the Johnny-Come-Lately myth (i.e., that black people are essentially newcomers to the Lutheran Church), and (3) the myth of the Unbridgeable Chasm (i.e., that the difference between Lutheranism and the black heritage is so great as to be unbridgeable). Not infrequently, these myths actually have been used as theories (tools) to study and explain black Lutheranism in the New World. Taken seriously, these myths suggest that the Lutheran Church has had little, if anything, to do with black people in the New World.

These myths/theories are not supported by the facts. Collectively, they are an uncritical application of the master-slave theory of the evangelization of black people to the Lutheran experience. They have gained some acceptance for two reasons. First, the theories appear to be valid because black Lutheranism has been studied in a highly fragmented way. Second, the theories are an attempt to respond to the accusation that Lutherans were inactive and/or ineffective in evangelizing black people.

However, the above summary would indicate that the Lutheran Church can hardly be accused of either inaction or ineffectiveness in evangelizing black people. On the average, once every eight years beginning with 1669, Lutherans have launched a new and/or additional effort to work with black people somewhere in the New World. Reviewing the past three centuries, it must be conceded that Lutherans have amassed a considerable storehouse of experience in working with black people. Yet, the Lutherans' fragmented perception of that experience, coupled with the small number of black converts (132,000 in the U.S.), has led to rationalizations.

While the three theories offer little by way of explanation, one of them—the theory of the Unbridgeable Chasm—is useful for high-

231

lighting two important conditions in which the Lutheran Church has had to work. First, for two centuries, the Lutheran Church attempted to evangelize black people within the context of colonial slave societies, that is, within the context of socio-political systems that both demanded and offered powerful incentives to redefine the nature and destiny of black people in secular, racist terms. In the United States, that condition has not altogether disappeared. The second condition that has been a constant—and intimately related to the first—is that, in reaching out to black people, the Lutheran Church has been attempting to transmit its message (the Gospel and Lutheran theology) across cultural boundaries.

While we may appear to be suggesting that there is some merit in the theory of the Unbridgeable Chasm, that is not the case. Interestingly, if pushed to the wall, Lutherans themselves would categorically reject any such notion; they have long been committed to the proposition that, without exception, the Gospel is clearly intended for all people. Lutherans are equally committed to the concept of the Gospel as transcultural, i.e., equally intended for and effective within all cultures.[1]

The data presented above reveals that decisive social and cultural differences did not necessarily constitute an insurmountable barrier to the evangelization of black people in the New World. On the contrary, as we look at Lutheran work in four different societies (the U.S., the Danish West Indies, Guyana, and Surinam), the Lutheran Church appears at times, on the one hand, to have been *most effective* and then again *least effective* in working with black people when the social and cultural barriers were most pronounced.

For example, the Lutheran Church was most effective in (1) the Danish West Indies beginning in 1770, (2) the Old South beginning in 1816, (3) Surinam beginning in 1860, (4) North Carolina beginning in 1891, (5) Guyana beginning in 1880, (6) Alabama beginning in 1916, and (7) the North and West U.S. beginning in 1920.

On the other hand, the Lutheran Church was least effective in (1) the U.S. North beginning in 1669, (2) the Georgia Salzburgers in 1750, (3) the Danish West Indies from 1755 to 1770, (4) the Old South from 1865 to 1891, (5) Guyana from 1816 to 1875, and (6) the work of the American Lutheran Church in the U.S. from 1890 to 1960.

From the above examples, two groups, the Danes in the West

Indies and the Georgia Salzburgers, typify the vastly divergent ways in which the Lutheran Church has worked with black people. Work in the Danish West Indies (1770–) illustrates an effective approach that acknowledged the differences in culture; work by the Salzburger Lutherans (1750) illustrates the least effective approach.

The Danish West Indies. The following methods, attitudes, and conditions characterized work in this area:

1. The motivation for evangelizing black people was seen as an important goal in itself.
2. The evangelizing group consciously recognized the decisive social and cultural differences between itself and those black people to be evangelized.
3. They were aware of the difference between the Gospel and culture, and they consciously rejected the notion of cultural conversion.
4. Evangelization was aimed at the indigenization of the Lutheran tradition within the black community/culture:
   a. They communicated in the language of the people being evangelized.
   b. Worship was adapted to the culture of the worshiping community.
   c. Separate congregations and worship services were organized for black converts.
   d. The black people who were brought into the church were permitted and encouraged to play significant roles in the institutional life of the church.
5. They concentrated on an urban black population (non-European).
6. Control of the program of evangelization was relatively free/independent/isolated from the influence of local white Lutherans.
7. While the Danish West Indies was a slave society, it was characterized by some moderation of institutional racism, flexibility, and by the possibility for some social mobility for black people. Witness the growing number of black people who achieved freedom.
8. The overwhelming majority of the black people brought into the Lutheran Church were not the slaves of Lutheran masters.

233

9. The Church provided free education for black children, both slave and free.

The Salzburger Lutherans. The following were characteristic of evangelizing efforts in Georgia:

1. The evangelizing group consciously recognized the decisive social and cultural differences between itself and the black people to be evangelized.
2. They lacked an awareness of the difference between the Gospel and culture. They assumed that the culture of the evangelizing group was the best way to introduce black people to the Gospel and the church.
   a. Black people (mostly children) worshiped together with Euro-Americans.
   b. This tended toward the denigration of black people and their way of life.
3. The evangelizing and evangelized groups were largely rural.
4. Control of the program of evangelization was immediately under local whites.
5. The Salzburgers rationalized that the purpose for introducing slavery into the colony was evangelization.
6. All of the black people brought into the Lutheran Church were the slaves of Lutheran masters.
7. The Church provided free education for black slave children.
8. The slave society was characterized by caste relationships and growing rigidity of social positions, with little provision for the freedom of black people.

One should not look at a given trait or condition either as absolute or as a matter of all-or-nothing. Additionally, it would be misleading to suggest that a group had to exhibit all of the methods and attitudes of the Danes to be effective, or that all of the methods and attitudes of the Salzburgers would have to be present to be ineffective. For example, even though the Lutheran Church ordinarily was most effective in urban areas and least effective in rural areas, it was very effective in rural Alabama (in part because evangelization was carried out largely by black people themselves). The successful North Carolina field in 1891 was also largely rural. As in Alabama, much of the effort at evangelization was initiated by black people themselves, some of whom had been members of the Lutheran Church before the outbreak of the Civil War.

What appears to be the most critical issue in the Lutheran effort to evangelize black people is to recognize the need to reach across cultural boundaries, recognizing cultural differences and responding to them appropriately. Both the Georgia Salzburgers and the Danes clearly recognized the cultural differences between themselves and the people they sought to evangelize. However, they defined differently what they saw, and each responded in different ways.

The Salzburgers saw the differences between themselves and black people as insurmountable. Henry Newman, the man to whom Boltzius regularly reported, spoke of that difference as "a bypass which nature hath interwoven in their very constitution." Even though Boltzius freely admitted that slavery was quite immoral, he was nevertheless caught in the trap of cultural racism. (That seems clear from his earliest correspondence almost two decades before launching his program of evangelization.) And in espousing cultural racism, he was caught in an even more devastating trap, namely, the inability to understand properly the very nature of the Gospel he sought to share. The Salzburgers concluded, therefore, that the only way to share the Gospel with black people was to wipe out cultural differences.

The Danes ultimately chose to work *inside* those differences, i.e., inside the context of black culture. In a word, the Danes opted for indigenization.

Every cultural group sees, thinks, organizes, and synthesizes its views of everything in the universe in its own unique way. Therefore evangelization, to be indigenous, must take place within the group's world view, working within that group's "meaning system," within its modes of confronting the world, dealing with the major issues of life as the group understands them and must deal with them. Indigenization of the Gospel means recognizing that the Gospel (including Lutheran doctrine) is transcultural.

The distinction between bringing the Gospel into the community and indigenization is important. Recall the fact that, formally, there was only one St. John's Lutheran congregation in Charleston, SC, but as one observer noted, there were in reality two congregations, one black and the other white. St. John's, Charleston, was almost an exact duplicate of what the Danes had done in the West

235

Indies—two separate congregations within one parish. But there were important differences. At St. John's it was not institutional Lutheranism that initiated the effort to bring black people into the Lutheran Church. Bachman's correspondence rather clearly indicates that black people invited themselves into the Lutheran Church. To Bachman's credit, he did not, as Boltzius did, see some kind of insurmountable barrier between black people and the Lutheran tradition. Rather, he let blacks themselves undertake the process of indigenizing the Gospel. And they were quite successful at it, enough so even to send a missionary to Africa. Recall that they did that on their own, despite Bachman's rather lukewarm stance about the matter.

The Salzburgers' strategy, the alternative to indigenization, attempted to evangelize with means and a medium that are foreign to the group. If any are to be won, they themselves are forced to "translate" what they hear from one medium to another. If the evangelized group is bicultural and/or somewhat willing to translate from one cultural context to another, there may be some measure of success. On the other hand, indigenization brings with it two cautions. First, in translating the Gospel from one culture to another, the message must be communicated clearly and unambiguously, with its full meaning. St. Paul raised this issue in his first letter to the church at Corinth (1 Cor. 14). Second, in communicating the message, one must get at the very heart and core of a people's life, going beyond their exterior facade.

Before the Civil War, black Lutheranism in the U.S. was a southern phenomenon; and black Lutherans, in every instance, were members of white congregations. Jehu (John) Jones' attempt to organize an independent black Lutheran congregation in the North in the 1830/40s failed.

The Civil War marked a significant change in U.S. black Lutheranism. Black people were in effect put out of the Lutheran Church in the South, told to organize separate congregations as well as a separate ecclesiastical structure, and, practically speaking, to do this on their own, without white resources. North Carolina Lutherans were ambivalent about this. Because there had been no preparation for the change, they looked on somewhat painfully as black Lutheranism in the United States almost became extinct.

Despite this trend, separate congregations for black and white

Lutherans became the accepted organizational policy of the Lutheran Church. For two years, 1889 to 1891, there was even a separate black Lutheran ecclesiastical organization, the Alpha Evangelical Lutheran Synod of Freedmen in America.

The policy of the Salzburgers was the same as that which characterized much of the rebirth of black Lutheranism discussed in chapter 9. Much of that "rebirth" proceeded on the assumption that spiritual conversion was contingent on cultural conversion. That assumption is theologically untenable and psychologically and socially unacceptable. Therefore, the "great debates" that followed the "rebirth" were inevitable and were not resolved by the newly adopted policies of *integration* or *inclusiveness*, because they were understood to mean that spiritual conversion was contingent on cultural conversion. And this was to take place, not in separate congregations, but *inside* integrated/inclusive congregations.

In 1957, while presumably pursuing a policy of integration, the ALC invoked the myth of the Unbridgeable Chasm as the rationale for "giving away" its black brethren in Alabama. Shortly thereafter the Missouri Synod implicitly acknowledged that integration was not working: the number of black Lutherans in their midst was not even keeping up with the rate of natural increase in the black population. In the twentieth century, the Lutheran Church continued its attempt at cultural conversion, but that has been obscured largely by the adoption of policies with the label *integration,* (introduced in 1947) and *inclusiveness* (adopted in 1964). In both instances, those policies dealt primarily with structural issues, designed to bring black people inside the organizational structure of the church. By the mid-1980s there was actually a significant decrease in the number of black people who held membership in the Missouri Synod.

Forthrightly stated, integration/inclusiveness (as understood and practiced by the Lutheran Church) would say that black people may come into the church if they will hear the Gospel, speak the Gospel, and worship and live by the Gospel *as Euro-Americans do.* The black vote has been loud and clear on this point. They don't want to be integrated/included so much as they want to be empowered. It comes as no surprise, therefore, that after 300 years there are only 132,000 black Lutherans in the United States.

The fundamental issue Lutherans have grappled with in their

efforts to bring African-Americans inside mainline Christianity is by no means new. At the risk of oversimplifying matters, the issue is: Is the message of the Christian church an ethnic ideology and the church itself merely another ethnic enclave? Or, is it something beyond that?

The early Christian church, starting with the events surrounding Pentecost, was unmistakably clear about that issue. The burden of much of St. Paul's writing rejects the notion of Christianity as an ethnic (Jewish) ideology. Luther and the Reformers unequivocally rejected the notion of Christianity as an ethnic (Roman) ideology. For very sound theological reasons they tackled the problem of indigenizing both the Gospel and the institution of the church. If one takes Pentecost seriously, its meaning is inescapable. As one goes about the business of "making disciples of all nations," the message concerning Jesus Christ is not an ethnic ideology nor is the church to become an ethnic enclave. Luther and the Reformers understood that.[1] And the black Lutheran experience, at least from the perspective of African-Americans, has been an attempt to achieve that.

Appendices

Appendix A
Black Professional Church Workers in the
Synodical Conference, 1877–1915

Mr. Frank Alston. The first graduate of the teachers program at Immanuel College. Taught the advanced classes at Immanuel.

Rev. John Alston. Graduated from Immanuel College. Ordained in 1909.

Miss Wilmar Barnhardt. Graduated from Immanuel College teacher's program. Taught at Grace Church in Concord and St. Luke's in Spartanberg.

Mr. A. Berger. A graduate of Luther and Immanuel Colleges. Taught at Mt. Zion, New Orleans.

Rev. Eugene Berger. Taught in the Christian day school at Mansura from 1908 to 1910, while a student at Luther College. Ordained in 1911.

Miss Mary Brown. Graduated from Immanuel College. Taught at Immanuel School in Greensboro.

Mr. E. Buntrock. Attended the teachers seminary in Addison, IL. Commissioned as a teacher in 1898. Taught at Immanuel School in Greensboro.

Mr. N. P. Burkhalter. Attended the Springfield seminary for several years. Taught at Mt. Zion School in New Orleans in 1889.

Mr. Emmanuel Burthlong. Started teaching in the Christian day school at Mt. Zion at the age of 17 in 1890. He was one of the first black students to attend the Springfield seminary, admitted in 1891. He died in 1897, just a few months after graduating from the seminary.

Rev. Marmaduke N. Carter. Attended high school in Baltimore and Capital University in Columbus, OH. Taught school at Concord and then in Greensboro. Ended his career as pastor of St. Philip's in Chicago, IL.

Rev. James Doswell. Grew up in St. Matthew's Church, Meherrin, VA. Graduated from the Springfield seminary. Served Holy Trinity Lutheran Church in Springfield, IL.

Rev. Stuart Doswell. A cousin of the Rev. James Doswell. Grew up in St. Matthew's Church Meherrin, VA. Ordained 1902.

Rev. Fred Foard. A member of the first class at Immanuel College in Concord. Ordained in 1909. First parish: Concordia, Rockwell. Last Parish: St. Matthew's, Meherrin.

Miss Claudia Galloway. Taught at Immanuel School in Greensboro.

Rev. William O. Hill. Graduated from Immanuel College in 1911. Served Bethany Lutheran Church, Yonkers, NY.

Miss Elizah Johnston. Taught at St. John's in Salisbury, NC.

Miss Eleanor King. Graduated from Immanuel's teacher program.

Rev. W. H. Lash. Graduated from the Springfield seminary. Ordained in 1904. Served Concordia Church, Rockwell. He was an astute businessman.

Rev. Paul Lehman. Attended Luther College and graduated from Immanuel College. The son-in-law of the Rev. John McDavid. Taught at the College in Selma. Served parishes in North Carolina and California.

Rev. Otho R. Lynn. Graduated from Immanuel College. First president of the Selma Acadamy. Fondly called "Dean Lynn" by many. Served Grace Church in Greensboro.

Rev. John McDavid. Entered the Springfield seminary in 1892. Taught school before being ordained in 1905. Served congregations in North Carolina and California. Was considered a master carpenter and builder of many church facilities.

Miss Addie McTier. Taught at Mt. Calvary, Sandy Ridge.

Rev. C. R. March. Graduated from Immanuel College. Ordained in 1911. First parish was at Southern Pines.

Rev. Yuku Mohomed. Was alleged to be an African prince. Served Bethlehem church in Monroe, NC, for a short time.

Rev. Charles Pea. Was ordained with classmates F. Foard and J. Alston on July 4, 1909. Known throughout black Lutheranism as a persuasive preacher.

Miss Sophie Raymond. A graduate of the Immanuel College teacher's program.

Miss Sylvin Raymond. A graduate of the Immanuel College teacher's program.

Mr. E. W. Reid. Studied at the Springfield seminary and Dr. Martin Luther College, New Ulm, MN. Taught school both in Charlotte and Greensboro.

Mr. Peter Robinson. Grew up in St. Paul's, New Orleans. Started teaching at Trinity, New Orleans, in 1914.

Mr. Napoleon Seeberry. Attended Addison Teacher's Seminary and graduated from Luther College. Taught both at St. Paul's and Bethlehem schools in New Orleans.

Mr. E. Stoll. The first black student to attend Concordia Seminary, St. Louis, in 1913. In November of that year, he went to Greensboro to complete his theological education at Immanuel.

Miss Beulah Sutton. Graduated from the Immanuel College teacher program. Taught at Immanuel school in Greensboro.

Mr. J. F. W. Thalley. Attended the Springfield seminary for several years. Taught at St. John's School in Salisbury.

Rev. Lucius Thalley. Graduated from the Springfield seminary. Served Holy Trinity in Springfield from 1894 to 1902.

Rev. C. P. Thompson. Educated at Luther College. Ordained in 1910.

Rev. John Thompson.

Miss Edna Walters. Graduated from Luther College. Taught at St. Paul's School in New Orleans.

Miss Pearl Windsor. Graduated from Immanuel College's teacher program.

Miss Adeline Winn. Graduated from Luther College. Taught successively at St. Paul, Trinity, and St. John's in New Orleans.

Appendix B
Black Pastors Added to the Synodical Conference Roster, 1916–1927

Rev. Walter F. Carlson. Studied at Greensboro.

Rev. F. Cozart. Graduated from Immanuel College in 1922.

Rev. William Eddleman. Graduated from Immanuel College in 1925.

Rev. John W. Fuller. Attended Shaw University in Raleigh, NC. Graduated from Immanuel College in 1917.

Prof. Isaac Holness. Ordained and installed in Pilgrim, Birmingham in 1923.

Rev. Jesse A. Hunt. Graduated from Immanuel College in 1918.

Rev. James Samuel Montgomery.

Rev. Wilfred J. Tervalon. Graduated from Immanuel College in 1914.

Appendix C
Black Workers Serving in the American Lutheran Church, 1890–1948

Rev. Issac Rracey

Rev. M. Browning

Rev. Daniel R. Braxton

Rev. Ivory Cameron. Ordained in 1948.

Rev. Nathaniel Carter

Mr. Nelson G. Coleman

Mr. DeJarnett

Mr. Grover Dixon

Rev. Percy C. Dumas

Mr. Freeman

Mrs. Lulu Hassen

Mr. A. G. Huguley

Rev. Taylor Johnson

Rev. J. Lawrence

Rev. Percey McShan. Ordained in 1948.

Rev. Carrington March

Rev. Philo W. Phifer

Rev. Louis A. Routte

Mrs. Mary Singletery

Rev. W. C. Sowell. Ordained in 1949.

Rev. T. R. Speigner. Ordained in 1940.

Mr. Harvard Stephens

Mr. Gordon Stroud

Rev. R. S. Tarrant

Mr. George Taylor

Mrs. M. Williams

Appendix D
Stations Opened and Served by the American Lutheran Church, 1890–1930

1890 Our Savior—Suburbs of Baltimore, MD
1896 St. Philip's—Baltimore, MD
1915 St. Philip's—Prattville, AL
     Grace—Jackson, MS
1916 Trinity—Montgomery, AL
1917 Christ—Tuscaloosa, AL
1920 St. Matthew's—Booth, AL
1922 Martin Luther—Mobile, AL
1923 St. Mark's—Wetumpka/Atoka, AL
1924 St. Paul's—Clanton, AL

Appendix E
Stations Opened and Served by the Synodical Conference, 1878–1915

1878   St. Paul's—Little Rock, AR
      Mission—Mobile, AL
1880   Mount Zion—New Orleans, LA
      St. Paul's—New Orleans, LA
1881   St. Matthew's—Meherrin, VA
1885   Trinity—New Orleans, LA
1888   Bethlehem—New Orleans, LA
      Holy Trinity—Springfield, IL
1891   St. Paul's—Charlotte, NC
      Immanuel—Reimerstown, NC
1893   Mount Calvary—Mount Pleasant, NC
1894   Concordia—Rockwell, NC
      Zion—Gold Hill, NC
      Grace—Greensboro, NC
1895   St. John's—Salisbury, NC
1896   Mount Zion—Meyersville, NC
      Mission—Atlanta, GA
      Mission—Wilmington, NC
1898   Mount Calvary—Sandy Ridge, NC (now Mt. Calvary
        at Kannapolis)
      St. Peter's—Dry's Schoolhouse, NC
      St. James—Southern Pines, NC
1899   St. Paul's—Mansura, LA
1902   Mount Calvary—Sandy Ridge, NC
      Mount Olive—Catawba County, NC
      Bethlehem—Monroe, NC
1903   Grace—St. Louis, MO
1904   Mount Zion—The Rocks, NC
1905   Mission—Napoleonville, LA
1907   Mission—Conover, NC
1908   St. Luke's—High Point, NC
1910   Bethany—Yonkers, NY
1911   Mission—Albermarle, NC
      Bethel—Greenville, NC
1912   Trinity—New Orleans, LA

Redeemer—New Orleans, LA
1913   St. John's—New Orleans, LA
Mission—Winston-Salem, NC
Mission—Fayetteville, NC
Mission—Wilmington, NC
1914   St. Luke's—Spartanburg, SC

Appendix F
Stations Opened and Served by the Synodical Conference in Alabama, 1916–1931

1916   Christ—Rosebud
       St. Paul's—Oak Hill
       St. Andrew's—Vredenburgh
       St. James—Buena Vista
       Mt. Olive—Tinela
       Mt. Calvary—Tilden
       Our Savior—Possum Bend
       Mt. Carmel—Midway
1917   St. John's—Joffre
1918   Bethany—Nyland
1919   Grace—Ingomar
       Zion—Tait's Place
1920   Faith—Mobile
       Trinity—Selma
       Pilgrim—Birmingham
1922   Bethlehem—Holy Ark
       Our Redeemer—Longmile
       St. Peter's—Pine Hill
1923   St. Matthew's—Arlington
       Hope—Kings Landing
1924   Gethsemane—Hamburg
1924   Bethel—Rockwest
       Holy Cross—Camden
1925   St. Luke's—Lamison
       Ebenezer—Atmore
1926   St. Mark's—Ackerville
1927   Peace—Maplesville
1929   Messiah—Bashi
       St. Philip's—Catherine
1930   Concordia—Montrose
1931   Good Shepherd—Vineland

Appendix G
Black Pastors in the American Lutheran Church, 1980

1. William Bell
2. Daniel Block
3. Lonnie Branch
4. Charles Brown
5. Nelson Coleman
6. Harry Griffith
7. Isaiah Harriday
8. David Hill
9. Raymond LeBlack
10. Willard McKiver
11. William Mitchell
12. Eileen Hyacinth Murray
13. Louris Routte
14. Kenneth Sanders
15. Theodore Speigner
16. Nelson Trout

Appendix H
Black Pastors in the Lutheran Church in America, 1988

1. Christian G. Airey
2. Murel E. Beatty
3. Winston S. Bone
4. James M. Capers
5. Julius Carroll IV
6. Churchhill Carter
7. Lynell H. Carter
8. Vernon E. Carter
9. Michael L. Cobbler
10. James Davis, Jr.
11. Theodore E. Day
12. Edward H. Dixon
13. Joseph A. Donnella II
14. James B. Dookram
15. James K. Echols
16. Rudolph R. Featherstone
17. James E. Gunther
18. Choyce G. Hall
19. James C. Hawthorne
20. Sherman G. Hicks
21. Callon W. Holloway, Jr.
22. Gwendolyn Johnson-Bond
23. Claude H. Hoyner
24. John B. Junior
25. Massie L. Kennard
26. Gwendolyn S. King
27. Margaret E. Lane
28. Victor C. Langford III
29. Jean A. Lafond Lapointe
30. Raymond Legania
31. Charles Leonard
32. Craig J. Lewis
33. Alfred Little
34. Robert L. Lowe, Sr.
35. Cyril A. Lucas
36. Earlean Miller
37. Thomas J. Minor
38. Willie J. Nelson
39. John A. Parkinson
40. Albert Pero, Jr.
41. Richard J. Perry, Jr.
42. Claude T. Petersen
43. Eugene M. Powell
44. Cynthia A. Shuler
45. Mack H. Smith, Jr.
46. Cheryl A. Stewart
47. Richard N. Stewart
48. James R. Thomas
49. Richard M. Wallace, Jr.
50. Lee H. Wesley

Notes

Introduction

1. See, E. Clifford Nelson, ed., *The Lutherans in North America* (Philadelphia: Fortress Press, 1975), 74.
2. Traditionally, when African Americans do history, they don't write it. They do it orally.

Chapter 1: The United States Colonial North, 1669–1776

1. Israel Acrelius, *A History of New Sweden* (Philadelphia: The Historical Society of Pennsylvania, 1874), viii.
2. Abdel Ross Wentz, *Basic History of Lutheranism in America* (Philadelphia: Fortress Press, 1965), 13.
3. E. B. O'Callaghan, *History of New Netherland or New York under the Dutch* (New York: Appleton & Co., 1946), 1:110–11.
4. By 1626, the Dutch had trading posts at Fort Orange (the present site of Albany), Fort Nassau (on the Delaware River opposite the present day Philadelphia), at the mouth of the Connecticut River, and New Amsterdam (Manhattan Island).
5. O'Callaghan, *History of New Netherland*, 385.
6. A. Leon Higginbotham, Jr., *In the Matter of Color, Race and the American Legal Process: The Colonial Period* (New York: Oxford University Press, 1978), 108, contends that "slavery as it existed in every other colony, did not come into being while the Dutch governed New Netherland.... Slavery in the Dutch colony never granted the master rights of absolute possession over the slave; it constituted only a labor obligation.... New Netherland remained one of the few colonies where slavery and freedom were not perceived as mutually exclusive conditions, but were instead inaccurate labels to describe blurred social distinctions and obligations of labor."
7. Edgar J. McManus, *A History of Negro Slavery in New York* (Syracuse: Syracuse University Press, 1970), 8.
8. O'Callaghan, *History of New Netherland*, 385.
9. Dingman Versteey, "The City of New Amsterdam," in Theodore M. Banta, *Yearbook of the Holland Society of New York, 1903* (New York: Knickerbocker Press, 1903), 196.
10. O'Callaghan, *History of New Netherland*, 385.
11. McManus, *Negro Slavery in New York*, 60.
12. Higginbotham, *In the Matter of Color*, 114.

13. Ibid., 114.

14. McManus, *Negro Slavery in New York*, 191–92.

15. Ibid., 194–95.

16. Higginbotham, *In the Matter of Color*, 113.

17. O'Callaghan, *History of New Netherland*, 345.

18. Harry J. Kreider, *Lutheranism in Colonial New York* (New York: Arno Press, 1972), 14.

19. Michael L. Cobbler, "One Blood, Many Colors" (January 15, 1986), 11.

20. Julius F. Sachse, *Justus Falckner, Mystic and Scholar* (Philadelphia, 1903), 102–3.

21. Aree van Guinea was a freed mulatto. In the literature, his name is sometimes spelled "Arie" and "van Genee." See: Simon Hart and Harry J. Kreider, trans., *The Lutheran Church in New York and New Jersey* (The United Lutheran Synod of New York and New England, 1962), 151, 175.

22. Ibid., 151.

23. Sachse, *Justus Falckner*, 104.

24. Lorenzo Johnson Greene, *The Negro in Colonial New England, 1620–1776* (New York: Columbia University Press, 1942), 274. Also in Humphreys, *An Account of the Endeavours of the Society for Propagation of the Gospel to Instruct the Negro Slaves of New York* (London, 1730), 27.

25. Pieter Christian was reportedly born in the 1860s in Madagascar.

26. Harry J. Kreider, *Lutheranism in Colonial New York*, 55.

27. Sachse, *Justus Falckner*, 106.

28. Delbert Wallace Clark, *The World of Justus Falckner* (Philadelphia: Muhlenberg Press, 1946).

29. Wilhelm Christoph Berkenmeyer, *The Albany Protocol*, 459.

30. Kreider, *Lutheranism in Colonial New York*, 56.

31. See St. Paul's letter to Philemon in the New Testament.

32. Berkenmeyer, *The Albany Protocol*, 271.

33. Kreider, *Lutheranism in Colonial New York*, 56.

34. Berkenmeyer, *The Albany Protocol*, 288.

35. H. M. Muhlenberg, Theodore G. Tappert and John W. Doberstein, trans., *The Journals of Henry Melchior Muhlenberg* (Philadelphia: Muhlenberg Press, 1942), 1: 669; 2:439; 3:120, 556, 595. Also M. L. Cobbler, "What Price Inclusion?" in *The Mt. Airy Parish Practice Notebook*, No. 19, Summer 1982, 2.

36. Ibid., No. 12, 2.

37. Muhlenberg, *Journals*.

38. Ibid., 1:330.

39. Ibid., 342.

40. Marcus Wilson Jernegan, *Laboring and Dependent Classes in Colonial America, 1607–1783* (Chicago: University of Chicago Press, 1931), 41.

Chapter 2: The Danish West Indies, 1713–

1. Jens Larsen, *Virgin Islands Story* (Philadelphia: Fortress Press, 1950), 30.
2. Ibid., 33.
3. Eva Lawaetz, *Black Education in the Danish West Indies from 1732 to 1853* (St. Croix: Friends of Denmark Society, 1980), 5–6.
4. Jens Larsen, *Virgin Islands Story*, 48.
5. Ibid., 61.
6. Author unknown, *A Proposal for Regulating the Situation of Negroes in the West Indies, etc.* (*Ordning of Vestindiske Forfatningsforholdangaaende Negerne med Mere*, 1826).

Chapter 3: The United States Colonial South, 1717–1781

1. William Edward Eisenberg, *The Lutheran Church in Virginia 1717–1962* (Roanoke, Virginia: The Trustees of the Virginia Synod, Lutheran Church in America, 1967), 5.
2. Ibid., 13.
3. Ibid., 47.
4. George Fenwick Jones, transcriber and editor, *Henry Newman's Salzburger Letterbooks* (Athens: University of Georgia Press, 1966), 7.
5. The Archbishop was Count Leopold Anton of Firmian.
6. Georgia was chartered in 1732.
7. Jones, *Salzburger Letterbooks*, 8.
8. Ibid.
9. Henry Newman was aware of the Salzburgers' dilemma. His letters were constantly filled with reminders to treat the first transport "well" so that they will encourage other Salzburgers to follow them to Georgia. See Newman's first letter, dated December 11, 1733, in Jones, *Salzburger Letterbooks*, 79, 80.
10. On the way from the continent to North America, the Salzburgers stopped at Dover, England. Everyone, including children, were given spending money. See Henry Newman's letter to Professor Francke in Germany, dated December 21, 1733, in George Fenwick Jones, *Salzburger Letterbooks*, 85, 86.
11. Higginbotham, *In the Matter of Color*, 218, 219.
12. As a religious community, each individual was required to subscribe to the Augsburg Confession, the Symbolical Books, as well as a code of regulations drawn up by three men: the Rev. Samuel Urlsperger of Augsburg, the Rev. Frederick Ziegenhagen of London, and the Rev. Gotthelf Augustus Francke of Halle. The regulations were prepared in 1733 and continued in force (with some later modifications made principally by Henry Muhlenberg in 1744). See P. Strobel, *The Salzburgers*, 93.
13. Ibid., 91.
14. Theodore Ahrendt, *The Lutherans in Georgia* (Chicago: Adams Press, 1979).
15. Both Boltzius and Gronau were appointed to their positions by Francke in Halle. Initially, Gronau was to serve as a catechist. He was later appointed pastor and assistant to Boltzius. The SPCK initially promised to pay him 30

pounds per year. See Jones, *Salzburger Letters*, 69. Gronau died in 1744; Boltzius in 1765.

16. George Fenwick Jones, ed.; Hermann J. Lacher, trans., *Detailed Reports on the Salzburger Emigrants who Settled in Georgia. Edited by Samuel Urlsperger,* Vol. I, 1733–1734.

17. Ibid., 57.

18. Ibid., 69.

19. Ibid., 89.

20. Ibid., 104.

21. Regrettably, such culturally-conditioned bias frequently is expressed by whites, blacks, and all ethnic groups.

22. Jones, *Reports on the Salzburger Emigrants.*

23. John Vat's letter was written on May 30, 1735. See Jones, *Reports on Salzburger Emigrants*, 583.

24. Kenneth Coleman, ed., *A History of Georgia* (Athens: University of Georgia Press, 1977), 36.

25. Footnotes #193 and #194 in Jones, *Reports on Salzburger Emigrants*, IV, 181.

26. W. D. Weatherford, *American Churches and the Negro* (Boston: Christopher Publishing House, 1957).

27. Jones, *Reports on Salzburger Emigrants.*

28. Ibid., 586.

29. Ibid., 194, 195.

30. Weatherford, *American Churches*, 140, 141.

31. A. G. Voigt, trans. and C. A. Linn, ed., *Ebenezer Record Book.* (Savannah, Ga.: C. A. Linn, Archivist, publisher, Evangelical Lutheran Synod of Georgia and Adjacent States, 1929), 32.

32. See Table 3: The Black Population in Colonial Georgia, 1740–1780.

33. Marcus Wilson Jernegan, *Laboring and Dependent Classes in Colonial America, 1607–1783* (New York: Frederick Ungar Publishing Co., 1960), 33, 34.

34. E. Clifford Nelson, ed., *The Lutherans in North America* (Philadelphia: Fortress Press, 1975), 74.

35. Henry Melchior Muhlenberg, *The Journals of Henry Melchior Muhlenberg*, Theodore G. Tappert and John W. Doberstein, trans. (Philadelphia: The Muhlenberg Press, 1942), 738.

36. Jones, *Salzburger Letterbooks*, 16.

37. Marcus Wilson Jernegan, *Laboring and Dependent Classes*, 33, 34.

38. Higginbotham, *In the Matter of Color,* 258.

39. The following were Rabenhorst and Lemcke's slaves who were baptized: #621 Catharine, #622 Hannah, #640 David, #654 Elierser, #704 Christian, #705 Simeon, #705 Judith (Simeon and Judith were twins and cited as a single entry), #825 Christian Candace, #697 George, Nathan, #797 Jojada, and #872 Phoebe.

40. See Appendix, Baptismal entry #828.

41. Promiscuity has always been a part of society. In this instance, promiscuity across racial lines had even more serious consequences.

Chapter 4: Surinam, 1791–

1. Cornelius C. Goslinga, *A Short History of the Netherlands, Antilles, and Surinam* (Boston: Martinus Nijhoff, 1979), 109.
2. Ibid., 105.
3. Ibid., 109.
4. Ibid., 115.
5. Richard Price, *Guiana Maroons: A Historical and Bibliographical Introduction* (Baltimore: The Johns Hopkins University Press, 1976), 9.
6. Ibid., 1, 2.
7. Ibid., 17–19.
8. Ibid., 21.
9. J. Wolbers, *Geschiedenis van Suriname* (Amsterdam: S. Emmering, 1861), 201. Cited by V. Naffiers.
10. Paul Beatty, *A History of the Lutheran Church in Guyana* (South Pasadena: The William Carey Library, 1970), 13.
11. Vernon H. Naffier, "Historical Sketch of Lutheranism in the Caribbean" (Unpublished paper, 1987), 2, 23.
12. Ibid., 2/22.
13. Leo King, *Evangelish Lutherse Kerk: 240 Jaar*, A 1981 anniversary booklet, and *Evangelish Lutherse Kerk: 245 Jaar*, A 1985 anniversary booklet (Paramaribo, Surinam: n.pub.).
14. Ibid.
15. Beatty, *Lutheran Church in Guyana*, 35.
16. Naffier, "Lutheranism in the Caribbean," 6/26.
17. Ibid.
18. Ibid., 8/28.

Chapter 5: Guyana, 1818–

1. Beatty, *Lutheran Church in Guyana*, 24.
2. Ralph J. White, *Six Years in Hammock Land* (Philadelphia: The United Lutheran Publication House, 1922), 45.
3. Beatty, *Lutheranism in Guyana*, 17, 18.
4. Ibid., 22.
5. White, *Hammock Land*, 46.
6. Beatty, *Lutheranism in Guyana*, 28.
7. C. T. Benze, ed., *The Lutheran Church in British Guiana* (n.pub., n.d.), 6. The contents suggest a 1940 publication date. The publication may be found in the Lutheran Theological Seminary Library, Philadelphia, PA.
8. Beatty, *Lutheranism in Guyana*, 35.
9. In the five-year period, 1824–1829, the membership of the Methodist congregation reached 3,000, almost all of which was black. Slaves who had been kept away from Christian worship were gathering in large numbers to hear whatever preacher came along. Beatty, 35.

10. Ibid., 104.

11. Vere T. Daly, *A Short History of the Guyanese People* (Georgetown, Guyana, 1966), quoted by Beatty, op. cit., 99.

12. G. Pearson, "The Negro's Grievance." *West Indian Quarterly* (1885–1886): 141–42, quoted in Daly, 298, and Beatty 84, 85.

13. Daly, *Guyanese People*, 298, quoted in Beatty, 85.

14. The records available are not entirely clear as to when Rev. Riach served the Berbice congregation. Given the 25-year occupancy of the church building by the Methodists, it seems likely that the Pastor Riach served the Lutherans some time during the 1940s. Beatty seems to confirm this, suggesting that Riach served the congregation from 1842 to 1846. See Beatty, *Lutheran Church in Guyana*, 130.

15. J. R. Mittelholzer, "Ebenezer Evangelical Lutheran Church, Berbice, British Guiana, S.A." in *History of the Evangelical Lutheran Synod of East Pennsylvania, 1842–1892* (Philadelphia: n.pub., n.d), 318.

16. Mittelholzer, *Ev. Luth. Synod of East Pennsylvania*, 309.

17. One commentator reports that Mittelholzer "was a type of peculiar blend, found in certain parts of South America, where the color line and race prejudice are largely obliterated. His physical features plainly betrayed the strain of his parentage." S. D. Daugherty, *South America's New Day* (Philadelphia: United Lutheran Church in America, n.d.) 11.

18. Beatty, *Lutheran Church in Guyana*, 63.

19. J. R. Mittelholzer, *Ev. Luth. Synod of East Pennsylvania*, 320.

20. Ibid., 320.

21. Beatty, *Lutheran Church in Guyana*, 65.

22. A catechist is a layperson who serves as a full-time church worker under the supervision of an ordained minister, and who usually performs many pastoral functions except baptisms, marriages, confirmations, and funerals.

23. New Amsterdam was the capital of the three colonies until the British takeover. Under British rule, Georgetown became the capital of British Guiana.

24. Mittelholzer, with his wife's assistance, supported himself during that three-year period of persecution by running the Academy.

25. R. J. White, *Hammock Land*, 55.

26. Ibid., 63.

27. *Board of Foreign Missions, General Synod of the Evangelical Lutheran Church in the United States of America, Thirty-Eighth Report, 1915*, 69. Cited in Beatty, *Lutheran Church in Guyana*, 78.

28. Beatty, 79.

29. Ibid., 79.

30. Ibid., 78.

31. Ibid., 104.

32. Alexander Sutherland McDonald, "A Divided Church in a Divided Nation: British Guiana." S.T.M. Thesis, Union Theological Seminary, New York, 1960, 111. Cited in Beatty, 102.

33. Beatty, 97.

34. Ibid., 114.
35. Ibid., 119.

Chapter 6: The Southern Slave States, 1774–1865

1. Pierre L. van den Berghe, *Race and Racism: A Comparative Perspective* (New York: John Wiley & Sons, 1967), 77, 78.

2. Hugh George Anderson, *Lutheranism in the Southeastern States, 1860–1886: A Social History* (The Hague: Mouton, 1969), 13.

3. Ibid., 13.

4. Ibid., 13.

5. Cited in the record book of St. John's Lutheran Church, and in Theodore G. Tappert and John W. Doberstein, trans., *The Journal of Henry Melchior Muhlenberg* (Philadelphia: Muhlenberg Press, 1942), II, 574, 575.

6. *Minutes of the Evangelical Lutheran Synod of North Carolina Seventh Convention at Guildford County* (Newberry: Aull & Houseal, 1894). Translated from the German Protocol-Peschau.

7. *Kurzer Bericht von den Konferenzen, 1810* (New Market), 1811.

8. *Minutes of North Carolina*, 1813–1826.

9. *History of the Lutheran Church in South Carolina*. Prepared and edited by The History of Synod Committee (Columbia, SC: The South Carolina Synod of the LCA, 1971), 238.

10. Gottlieb Schober, *A Comprehensive Account of the Rise and Progress of the Blessed Reformation of the Christian Church by Dr. Martin Luther* (Baltimore: Schaeffer & Maund, 1818), 167.

11. *North Carolina Historical Review,* October 1973, 307 and 317.

12. Jacob L. Morgan, Bachman S. Brown, and John Hall, eds., *History of the Lutheran Church in North Carolina, 1803–1953* (Published by the United Evangelical Lutheran Synod of North Carolina), 82.

13. *Extracts from the Minutes of the Evangelical Lutheran Synod for North Carolina and Adjacent States, June 2, 1822,* 9.

14. *Minutes of the Sixty-first Annual Convention of the Evangelical Lutheran Synod and Ministerium of North Carolina, 1864,* 10.

15. *Minutes of the Evangelical Lutheran Synod and Ministerium of North Carolina and Adjacent Parts.* Convened at St. John's Church, Cabarrus County, NC, May 1837 (Salisbury: Western Carolina Office, 1837), 12.

16. *Friendship Lutheran Church—History of the Congregation,* 20. Unpublished document of the Friendship Lutheran Church in Taylorville, NC.

17. Socrates Henkel, *History of the Evangelical Lutheran Tennessee Synod* (New Market, VA: Kendel & Co., 1890), 53–164.

18. William Edward Eisenberg, *The Lutheran Church in Virginia, 1717–1962* (Roanoke, VA: The Trustees of the Virginia Synod, Lutheran Church in America, 1967), 218.

19. Richard C. Wade, *Slavery in the Cities: The South 1820–1860* (New York: Oxford University Press, 1964), 244.

20. George F. Jones, ed. and Hermann J. Lacher, trans., *Detailed Reports of the*

Salzburger Emigrants who Settled in America, Edited by Samuel Urlsperger (Athens: University of Georgia Press, 1968), I, 117.

21. Wade, *Slavery in the Cities*, 53.

22. Ibid., 41.

23. Ibid., 51.

24. Ibid.

25. Ibid., 248.

26. E. Horace Fitchett, "The Origin and Growth of the Free Negro Population of Charleston, South Carolina," *Journal of Negro History*, Vol. 26, 1941, 435–436.

27. *Minutes of an Extra Meeting of the Vestry, Wardens & Congregation of the Lutheran Church of German Protestants on Monday, February 5, 1816,* St. John's Lutheran Church, Charleston, South Carolina.

28. R. M. Bost, "The Reverend John Bachman and the Development of Southern Lutherans." A dissertation, Yale University, 1963, 388.

29. Benjamin Kurtz, *The Lutheran Observer*.

30. *The Missionary*, II, No. 46, 181.

31. Bost, "The Rev. John Bachman," 389, footnote 34.

32. Bill Kovarik, "Housing Authority Offers Old Cemetery For Sale," *The Charleston Post-Courier*, January 7, 1983.

33. *Minutes of the Thirty-fifth Meeting of the Evangelical Lutheran Synod and Ministerium of South Carolina and Adjacent States, October 28, 1858,* 28.

34. *Extracts of the Minutes of the Fourteenth Synod and Ministerium of South Carolina and Adjacent States, Charleston, 1837,* 37, 38.

35. *Extracts from the Transactions of the German and English Lutheran Synod for North Carolina and Adjacent States, 1820,* 12.

36. *History of the Lutheran Church Church in South Carolina,* 241.

37. Ibid., 244.

38. Fitchett, "Origin and Growth of Negro Population," 435, 436.

39. *History of the Lutheran Church in South Carolina,* 269.

40. Digest of the Ordinance Charleston, 1783–1844, 380. "Ordinance passed December 19, 1835. Sec. V. That it shall not be lawful for any free Negro or person of Color, who has left the State at any time previous to the passing of this Act, or for those who hereafter leave the State, ever to return again into the same without being subject to the penalties of the first section of this Act as fully as if they had never resided therein." Quoted by E. Horace Fitchett, "Origin and Growth of Negro Population" cited above, 436.

41. *History of the Lutheran Church in South Carolina,* 269.

42. Bishop Daniel Alexander Payne, *Recollections of Seventy Years* (New York: Arno Press & The New York Times, 1968), 44–46.

43. *History of the Lutheran Church in South Carolina,* 272, 273.

44. Michael L. Cobbler, "Three Early Black Leaders,' *A Study of Black Lutheran Congregations* (Institute for Mission in the U.S.A., Wayne C. Stumme, Director, 1987), 26.

45. *History of the Lutheran Church in South Carolina,* 242, quoting the South Carolina Synod Minutes, 1835, 8.

46. Report of the Rev. J. Crim to the South Carolina Synod, November 8, 1838. South Carolina Synod Archives.

47. *Minutes of the Evangelical Lutheran Synod and Ministerium of South Carolina and Adjacent States, 1859,* 5. In that year the plantation missionary reported that he had received 24 whites and 20 blacks into the faith.

48. *History of the Lutheran Church in South Carolina,* 244.

49. *Minutes of the Twenty-fifth Meeting of the Evangelical Lutheran Synod and Ministerium of South Carolina and Adjacent States.* Convened at St. Mark's Church, Edgefield, SC. (Charleston: Steam-Power Press of Walker and James, 1852), 9, 10.

50. *Minutes of the Twenty-fifth Meeting of the Evangelical Lutheran Synod and Ministerium of South Carolina and Adjacent States,* 9, 10.

51. *Minutes of the South Carolina Synod and Ministerium, 1858.*

52. Ibid., 1859.

53. *The Missionary,* II, No. 46, 181. The Rev. John Bachman was the chief Lutheran defender of slavery in the South.

54. Ahrendt, *The Lutherans in Georgia,* 31.

55. *The Lutheran Observer,* 22, No. 42, October 13, 1854, 116.

56. Ahrendt, *The Lutherans in Georgia,* 33.

57. Ibid., 35.

Chapter 7: Jehu Jones and the First All-Black
Lutheran Church, 1832–1849

1. Records of St. John's Lutheran Church, Charleston, SC. Jones' father is said to have owned a hotel in Charleston and was a man of comfortable means.

2. A personal conversation with Mr. George Bonnett, a member of St. John's Lutheran Church, Charleston, SC, October 28, 1988.

3. Edward D. Smith, *Climbing Jacob's Ladder* (Washington and London: Smithsonian Institution Press, 1988), 56.

4. Edward Raymond Turner, *The Negro in Pennsylvania: Slavery—Servitude—Freedom, 1639–1861* (New York: Arno Press & The New York Times, 1969), 136.

5. Theo. Hershberg, "Free Blacks in Antebellum Philadelphia: A Study of Ex-Slaves, Freeborn and Socioeconomic Decline," *Journal of Social History,* 5, 1971–72, 195.

6. Ibid.

7. Ibid.

8. The building is still standing today, although extensively remodeled and with a new front. The cornerstone, now located inside the main entrance, indicates that the building was dedicated in 1834. That date refers to the time when the congregation was organized.

9. Jehu Jones letter of May 2, 1836, to *The Lutheran Observer,* III, No. 37, May 6, 1836.

10. Ibid.

11. Ibid., letter of January 16, 1837, VI, No. 24, February 3, 1837.

12. Ibid., letter of April 19, 1839, V, No. 37, May 4, 1838.

Chapter 8: The Old Lutherans in the South, 1865–1891

1. *South Carolina Synod Minutes,* 22.

2. *The Lutheran Visitor,* April 27, 1877.

3. Ibid., June 6, 1880.

4. *History of the Lutheran Church in South Carolina,* 308.

5. *Minutes of the Meeting of the Vestry of St. John's Lutheran Church, Charleston, South Carolina, April 8, 1870.*

6. St. John's Lutheran Church, *Minutes, 1883–1913,* April 21, 1911, meeting.

7. St. John's Lutheran Church, *Minutes,* October 13, 1911, meeting.

8. *The Charleston Post-Courier,* September 18, 1957.

9. Bill Kovarik, "Housing Authority Offers Old Cemetery For Sale," *The Charleston Post-Courier,* January 7, 1983.

10. Richard C. Dickinson, *Roses and Thorns* (St. Louis: Concordia Publishing House, 1977), 24, 25.

11. Ibid., 25.

12. *Minutes of the South Carolina Synod and Ministerium, August 25, 1870,* 27.

13. Ibid., 1880 Convention.

14. *Minutes of the Seventieth Convention of the North Carolina Synod, April 30–May 5, 1873,* 27.

15. Ibid., The Seventy-first Convention, April 29–May 3, 1874, 26.

16. *Life Sketches of Lutheran Ministers of the North Carolina and Tennessee Synods, 1773–1965* (North Carolina Synod, 1966), 238.

17. Dickinson, *Roses and Thorns,* 25.

18. Ibid., 25.

19. William Edward Eisenberg, *The Lutheran Church in Virginia, 1717–1962* (Roanoke, VA: Trustees of the Virginia Synod, Lutheran Church in America, 1967), 218.

20. Thomas Noon, *Concordia Historical Institute Quarterly,* 50, No. 2, 59, 60, quoting the 65th annual convention of the Maryland Synod, 1884, p. 16.

21. Ibid., 60.

22. *Minutes of the Eighty-sixth Convention of the North Carolina Synod,* 1889.

23. Smith, *Climbing Jacob's Ladder,* 101.

Chapter 9: The Rebirth of Black Lutheranism, 1877–1950

1. The Synodical Conference was founded November 11–13, 1871, and originally consisted of the Illinois, Minnesota, Missouri, Norwegian, Ohio, and Wisconsin Synods. Its first meeting was held January 11–13, 1872.

2. F. Dean Lueking, *Mission in the Making* (St. Louis: Concordia Publishing House, 1964), 85.

3. Ibid., 93

4. Ibid., 94

5. Ibid., 94.

6. Ibid., 101.

7. Ibid., 102.

8. Ibid., 133.

9. The Rev. Edwin Thompson was not from Mansura. His home was New Orleans. Since his father was from Mansura, he is traditionally counted as part of the "Mansura Maffia." Mr. Otis Demouy, also from Mansura, graduated from Immanuel, but did not enter the ministry.

10. Michael Cobbler.

11. Dickinson, *Roses and Thorns*, 156.

12. Ervin E. Krebs, *The Lutheran Church and the American Negro* (Columbus, Ohio: Board of American Missions, American Lutheran Church, 1950), 20.

13. N. J. Bakke, *Our Colored Mission* (St. Louis: Concordia Publishing House, 1914), 50.

14. Ibid., 49.

15. Lueking, *Mission in the Making*, 116.

16. Bakke, *Our Colored Mission,* 51.

17. Ibid., 51.

18. Ibid., 86.

19. Ibid., 72.

20. Ibid., 65.

21. Lueking, *Mission in the Making*, 111.

22. P. W. Phifer died in 1911.

23. Lueking, *Mission in the Making*, 117.

24. Bakke, *Our Colored Mission*, 54.

25. Ibid., 56.

26. Ibid., 57.

27. Ibid., 58.

28. Ibid., 59.

29. Ibid., 61.

30. Ibid., 63.

31. Ibid., 68.

32. Ibid., 70.

33. Christopher F. Drewes, *Half a Century of Lutheranism among our Colored People* (St. Louis: Concordia Publishing House, 1927), 20.

34. Dickinson, *Roses and Thorns*, 156.

35. An interview with the Rev. Dr. Howard Foard, son of student F. Foard.

36. John F. Nau, *Nau! Mission Inspired* (St. Louis: Clayton Publishing House, 1978), 55.

37. Mr. Stoll is said to have originally gotten into Concordia Seminary, St. Louis, because they didn't know he was black. He was reportedly sent to Immanuel after his race was discovered.

38. Krebs, *Lutheran Church and the Negro*.

39. Ibid.

40. Drewes, *Half a Century of Lutheranism among Colored*, 56.

41. Ibid., 66.

42. Rosa Young, *Light in the Dark Belt* (St. Louis: Concordia Publishing House, 1950), 56.

43. Daniel Wiseman came to Brooklyn from the Danish West Indies in 1872.

44. Krebs, *Lutheran Church and the Negro*.

45. Bakke, *Our Colored Mission*, 44.

46. Drewes, *Half a Century of Lutheranism among Colored*, 52.

47. Krebs, *Lutheran Church and the Negro*, 25, 26.

48. *Minutes of the Thirty-fifth Evangelical Lutheran Synodical Conference of North America at Indianapolis, Indiana, August 6–11, 1936*, 13.

49. Annual institutes on race relations had been conducted primarily in St. Louis and Chicago beginning in 1945. In 1950, LHRAA went national, and institutes were held annually at Valparaiso University in Indiana. In 1958, Dr. Clemence Sabourin of New York City became the first black person to serve as LHRAA's president.

   For additional information on Missouri's work in Nigeria see:

   Paul M. Volz, *The Evangelical Lutheran Church of Nigeria, 1936–1961* (Calabar, Nigeria: The Hope Waddell Press, 1961).

   Dr. Edet William Amakpa, Rt. Rev. A. T. U. Ekong, N. M. Uko, and O. C. Williams, *A Short History of the Lutheran Church of Nigeria* (Obot Idim, P.A.-UYO: The Lutheran Press, n.d.).

Chapter 10: The Great Debates, 1930–1964

1. The merger of the Joint Synod of Ohio, the Buffalo Synod, and the Iowa Synod as the American Lutheran Church took place in 1930.

2. Krebs, *The Lutheran Church and the Negro*, 50.

3. Ibid., 50, 51.

4. *Statistical Yearbook of the Lutheran Church—Missouri Synod, 1932*, 144.

5. *Proceedings of the ULCA Convention, 1938*, 52.

6. *Proceedings of the ULCA Convention, 1940*, 65.

7. Krebs, *Lutheran Church and the Negro*, 65.

8. Ibid., 72.

9. Sr. Cecilia R. Wilson, "The United Lutheran Church in America's Ministry to Southern Blacks from 1936–1962: An Investigative Overview," 1985, 24. An unpublished independent study paper.

10. Dickinson, *Roses and Thorns*, 77.

Chapter 11: Integration, Inclusiveness, or What? 1947–1990

1. Thomas Coates, *The Human Relations Association of America: A Historical Summary* (Published by the Association, n.d.), 3.

2. *Proceedings of the 1956 Convention of the Lutheran Church—Missouri Synod*, St. Paul, MN.

3. Ibid.

4. Resolution 4-09, Proceedings of the 1979 Convention of the Lutheran Church—Missouri Synod, St. Louis, Missouri.

5. *What Synod Says . . . Synodical Resolutions 1975 . . . About Multicultural Ministry* (St. Louis: Board for Parish Services, The Lutheran Church—Missouri Synod, n.d., no page given).

6. Ibid.

7. Ibid.

8. *A Preliminary Report of the Review of District, College, and Agency Data.* A report prepared for the summit conference of synodical leaders involved in black ministry, St. Louis, MO, January 31–February 2, 1986.

9. *Minutes of the Board of American Missions,* American Lutheran Church, October 1956.

10. Ibid., 1957.

11. Ibid.

12. Ibid., 1958.

13. *Proceedings of the Forty-fifth Convention, Lutheran Synodical Conference, 1958,* 48.

14. *Minutes of the Board of American Missions, American Lutheran Church, April 1958,* and *Proceedings of the Forty-fifth Convention, Lutheran Synodical Conference, 1958,* 49.

15. *The Second Biennial Convention of the Lutheran Church in America, 1964.*

16. Ibid.

17. The 1967 Consultation of the Coordinating Committee of the Lutheran Church in America.

18. Bylaw adopted at the 1972 Lutheran Church in America convention.

19. "Goals and Plans for Minority Ministry—LCA 1978–1984."

20. Ibid.

21. A conversation with the Rev. Craig Lewis, October 1988.

Chapter 13: Conclusions

1. What Luther and the Reformers *did* is as important as what they *wrote.* They sought to speak their message "inside" the community they served. In translating the Bible into German, creating the German mass, and developing a hymnology from the music of the people, they created an indigenous church.